Linguistics, Philosophy, and Montague Grammar

Linguistics, Philosophy, and Montague Grammar

Edited by
Steven Davis and Marianne Mithun

University of Texas Press, Austin and London

In memory of Michael Bennett

Library of Congress Cataloging in Publication Data

Conference on Montague Grammar, Philosophy, and
    Linguistics, State University of New York at
    Albany, 1977.
    Linguistics, philosophy, and Montague grammar.

    1. Montague grammar — Congresses. 2. Languages
— Philosophy — Congresses. I. Davis, Steven.
II. Williams, Marianne Mithun. III. Title.
P158.5.C6   1977   415   79-13975
ISBN 0-292-74625-3

Requests for permission to reproduce material from this work
should be sent to Permissions, University of Texas Press,
Box 7819, Austin, Texas 78712.

Contents

Preface

The papers in this volume were presented at a conference on
Montague Grammar, Philosophy, and Linguistics, held at the
State University of New York at Albany in April 1977. Other
papers prepared for the conference which do not appear here
include "Diachronic Evidence of Non-Uniqueness in Montague
Grammar" by Josh Ard, "Questions Revisited" by Lauri Karttunen,
"Inception, Incorporation, and Causation in Montague Grammar"
by Marianne Mithun and Richmond Thomason, "Some Methodological
Remarks on Semantics" by Richmond Thomason, "A Fragment of
Serbo-Croatian in Montague Grammar" by Sarah Thomason and
Richmond Thomason, and "A Semantics for Almost" by Ivar
Tönisson.

The purpose of the conference was to bring together
linguists and philosophers currently engaged in developing
the theoretical framework of Montague grammar to share their
recent work. The discussion was intense and informative for
all, and we are very grateful to the Conversations in the
Disciplines Program, administered by the Office of Educa-
tional Services of the State University Central Administration,
for making it possible.

We wish to thank David Malloy for his assistance in
proofreading the manuscript.

In McCawley's, Parsons's, Siegel's, and Bennett's papers,
boldface is indicated by tildes under expressions.

We have dedicated our book to the memory of Michael
Bennett, who died suddenly in January 1979. His death is the
loss of a valuable contributor to research on Montague grammar
and of a friend.

Introduction

Since the first publication of Montague's "Proper Treatment
of Quantification in Ordinary English" (PTQ) in 1970, work on
Montague grammar has followed two principal lines of development. On one side, the framework has been revised to accommodate the insights of linguists into the nature of human
language, particularly in the area of syntax. On the other,
both linguists and philosophers have tested and extended the
theory to account for data beyond that treated in Montague's
fragments. The first three papers in this volume deal primarily
with the first area, the others primarily with the second.

Bach notes that most comparisons of transformational and
Montague grammars have been based on "standard" (post-*Aspects*)
versions of transformational grammar. Since the classical
(pre-*Aspects*) version bears a closer resemblance to Montague
grammar in many ways, and since it is more restrictive than
the standard versions, and thus preferable, Bach outlines a
theory of syntax based on the classical version, which he then
compares to a grammar which is almost equivalent to PTQ in
"strong generative capacity" (in the sense of Cooper and
Parsons 1976).

Partee addresses a major concern of linguists not generally
shared by logicians: that of constraining as narrowly as
possible the class of possible grammars of human language.
She notes that while Montague's theory of grammar incorporates
strong constraints on the relation between syntactic and
semantic rules, it has almost no constraints on the form of
syntactic or semantic operations. Partee takes on the task of
further constraining the syntax. She first proposes several

modifications in Montague's syntactic component. These include
the use of labeled brackets, the introduction of syntactic
"features" as recursively defined properties of expressions,
relaxation of the requirement that syntactic operations be
total functions, and the concomitant addition of "structural
analysis statements" to syntactic rules and the separation of
syntax and morphology. She then suggests the following constraints on the syntax: (C1) no internal structure building;
(C2) no extrinsic rule ordering; (C3) no obligatory rules;
(C4) no purely abstract morphemes; and (C5) no appeal to derivational history. She proposes that syntactic operations be
required to be expressed as a composition of subfunctions,
the subfunctions representing language particular recurrent
operations which are definable as a composition of primitive
operations. She presents a stock of these primitive operations
and a framework containing these modifications and constraints,
then reconsiders the fragment of English in PTQ in light of
this framework.

McCawley opens by comparing the bases of transformational
and Montague grammars: the types and domains of their rules.
After examining Montague's treatments of Raising and the
auxiliary verb system in English, and comparing them to
alternative transformational analyses, McCawley suggests some
revisions of Montague grammar, to capture certain strengths
of the transformational model. These include adjustments in
the individuation of rules, interactions among rules, and
the local well-formedness constraint.

A prerequisite to judging the success of the Montague model
in achieving the goals of linguists and logicians is the
application of it to a sufficiently wide range of phenomena
within the concerns of each. The papers by Parsons, Dowty,
Groenendijk and Stokhof, Bennett, Siegel, and Waldo in this

volume present extensions of the model to account for data beyond that considered by Montague.

Parsons investigates the theoretical consequences of incorporating type distinctions into ordinary English. He is motivated by the hypothesis putatively demonstrated by the Russell Paradox, that any language rich enough to contain talk about properties must either incorporate type distinctions or else run the risk of inconsistency. He considers what English would be like if it did include such distinctions, although it is commonly assumed not to. Parsons extends the system of PTQ to include explicit talk about properties by exploiting the underlying type system of Montague's intensional logic. The proposed modifications of the syntax keep the types hidden for the most part. They have no effect on the pronunciation of sentences, and they surface only in the occasional ill-formedness of sentences that seem somewhat odd, while appearing generally well-formed. The resulting modified syntax closely resembles parts of the Chomskyan model.

Dowty investigates the ramifications of Thomason's treatment of passive sentences on the description of Dative 'Movement' (1974; 1976; Mss). Thomason treats Passive as an operation on transitive verbs rather than as a transformation on complete sentences. However, if Dative 'Movement' is taken to be a sentence transformation, then Thomason's theory cannot explain the two passive forms that dative sentences have, for example, 'A book was given to Mary by John' and 'Mary was given a book by John'. Dowty's solution is to treat Dative 'Movement', as well, as an optional operation on verbs, called the *category changing method*, rather than on sentences, and to order it before Thomason's Passive. One of the advantages of replacing operations on sentences with operations on verbs is that it is possible in certain cases to regard such an

operation as a word formation rule rather than a syntactic
rule. Dowty offers evidence that Dative has a number of
characteristics which are taken to distinguish word formation
rules from syntactic rules.

The second part of Dowty's paper introduces a general
theory of word formation for Montague grammar. He adopts
Montague's method of syntactic formation and semantic interpretation for formalizing a 'lexical component', but assigns
to this component the generation of the set of 'possible
lexical items' out of which expressions may be taken to be
introduced as basic expressions of the English grammar. As
Dative 'Movement' will have exactly the same form in this
theory whether it is regarded as a syntactic or a lexical
rule, the treatment of the first part of the paper survives
intact, except that the initial states of derivations are now
lexical derivations. Finally, Dowty suggests that the category
changing method might profitably be applied to other transformational problems in English syntax, such as the Raising rules.

Groenendijk and Stokhof discuss the generation of infinitives
in Montague grammar. In their proposal, infinitives are translated into expressions which directly denote propositions.
In addition, these expressions contain, in subject position,
a new type of expression in intensional logic, the denotation
of which depends upon the context of the infinitive. This
context is determined by the expressions in the matrix
sentence in which the infinitive occurs, and it consists of
the entities which these expressions denote. They contrast
their treatment of infinitives with that of Thomason (1974) in
which infinitives denote properties rather than propositions.
Thomason relates infinitives to propositions, but only
indirectly through meaning postulates. Groenendijk and
Stokhof maintain that Thomason's view contains unmotivated

syntactic complications which theirs avoids, since their view
does not need meaning postulates to account for the relation
between infinitives and propositions. They further suggest
that their notion of context might be fruitfully applied to
such constructions as 'John gives a book', reflexive and nonreflexive anaphoric pronominal reference, and quantified
term phrases.

Bennett examines the behavior of mass nouns and mass terms
within the Montague framework. He first distinguishes the two.
Mass nouns are like count nouns in that they take quantifiers
to form terms. Mass terms are proper names of substances.
He rejects with Montague the idea that every mass noun phrase
corresponds to a mass term, but departs from Montague's view
that mass terms denote properties of individuals. One argument
against this is based on Kripke's (1972) views about reference.
This argument supports Parsons's (1970) thesis that mass terms
denote basic individuals. Bennett concludes with a discussion
of the dependence of nondenoting mass and count noun phrases
upon nondenoting mass and species terms.

Siegel incorporates measure adjectives into a revised
version of Montague grammar. Measure adjectives are adjectives
like 'tall' which cannot be interpreted straightforwardly
because their extensions depend upon such things as the determination of a measurement scale, a comparison class, and a
norm for the measured property. Siegel argues that measure
adjectives constitute a special class of the simple predicate
adjectives that are usually called absolute adjectives.
Measure adjectives share the syntactic and the extensional
semantic behavior predicated within the Montague framework
for absolute adjectives such as 'carnivorous', that is, for
one place predicates on individuals. They differ from other
absolute adjectives only because they are vague in certain

predictable ways. Theories of interpretation of measure
adjectives indicate that the vagueness must be cleared up in
the context of use, not in the grammar. From this, she
concludes that although measure adjectives have generally
been considered to be relative, not absolute adjectives,
there is no need to violate the syntax-semantics correspondence by classifying them with the other relative adjectives,
like 'former', which are syntactically ad-common-nouns, not
predicates, and semantically operate on properties rather
than individuals.

Waldo applies the Montague model to sortally incorrect
sentences, those which are syntactically well-formed but
semantically deviant because they predicate of an object an
inappropriate property. 'The theory of relativity is shiny'
is such a sentence. Waldo first proposes a grammar which
generates and allows for the interpretation of a range of
sortally incorrect sentences. He next shows that sortally
incorrect sentences turn out to be semantically deviant by
introducing partial functions into the semantics, so that
subject-predicate sortally incorrect sentences are interpreted as having no truth value. In order to retain as much
classical logic as possible, he uses the method of super-
valuations. In a final section, he demonstrates the operation
of the fragment on sortally incorrect sentences and shows how
the semantics can deal with nonreferring definite descriptions.

In extending the Montague framework to account for previously undiscussed aspects of natural language, these papers
raise at least as many questions as they address. At the same
time, they bring the goals of both linguists and logicians to
the development of the model. It is hoped that this inter-
disciplinary communication will continue fruitfully.

References

Cooper, Robin, and Terence Parsons. 1976. "Montague Grammar, Generative Semantics, and Interpretive Semantics." In Barbara H. Partee, ed., *Montague Grammar*. New York: Academic Press.

Kasher, Asa. 1976. "Logical Rationalism: On Degrees of Adequacy for Semantics of Natural Languages." *Philosophica* 18: 139 – 157.

Kripke, Saul. 1972. "Naming and Necessity." In D. Davidson and G. Harmon, eds., *Semantics of Natural Language*. Dordrecht: D. Reidel Publishing Co.

Montague, Richard. 1974. "The Proper Treatment of Quantification in Ordinary English." In Richmond Thomason, ed., *Formal Philosophy: Selected Papers of Richard Montague*. New Haven: Yale University Press.

Parsons, Terence. 1970. "An Analysis of Mass Terms and Amount Terms." *Foundations of Language* 6: 362 – 388.

Thomason, Richmond. 1974. "Some Complement Constructions in Montague Grammar." In *Proceedings from the 10th Regional Meeting of the Chicago Linguistic Society*, pp. 712 – 722.

———. 1976. "Some Extensions of Montague Grammar." In Barbara H. Partee, ed., *Montague Grammar*. New York: Academic Press.

———. Ms. May 1976. "Montague Grammar and Some Transformations."

———. Ms. June 1976. "On the Interpretation of the Thomason 1972 Fragment."

Linguistics, Philosophy, and Montague Grammar

1

Montague Grammar and Classical Transformational Grammar

Emmon Bach

0. *Introduction.*

In an important paper, Cooper and Parsons (1976) have shown
how to obtain transformational grammars of two kinds that are
strongly equivalent to a fragment of English grammar given by
Montague (1973) (henceforth PTQ, with references to the
reprint in Montague 1974). By 'strongly equivalent' they mean
that the pairings of English sentences and their interpretations differ only when one of the systems gives an interpretation which is logically equivalent to an interpretation
given by the other. Both grammars are variants of the form of
transformational grammar which developed after the publication of Chomsky's *Aspects* (1965). It has been remarked that
the earliest versions of transformational grammar (Chomsky
1975a [1955], 1957) were closer in spirit and in detail to
the system of Montague grammar than later versions of the
theory (the 'standard' theory of Chomsky 1965 and its derivatives). The points of resemblance are three: (1) the classical
theory included the notion of a 'transformation marker'
(T-marker), which is in some ways like the analysis trees of
Montague grammar (Partee 1975). (2) The systems of 'semantic
theory' envisaged for the theory of Katz and Fodor 1963 (but
not later writings by Katz, or Katz and Postal 1964) included
a type of 'projection rule' (Type 2) which is very close to

the translation rules of PTQ. (3) Earlier transformational
grammars observed a kind of 'local grammaticality' which is
parallel to but not in general identical with the 'well-
formedness constraint' usually observed in Montague's fragments and considered important by more recent workers in this
tradition.[1]

Since a good deal of the motivation that went into the
revision of transformational theory undertaken in *Aspects*
arose from the attractiveness of a hypothesis that appears to
be wrong (the 'Katz-Postal' hypothesis), it would seem to be
worthwhile to explore the earlier model once again. Moreover,
studies of the generative capacity of the 'standard' theories
have shown that they are too powerful, since they are equivalent in power to various systems defining all recursively
enumerable sets (Peters and Ritchie 1973a). The 'classical'
theory can be shown to be weaker. The power of the modified
system explored here is unknown.

The least satisfactory aspect of all transformational
theories has been their treatment of quantification. The
present paper is devoted to exploring a modification of the
classical theory that makes it possible to handle quantification in a way that parallels the treatment in PTQ almost
exactly. The particular grammar given below satisfies a
'local grammaticality' constraint with the sole exception
that some structures are generated which underlie no well-
formed expressions of English, since they contain variable
elements which are 'filtered out' by the transformational
component. It should be noted that all versions of interpreted
transformational grammars use infinite sets of variables; the
differences only arise as to the place in the systems of
representation where these variables are used.

In Section 1 I sketch a general theory of modified
transformational grammars of the sort just alluded to. We may
call them KT-grammars (where KT is mnemonic for the idea of a
Kernel set of basic structures that is extended by a Transformational component). In Section 2, I give a KT-grammar for
the fragment of English described in PTQ. In 3 I undertake
a comparison of the two grammars, and in 4 I introduce some
improvements that carry the grammar a little closer to descriptive adequacy and extend its coverage of English grammar.

1. *General Theory of KT-Grammars.*

A KT-grammar is a formal system (Smullyan 1961) which defines
an infinite set of pairs, each consisting of a syntactic
structure and a translation of the structure into an interpreted intensional logic. The syntactic rules of each grammar
are of several kinds: the kernal rules which correspond
roughly to context-free rewriting rules in a phrase-structure
grammar; several types of transformational rules which
convert and combine structures defined by the kernel rules
into a larger set of structures that underlie (in part)
sentences and noun phrases of the language described. By
'structure' I mean a string of symbols which are either
members of the vocabulary of the language or members of a
finite set of labeled brackets. For each syntactic rule we
require that there be a unique translation rule which is a
function from the translations of the input structures to the
translation of the structures obtained by applying the
syntactic rule.

The system differs from classical transformational theory
in several ways:

1. Classical systems define a language as a set of sentences. KT-grammars define a language as a set of sentences

and noun-phrases.

2. Correspondingly, KT-grammars include not only transformations for embedding transforms of sentences into sentences but also transformations for embedding noun-phrases into sentences.

3. KT-grammars supplement the finite vocabularies of classical systems with an infinite set of indexed pro-forms of several types. These pro-forms (which are translated into expressions containing variables in the intensional logic) are used not only for ordinary quantification of noun-phrases (as in PTQ), but also as substituents for other types of embedding rules (like the 'dummy symbols' of Fillmore 1963).

4. The sets of rules of classical grammars (and 'standard' grammars) are finite; those of KT grammars are infinite, since some of the 'rules' are actually rule schemata. That is, I allow rule schemata of the form

$$\ldots \text{ pro-form}_i \ldots$$

where the grammar includes an infinite number of indexed pro-forms, *pro-form*$_1$, *pro-form*$_2$, ... Such a schema then stands for the infinite set of rules gotten by replacing 'i' by some integer. In this respect they are like Montague grammars.

In addition, I allow (but do not use here) conjunction rules which apply to an indefinite number of instances of structures meeting the conditions of the rule. Such rules have been used in informal presentations of the standard theory as well as the classical theory.

I depart from more traditional formulations in several further ways. Rather than defining derivations and several levels of syntactic structure to which rules of interpretation apply, I give direct recursive definitions for the

generated objects, each a pair consisting of a syntactic
structure and its translation. Further differences in details
will be noted below.

Each grammar makes use of a number of different sets of
symbols, of which some are given by the general theory for
every grammar and some are particular to a grammar. The
former includes a finite set of labeled right and left
brackets, including in particular $'[_S'$, $']_S'$, $'[_{NP}'$, $']_{NP}'$,
and two infinite sets of 'meta-variables' which are (i) variables standing for arbitrary strings of symbols and brackets
(including the null string e), and (ii) variables which stand
for arbitrary well-formed labeled bracketings.

The particular vocabularies include a set of kernel-
terminal elements and a partially overlapping set of T-terminal elements, elements which are terminal for the transformational component. The former but not the latter includes an
infinite set of indexed pro-forms of various kinds, including,
in particular, pro-sentences and pro-noun-phrases. I define
the language generated by the grammar as that set of strings
over the T-terminal vocabulary which is obtained by removing
all brackets from the first member of a pair included in the
set of structural descriptions of sentences and noun phrases
(syntactic structure plus translation) defined by the grammar.

In addition, I make use of a suggestion of Partee's (1978)
and define recursively certain properties of expressions of
the syntax for gender, case-marking and verb-morphology. Some
of the rules which do this and spell out the effects are
included in a list set of rules (M-rules) which map the
output of the transformations into well-formed English
sentences.

The grammar will then take the following form:

Lexicon: a listing of lexical items each given with its assignment to a syntactic category and a translation into intensional logic.

Kernel rules: a recursive definition of a set of pairs, the first being a syntactic structure (labeled bracketed string), the second its translation into intensional logic. These are the *kernel structural descriptions*.

Transformations: rules which extend the set of structural descriptions for noun-phrases and sentences. These transformations fall into four types:

Preliminary singulary transformations which apply to simple structural descriptions which underlie kernel sentences and noun-phrases and which apply to embedded structures before they are embedded and to their matrices after embedding.

Embedding transformations which substitute transforms of sentences for various kinds of indexed pro-forms or substitute noun-phrases for indexed pro-noun-phrases.

Conjoining transformations which form coordinate structures or reduce coordinate structures.

Final singulary transformations and morphological rules which are extrinsically ordered and apply after all other rules to map the set of outputs from the previous rules into English sentences.

I shall not give an explicit formalization for the general theory of grammars of this kind (since I think it's too early to make a lot of particular decisions about the general theory). However, the grammar given in the next section is intended to be completely explicit and to be understood as it stands. This aim leads to a rather cumbersome formulation for a number of rules, which could be simplified considerably

if the grammar were embedded, as it should eventually be, in
a general theory of grammars of this kind. I'll point out
places where I think such simplification can be expected to
be possible. I hope that the fragment will meet the objections
of people like Montague and Michael Bennett, who have com-
plained about the inexplicitness of transformational grammars.

2. *A KTG for PTQ.*

The following grammar G is (with the exceptions noted at the
beginning of Section 3) strongly equivalent to PTQ. For the
intensional logic I will simply adopt without change the
language of PTQ, Section 2, and its interpretation.

2.1. *Lexicon.*

The lexicon of G is a set of triples, the first an expression,
the second a category label (to be used to define the set of
labeled brackets), and the third a translation of the expres
sion into the intensional logic. The basic bracket labels for
lexical elements correspond to the basic categories of PTQ
as follows:

G	PTQ
Vi	B_{IV}
N	B_T (!)
Vt	B_{TV}
AvV	B_{IAV}
CN	B_{CN}
AvS	$B_{t/t}$
Prep	$B_{IAV/T}$
Vthat	$B_{IV//t}$
Vto	$B_{IV/IV}$

From the point of view of transformational grammar certain
phrase-types of PTQ are superfluous (for this fragment but not
necessarily for a richer one) and are hence omitted. They are
the phrase types corresponding to Vt, AvS, Prep, Vthat, and
Vto. For all others we include among the bracket labels for
every X on the above list a label KP (corresponding to P_X for
B_X as above). In addition, I use S corresponding to P_t and
Aux with no corresponding category in PTQ.

I will not give a complete lexicon. With the exception of
pronouns (given below) it consists of the set of basic expressions of PTQ, each followed by a label according to the above
table and its translation according to the translation rules
of PTQ (but *that* and *to* are introduced by rules rather than
as part of a basic expression). For example, the lexical entry
for *find* is this:

$$\langle \text{find, Vt, find'} \rangle$$

I use the following indexed pro-NP's (reasons for the
particular choices will be made clear below):

$$\left. \begin{array}{l} \langle \text{her}_{6i} \quad\quad \text{N, } \hat{P} \, P \, \{x_{6i}\} \rangle \\[2mm] \langle \text{him}_{6i + 2}, \text{ N, } \hat{P} \, P \, \{x_{6i + 2}\} \rangle \\[2mm] \langle \text{ it}_{6i + 4}, \text{ N, } \hat{P} \, P \, \{x_{6i + 4}\} \rangle \end{array} \right\} \quad i = 0, 1, 2, \ldots$$

(The individual concept variables introduced in the rules
below will be chosen from the set x, y, x_5, x_7, ...)

In addition to the above variables for individual concepts,
the rules will introduce the following variables:

$$\text{that}_i \quad\quad \text{translated as } p_i \text{ (propositional variables of type}$$
$$\langle \text{s, t} \rangle)$$

$$\left. \begin{array}{l} \text{such}_i \\ \text{to}_i \\ \text{one}_i \end{array} \right\} \quad \text{translated as } q_i \text{ (variables over properties of}$$
$$\text{individual concepts:}$$
$$\langle \text{s, } \langle\langle \text{s, e} \rangle, \text{ t} \rangle\rangle)$$

(These are of the same type as Montague's P, Q, and I'll
assume that they are disjoint from these by letting P, Q,
etc., be indexed by even numbers, the above by disjoint sets
of odd numbers.)

2.2. *Kernel Rules*

The set of *kernel structural descriptions* of G is the smallest
set $SD_K(G)$ defined by the *lexicon* and the rules KR0 - 7.

KR0. If $\langle \alpha, A, \alpha' \rangle$ is in the lexicon of G,
then $\langle [_A \alpha], \alpha' \rangle$ is in $SD_K(G)$.

(This is a general rule for any grammar and would be part of
the definition of a grammar and its language according to a
fully formalized general theory.)

The following rules are part of the particular grammar G.
I will give them in an abbreviated form which can be made
clear by giving the 'official' form of the first rule (it's
easy but tedious to spell out this abbreviation explicitly).
(I omit labels on right brackets when it's clear.[2])

If $\langle [_{AvS} X_1], \ \alpha \rangle \in SD_K(G)$, then $\langle [_S [_{AvS} X_1] \ \text{that}_i],$
$\alpha(p_i) \rangle \in SD_K(G)$.

KR1.

S → AvS that$_i$ $\qquad\qquad\qquad\qquad$ AvS'(p_i)

KR2.

$$
S \ \rightarrow \ NP \ Aux
\begin{cases}
Vip \\
to_{6i + 1}
\end{cases}
\qquad
\begin{array}{l}
\text{(a)} \ NP'(^{\wedge}ViP') \\
\text{(b)} \ NP'(q_{6i + 1})
\end{array}
$$

KR3.

$$\text{ViP} \rightarrow \begin{cases} \text{Vto to to}_{6i+1} \\ \text{Vthat that that}_i \\ \text{Vt NP} \\ \text{Vi} \\ \text{to}_{6i+1} \text{ AvVP} \\ \text{be a CNP} \end{cases}$$

(a) $\text{Vto'}(q_{6i+1})$

(b) $\text{Vthat'}(p_i)$

(c) $\text{Vt'}(^\wedge\text{NP'})$

(d) Vi'

(e) $\text{AvVP'}(q_{6i+1})$

(f) CNP'

KR4.

$$\text{AvVP} \rightarrow \begin{cases} \text{AvV} \\ \text{Prep NP} \end{cases}$$

(a) AvV'

(b) $\text{Prep'}(^\wedge\text{NP'})$

KR5.

$$\text{NP} \rightarrow \begin{cases} \text{NP or NP} \\ \text{N} \\ \begin{cases} \text{every} \\ \text{the} \\ \text{a} \end{cases} \text{CNP} \end{cases}$$

(a) $P[\text{NP}_1'(P) \vee \text{NP}_2(P)]$

(b) N'

(c) $\hat{P} \wedge x [\text{CNP'}(x) \rightarrow P\{x\}]$

(d) $\hat{P} \vee x [\wedge y[\text{CNP'}(y) \leftrightarrow x = y]$ & $P\{x\}]$

(e) $\hat{P} \vee x [\text{CNP'}(x)$ & $P\{x\}]$

KR6.

$$\text{CNP} \rightarrow \begin{cases} \text{CNP such}_{6i+3} \\ \text{one}_{6i+5} \\ \text{CN} \end{cases}$$

(a) $x[\text{CNP'}(x)$ & $q_{6i+3}\{x\}]$

(b) $x[q_{6i+5}\{x\}]$

(c) CN'

KR7.

Aux → Pres   no translation rule

Here and below I assume that improper binding of variables will be avoided by replacing a translation by a logically equivalent one by changing the subscripts on variables which are bound in an expression to be combined with another expression whenever the second expression contains variables (of the same type) with the same subscript. E.g., when we combine an expression ϕ containing a bound variable u with an expression containing u_i (free or bound), we change the first expression ϕ by substituting u_m for u_i throughout ϕ

where m is the least odd or even integer such that u_m occurs in neither expression, according as i is odd or even and $m = i$ (modulo 6). Details of the rules will be commented on below in Section 2.4.

2.3. *Transformations*.

The transformations will be given in an explicit form. The only abbreviations will be these.

(1) In place of '$[_A \, W_i \,]_A$' (where W_i is a variable over well-formed labeled bracketings) I will write 'A_i' (without subscript if only one such variable with a given bracket label occurs).

(2) I will use numbered curly braces to abbreviate sets of partially similar rules in a way that is familiar in the linguistic literature:

$$\cdots \quad \left\{ \begin{matrix} X \\ Y \\ _i \, Z \end{matrix} \right\}_i \quad \cdots \quad \left\{ \begin{matrix} A \\ B \\ _i \, C \end{matrix} \right\}_i \quad \cdots$$

abbreviates the three rules or statements

$$\cdots \, X \, \cdots \, A \, \cdots$$
$$\cdots \, Y \, \cdots \, B \, \cdots$$
$$\cdots \, Z \, \cdots \, C \, \cdots$$

(3) pro_i is an abbreviation for

$$\left\{ \begin{matrix} him_i \\ her_i \\ _j \, it_i \end{matrix} \right\}_j$$

Readers of the linguistic literature should be warned that the formalism departs from the usual formalism in this respect: When we have a rule starting 'If $\langle \, [_S \, A \, B \, X], \, \alpha \rangle$ is

in SD(G)' where A, B are bracket labels or brackets or
constants, then the description is not met by any labeled
bracketed strings in which something, even only brackets,
separates A and B. (I relax this somewhat in the M-rules.)

(4) X, X_1, X_2, ... are 'meta-variables' standing for
arbitrary strings of elements and brackets and W, W_1, W_2, ...
are variables for arbitrary well-formed labeled bracketed
strings.

Finally, I assume throughout a general convention by which
the structure appearing in the then-clause of a rule is to
be the reduction of the structure actually given (see Peters
and Richie 1973a), that is the result of applying the
following reduction *red* until no longer applicable:

1. *red* ($[_A \ ]_A$) = e (the empty string)
2. *red* ($[_A[_AW]_A]_A = [_AW]_A$) (where W is as usual
a well-formed labeled
bracketing).

By (1) we eliminate 'empty brackets'; by (2) we eliminate
redundant labeled brackets.

The set of transformationally extended structural descriptions of G is the smallest set $SD(G)$ such that its membership
follows from T0 - 12 and M1 - 10.

T0. If $\langle [_{NP} X], \alpha \rangle$ is in $SD_K(G)$, then it is in $SD(G)$ also.

If $\langle [_S X], \phi \rangle$ is in $SD_K(G)$, then it is in $SD(G)$ also.

(Again, this is to be part of the general theory of KT-
grammars. This rule says that every kernel NP or S structure
is also in the set to be transformationally extended.)

2.31. *Preliminary Singulary Transformation*

T1. Future tense:

If $\langle [_S$ NP $[_{Aux}$ Pres$]$ ViP$]$, $\phi \rangle \in$ SD(G), then

$\langle [_S$ NP $[_{Aux}$ will$]$ ViP$]$, W $\phi \rangle \in$ SD(G).

T2. Perfect tense:

If $\langle [_S$ NP $[_{Aux}$ Pres ViP$]$, $\phi \rangle \in$ SD(G), then

$\langle [_S$ NP $[_{Aux}$ Pres have$]$ ViP$]$, H $\phi \rangle \in$ SD(G).

T3. Negative:

If $\langle [_S$ NP Aux ViP$]$, $\phi \rangle \in$ SD(G), then

$\langle [_S$ NP Aux not ViP$]$, $\neg$ $\phi \rangle \in$ SD(G).

T4. Pronominalization (obligatory):

If $\langle [_S$ X$_1$ pro$_i$ X$_2$ pro$_i$ X$_3]$, $\phi \rangle \in$ SD(G)

$\langle [_S$ X pro$_i$ X$_2$ pro X$_3]$, $\phi \rangle \in$ SD(G)

where *pro* is *him* if *pro$_i$* is *him$_t$*

her if *pro$_t$* is *her$_i$*

it if *pro$_i$* is *it$_i$*.

This rule is assumed to iterate until no longer applicable.

2.32. *Embedding Rules*

For the purposes of the embedding transformations, I assume
the following recursive definition of *gender*:

1. *man, John, Bill, him$_i$* are Masculine.
2. *woman, Mary, her$_i$* are Feminine.
3. *it$_i$* and all other members of CN are Neuter.
4. Let α range over Masculine, Feminine, or Neuter.

   If X$_1$ is α, so are
   (i) $[_{CN}$ X$_1]$

(ii) $[_{CNP}[_{CN} X_1]]$

(iii) $[_{CNP}[_{CNP}X_1] X_2]$ (where the whole thing is a well-formed lb)

(iv) $[_{NP} X_2 [_{CNP} X_1]]$ (where the whole thing is a well-formed lb)

(v) $[_N X_1]$

(vi) $[_{NP} X_1]$.

(I leave unsettled the question of the status of phrases like *John or Mary*.) If two expressions are both Masculine, Feminine, or Neuter, we say that they *agree in gender*.

T5. *That*-embedding:

(a) If $\langle [_S \text{AvS that}_i], \phi \rangle$ and $\langle S, \psi \rangle \in SD(G)$

then $\langle [_S \text{AvS S}], \lambda p_i \phi (^\wedge\psi) \rangle \in SD(G)$.

(b) If $\langle [_S \text{NP} [_{Aux} \text{Pres}] [_{ViP} \text{Vthat that that}_i]], \phi \rangle$

and $\langle S, \psi \rangle \in SD(G)$,

then $\langle [_S \text{NP} [_{Aux} \text{Pres}] [_{ViP} \text{Vthat that S}]]$,

$\lambda p_i \phi (^\wedge\psi) \rangle \in SD(G)$.

T6. *To*-embedding:

(a) If $\langle [_S \text{NP} [_{Aux} \text{Pres}] \text{to}_i], \phi \rangle$ and

$\langle [_S[_{NP}[_N \text{pro}_j]] [_{Aux} \text{Pres}] \text{ViP}], \psi \rangle \in SD(G)$

then $\langle [_S \text{NP} [_{Aux} \text{Pres}] \text{ViP}], \lambda q_i \phi (\hat{x}_j \psi) \rangle$

$\in SD(G)$ where *NP* and *pro$_j$* agree in gender.

(b) If $\langle [_S \text{NP} [_{Aux} \text{Pres}] [_{ViP} \text{Vto to to}_i]], \phi \rangle$ and

(second member as in (a)) $\in SD(G)$

then $\langle [_S$ NP $[_{Aux}$ Pres$]$ $[_{ViP}$ Vto to ViP$]$ $]$,

λ q_i ϕ $(\hat{x}_j$ $\psi))\in SD(G)$ where *NP* and *pro$_j$* agree

in gender.

(c) If $\langle [_S$ NP $[_{Aux}$ Pres$]$ $[_{ViP}$ to$_i$ AvS$]$ $]$, $\phi\rangle$ and

(second member as in (a)) $\in$ SD(G)

then $\langle [_S$ NP $[_{Aux}$ Pres$]$ $[_{ViP}$ ViP AvS$]$ $]$,

λ q_i ϕ $(\hat{x}_j$ $\psi))$ $\in$ SD(G) where *NP* and *pro$_j$*

agree in gender.

T7. Relative clause:

If $\langle [_A$ X$_1$ $[_{CNP}$ CNP such$_1]$ X$_2]$, $\phi\rangle$ and

$\langle [_S$ X$_3$ pro$_j$ X$_4]$, $\phi\rangle$ $\in$ SD(G)

where A = NP or S; and *pro$_j$* and *CNP* agree in gender

then $\langle [_A$ X$_1$ $[_{CNP}$ CNP such that $[_S$ X$_3$ pro X$_4]$ $]$ X$_2]$,

λq_1 ϕ $(\hat{x}_j$ $\psi))$ $\in$ SD(G) (and *pro* is as in T4).

T8. *One*-embedding:

If $\langle [_A$ X$_1$ one$_i$ X$_2]$, $\phi\rangle$ and $\langle [_S[_{NP}[_N$ pro$_j]$ $]$

$[_{Aux}$ Pres$]$ $[_{VP}$ be a CNP$]$ $]$, $\psi\rangle$ $\in$ SD(G)

where A = S or NP

then $\langle [_A$ X$_1$ CNP X$_2]$, λ q_i ϕ $(\hat{x}_j$ $\psi))$ $\in$ SD(G).

T9. Quantification:

If $\langle [_S$ X$_1$ pro$_i$ X$_2]$, $\phi\rangle$ and $\langle$NP, $\alpha\rangle$ $\in$ SD(G)

then $\langle [_S$ X$_1$ NP X$_2]$, α $(\hat{x}_i$ $\phi))\rangle$ $\in$ SD(G).

I require (as part of the definition of a KTG and its
operation) the following general conventions on generalized
transformations involving subscripted pro-forms:

Uniqueness convention: If an embedding transformation mentions one or more indexed pro-forms, then it is defined only for structures satisfying the rule in a unique way (that is for particular choice of i there can be only one occurrence of *pro-form$_i$* in the input structures).

This convention ensures that T4 must have been iterated exhaustively on an input structure before it is available for embedding into a structure by T6 (*to*-embedding), T7 (relative clause), or T8 (*one*-embedding) or before an NP can be embedded into it by T9 (quantification). It also ensures that one and only one occurrence of a given *that$_i$*, *to$_i$*, *such$_i$*, or *one$_i$* will be contained in the matrix for the embedding rules involving these pro-forms.

2.33. *Rules of conjunction and disjunction* (CT)

T10. *And*-conjunction:

If $\langle S_1, \phi \rangle$ and $\langle S_2, \psi \rangle \in SD(G)$
then $\langle [_S S_1$ and $S_2], \phi \wedge \psi \rangle \in SD(G)$.

T11. *Or*-conjunction:

Same as T9 but with *or* and $\vee$ replacing *and* and $\wedge$, respectively.

T12. Conjunction reduction (ViP conjunction):

If $\langle [_S[_S[_{NP}[_N pro_i]] [_{Aux} Pres] ViP_1$

$\left\{ \begin{matrix} and \\ or \end{matrix} \right\}_1$ $[_S[_{NP}[_N pro_i]] [_{Aux} Pres] ViP_2]], \phi \rangle$

$\in SD(G)$

then $\langle [_S[_{NP}[_N pro_i]] [_{Aux} Pres] [_{ViP} ViP_1 \left\{ \begin{matrix} and \\ or \end{matrix} \right\}_1$

$ViP_2]], \phi \rangle \in SD(G)$.

2.34. Final Singulary Transformations and Morphological Rules.

These rules deal primarily with getting the forms of pronouns
and the verbs to come out right. Again I make use of certain
recursively defined properties of expressions. Since these
rules deal with government, i.e., properties determined by
the external environment of the expressions in question, the
recursive definitions work 'top-to-bottom.'

M1. Nominative case marking:

If NP occurs in the environment: $[_S \ X_2 \ \rule{1cm}{0.4pt} \ X_3]$,
where $X_2 = e$ or *AvS*
then NP is Nominative.

M2. Finite verb marking:

If ViP occurs in the environment: $[_S \ X_2 \ [_{Aux} \ Pres]$
$\rule{1cm}{0.4pt} \ X_3]$,
then ViP is Third Person Singular Present and Pres
is deleted.

M3. Past participle marking:

If ViP occurs in the environment: $[_S \ X_2 \ have]_{Aux} \ (not)$
$\rule{1cm}{0.4pt} \ X_3]$,
then ViP is Past Participial.

M4. Property spreading:

(a) Let A = NP or VP and α = Nominative, Third Person
Singular Present, or Past Participial.
If $[_A \ A_1 \ \left\{ \begin{matrix} or \\ and \end{matrix} \right\} \ A_2]$ is α, so are A_1 and A_2.

(b) If $[_{NP} \ N]$ is α, so is N.

(c) If $[_{ViP} \ ViP \ AvVP]$ is α, so is ViP.

(d) If $[_{ViP}$ Vx X$_2$] is α, so is Vx where Vx = Vi, Vt, Vthat, Vto, or b.

M5. $[_S$ X$_1$ $[_{Aux}$ Pres] (not) X$_2$ be X$_3$] $\rightarrow$

$[_S$ X$_1$ $[_{Aux}$ be] (not) X$_2$ X$_3$]

when X_2 is a string of brackets.

M6. Do-support:

$[_S$ X$_1$ $[_{Aux}$ Pres] X$_2$] $\rightarrow$ $[_S$ X$_1$ $[_{Aux}$ Pres do] X$_2$]

M7. Have/do/be morphology:

Pres have $\rightarrow$ has
Pres do $\rightarrow$ does

M8. Pronoun morphology:

The Nominative forms of *her*, *him*, *her$_i$*, *him$_i$* are *she*, *he*, *she$_i$*, and *he$_i$*, respectively.

M9. Verb morphology:

(a) The Third Person Singular Present form of *be* is *is*; otherwise it is αs when α is in Vt, Vi, Vthat, Vto.

(b) The Past participial forms of *run, rise, find, lose, eat, be* are *run, risen, found, lost, eaten, been,* respectively; for all other members α of *Vt, Vi, Vthat, Vto* it is αd if α ends on a vowel; otherwise it is αed.

M10. *a/an* alternation:

a $\rightarrow$ an in the environment of a following vowel (this is a morphological rule applying to the morpheme 'a').

2.4. *Comments on the Grammar*

Lexicon. The basic form of pronouns is taken to be the non-nominative or objective form in line with what seems to be the correct and simplest treatment of English. Note that extending the grammar to cover other constructions will still give us the right forms (for colloquial English).

Syntactically distinct pro-forms of the same semantic type are given disjoint indices in order to make the statement of the rules simpler. Note, for example, that this device ensures that the uniqueness condition on embedding rules (a syntactic condition) has the consequence that the lambda-abstraction in the translation will never bind the translation of a syntactically different expression. For example, although *one$_i$* and *such$_j$* are of the same semantic type, a rule embedding for one will never 'catch' a translation of the other.

KR-rules. Some of the peculiar-looking rules are included to make sure we get a grammar as closely equivalent to PTQ as possible. Classical grammars did not treat in any detail some of the constructions included here, and the theory was somewhat equivocal (at least in practice) as to whether the set of kernel structures was to be finite or not. Our grammar would define a finite kernel language save for the inclusion of case (a) of KR5 (disjunction of NP's). This is necessary if we are to get the 'direct generation' reading of sentences like *John seeks Mary or Bill.*

The only substantive innovation is contained in KR3 (f), which provides a new translation for sentences like *John is a fish*: j*(^fish'). I have not provided any NP structure for the predicate nominal because it doesn't make any difference here (and I'm not too sure we need it in general, since predicate nominals are notoriously un-NP-like). It seems to

me likely that something like this treatment of *be* is required
for adjectives anyway, as a number of writers have suggested
(e.g., Lee 1974). This rule is required to get the effects of
common-noun quantification into the grammar (via *one*-embed-
ding). It is perfectly possible to write a rule within our
formalism that will assign an NP structure to the predicate
nominal, namely this:

$$\text{If } \langle \text{CNP}, \alpha \rangle \in SD_K(G),$$
$$\text{then } \langle [_{ViP} \text{ be } [_{NP} \text{ a CNP}] \ ], \alpha \rangle \in SD_K(G).$$

This shows that our formalism allows rules not statable in
the form of phrase-structure rules although the effect of the
rule could be achieved if the kernel rules were allowed to be
context-sensitive (an option usually deemed necessary in
classical grammars).

Transformations. The rules are stated in a detailed enough
fashion that certain orders of application are excluded
simply by the form of the rules. The following points are
worth noting:

T1 - 3 (the meaning-changing singulary transformations) are
stated in such a way that they can only apply to a simple
sentence before it is embedded or conjoined (except for the
case where T12 [conjunction reduction] has reduced a sentence
to a form in which there is a single *Pres*). This ensures that
we get the same relationships of scope for the sentential
operators ¬, W, H, and *necessarily* as in PTQ (with *necessarily* always outside the operators).

T5 - 6 (*that-* and *to*-embedding are stated in such a way
that embedding must take place before any of T1 - 3 can apply
to the matrix. This brings about for these rules an order of
application postulated as correct by Fillmore (1963) and for

which some evidence can be given. On the other hand T7 (relative clause) and T8 (*one*-embedding) as stated could be applied at any time subject only to the requirement (from the uniqueness condition) that if the second structure (the constituent) contains several like-indexed pro's, they must undergo T4 (pronominalization) before the rule can apply, and in the case of relative clauses, T1 - 3, and T5 and T6, cannot apply to a relative clause after it is embedded.

However, it is not the case that all and only the correct orders of application follow from the rules (I mean correct in the sense of getting a grammar equivalent to PTQ). For example, without some extrinsic ordering constraints it would be possible to form a future tense, then quantify in, then do negation, thus obtaining a translation for a sentence like the following not available from PTQ:

Every unicorn will not walk

$\neg$ [every unicorn' ($\hat{x}$ [W(walk' (x)]])]

I will thus assume that the rules are ordered in blocks (as in Fillmore's 1963 theory) at least in such a way that the PST must apply one after the other (if applied) before a sentence is subject to quantification and that after quantification a sentence cannot undergo the PST again unless by virtue of its being embedded in a larger structure (where only T4 might affect it). I have already stated that the M-rules are extrinsically ordered to apply after all others (and must themselves apply in the order given).

3. *Comparison of PTQ and G.*

In this section I will first discuss the relationship between the two grammars as far as their strong generative capacity (here: pairings of strings and translations) is concerned, then some general differences between the two models.

3.1. *Strong Equivalence.*

The language of G is the same as the members of P_t and P_T and the two grammars are strongly equivalent with the following exceptions:

1. $L(G)$ contains no strings with indexed pro-forms, that is, $L(G)$ is the set of *English* sentences and noun-phrases in P_t and P_T. This is because the indexed pro-forms are not in the T-terminal vocabulary of the grammar and hence by definition no strings containing them are either.

2. G does not assign readings to sentences or noun-phrases corresponding to vacuous applications of the rule S14, S15, S16 (quantification) in PTQ. This follows because the relevant rules are not functions from all members of the sets of expressions P_t, P_{CN}, and P_{IV} but only from the subset of these expressions which contain appropriate indexed pro-forms.

3. Similarly, $L(G)$ does not contain any sentences with relative clauses containing no pronouns such as *John loves a woman such that Bill is a fish.* This is so for the reason given under (2).

4. G makes available a reading for sentences like the following that is not available from PTQ:

Every woman does not love her (= herself).

By PTQ this can come only by quantifying in *every woman* (S14). Hence, there is no reading under which the negation operator is outside the scope of the subject NP, that is, no translation corresponding to the more natural English rendition *Not every woman loves herself* (cf. Partee 1975: and for some discussion Bach 1976, and below, Section 4.4).

5. The use of recursive properties of expressions in the M-rules makes it possible to correct two mistakes in PTQ. (i) My rules will get the right forms of verbs in conjoined verb phrases, and distinguish two structures in examples like these (see Bennett 1974):

> John walks and talks. (PTQ: John walks or talks.)
> John tries to walk and talk.
> John tries to walk and talks.

(ii) My rules will distribute the correct case forms of pronouns in disjoined NP's where PTQ incorrectly gives phrases like *see Mary or he*, *see Mary or he*₃ (Barbara Partee pointed out this error to me).

6. The dual treatment of *be* given here provides alternative readings for some sentences of PTQ. Although this detail was included primarily to allow the grammar to capture the results of common-noun quantification by S15 without getting some unwanted results (see discussion of *one*-embedding below), it does, I believe, have some independent justification. Although most sentences with *be* in PTQ will, by meaning postulate (2) (PTQ, p. 263), turn out to be equivalent to our translation, it seems to me that there is a sense of predicational sentences like *John is a fish* different from the one given by PTQ: 'there's a fish that John is identical with.' Notice the sentence *John wants to be a fish and eat it* which can arise by quantification into predicate nominal position in PTQ (and *G*). At best it seems to me that this sentence is peculiar and that its translation fits only one of the senses of the copular sentence *John is a fish*. Note further that PTQ (and *G*) allows a peculiar reading for *John isn't a fish* 'there's a fish that John isn't.' *G* allows the derivation of copular sentences which do not permit quantification into

the predicate nominal position. It seems to me doubtful that if Montague had been a native speaker of almost any language but English he would have treated *be* as a transitive verb.

With these exceptions, then, G bears the following relationship to PTQ.

I. $\langle X, \phi \rangle$ is a terminal structural description of G if and only if the debracketization of X, $d(X)$, is in P_t or P_T and there is a derivation from PTQ that assigns the translation ϕ (or a logically equivalent one) to $d(X)$.

Let's note first that there is no disambiguated language in this model, since we can have several different translations for the same syntactic structure. We can, however, borrow the notion of a transformation-marker from classical transformational theory and use the T-markers of a sentence as a disambiguated language for showing equivalence.

Let's define a *(generalized) T-marker* as a tree rooted in a terminal structural description of either a sentence or a noun-phrase, whose leaves are structures gotten from the lexicon by using rule KRO, and each subtree defined as follows: If a derivation uses a particular rule, then let the result of applying the rule be a tree whose root is the structural description corresponding to the *then* part of the rule, and whose immediate branches are the structural description(s) corresponding to the *if* part. For example, the T-marker for the simplest derivation of *John loves Mary* is shown below. (I call this structure a 'generalized' T-marker because it differs from the classical notion, which was a tree whose leaves were K-terminal structures and which included no information about the translation.)

$[_S[_{NP}[_N$ John]] $[_{ViP}$ $[_{Vt}$ loves] $[_{NP}[_N$ Mary]]]], j*($^\wedge$love($^\wedge$m*))

|

M-rules

|

$[_S[_{NP}[_N$ John]] $[_{Aux}$ Pres] $[_{ViP}[_{Vt}$ love]

$[_{NP}[_N$ Mary]]]], j*($^\wedge$love($^\wedge$m*))

|

$[_S[_{NP}[_N$ John]] Aux $[_{ViP}[_{Vt}$ love] $[_{NP}[_N$ Mary]]]],

j($^\wedge$love($^\wedge$m))

$[_{NP}[_N$ John]], j* $[_{ViP}[_{Vt}$ love] $[_{NP}[_N$ Mary]]], love' ($^\wedge$m*)

|

$[_N$ John], j* $[_{Vt}$ love] $[_{NP}[_N$ Mary]], m*

|

$[_N$ Mary], m*

The proof of (I) goes like this: It can be shown that every T-marker determines a unique terminal structural description. We define a mapping from T-markers into analysis trees which takes place in several stages:

(i) Given a T-marker *t*, we construct a T-marker *t'* which is just like *t* except that in place of branches rooted by S-structures and immediately dominated by structures that result from embedding for *one$_i$* or *to$_i$* we have branches containing CNP or ViP structures in place of the original S-structures. This T-marker is a T-marker that would have resulted from a grammar which embedded CNP's and ViP's and which contained quantification rules for getting NP's into those structures and which included such structures in the extended set of structural descriptions SD(G). For example,

a branch schematically represented as (a) will be mapped into
a branch of the form (b):

a.   [John Pres Vto to ViP], $\lambda q_1 \; \phi(\hat{x}_4 \; [\alpha[\hat{x}_j \; \psi])$

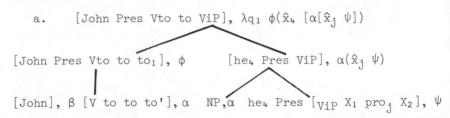

[John Pres Vto to to_1], ϕ [he₄ Pres ViP], $\alpha(\hat{x}_j \; \psi)$

[John], β [V to to to'], α NP,α he₄ Pres [$_{ViP}$ X₁ pro$_j$ X₂], ψ

b.   [John Pres Vto to ViP], $\lambda q_1 \; \phi(\hat{x}_4 \; [\; [\alpha \; [x_j \; \psi])$

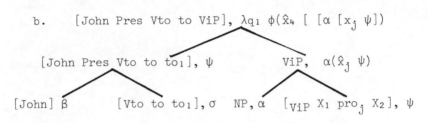

[John Pres Vto to to_1], ψ ViP, $\alpha(\hat{x}_j \; \psi)$

[John] β [Vto to to_1], σ NP, α [$_{ViP}$ X₁ pro$_j$ X₂], ψ

(ii) We then define a second mapping which converts the
results of (i) into a new set of T-markers which are just
like the old ones, but wherever we have a subtree dominated
by a structure resulting from embedding for *that$_i$*, *to$_i$*,
such$_i$, or *one$_i$*, we form a branch which results from replacing
the syntactic *pro-form$_i$* by the embedded structure throughout
the branch corresponding to the matrix and changing the new
leaves involving Vthat, AvVS, Vto, etc. to branches of the
form

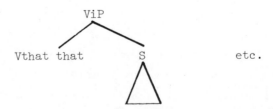

and deleting the branch for the embedded structures. To
continue the above example, this mapping will give the tree
(c) (leaving out the translations).

c.

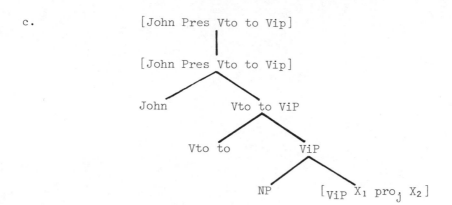

We now have a T-marker which would result from a grammar
with no embedding rules except quantification (into S, CNP,
ViP) (such a grammar, which is not exactly a KT-grammar, is
given in Appendix B). Moreover, the T-marker is a refinement
of the analysis tree from PTQ that the mapping will produce.

The chief complication in step (ii) involves making sure
that a free variable pronoun occurring in the embedded
structure does not get 'caught' accidentally by a quantification which has occurred in the matrix structure. To prevent
this (and we can always tell if it is going to happen) we
replace all pro_i's which have been bound in the matrix by
pro_n's where n is the least integer $= i$ (modulo 6) such that
pro_n occurs in neither the matrix structure nor the embedded
structure.

(iii) It is now possible to map the result of (ii) into
an analysis tree. The mapping is straightforward (let the map
of each node expression be the debracketization of the first
member of the pair, followed by the appropriate number for
Montague's syntactic functions, which is completely recover-
able from the form of the immediate branches). For the sample
T-marker given at the beginning of this discussion we would
have

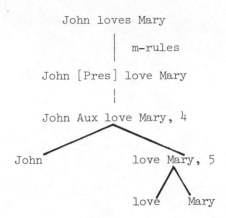

This leaves us with some single-branched subtrees resulting from pronominalization and the rules for tense and negation. The former will be of the form:

$$[X_1 \ pro_i \ Y \ pro \ \ldots \ pro \ \ Z]$$

$$[X_1 \ pro \ \ Y \ pro_i \ \ldots \ pro_i \ Z]$$

and occur immediately dominated by a node resulting either from quantification or relative clause formation. For these, we erase the upper structures in the single branched subtree.

Results of T1 - 3 will be single-branched structures like these:

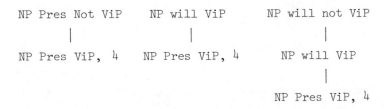

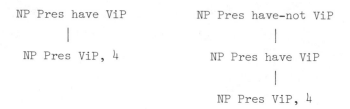

These we replace by the debracketization of the result of
applying Ml - 10 to the first member of the top structure and
write down the numbers 11, 12, 13, 14, and 15 respectively to
the right. Finally, we delete all nodes which have no numbers
with them except for the leaves (the basic expressions) and
connect the lines thus lopped.

The result of this mapping will be an analysis tree, and
PTQ will assign to it a translation which is logically equivalent to the translation given by G to the original T-marker
(with the exceptions noted above). This will be so because
the embedding rules for $such_i$, $that_i$, one_i, to_i all involve
lambda abstraction over a variable for senses of expressions
applied to the sense of the expression translating the
embedded structure.

The conversion c from M-trees to T-markers is an analogous
process which takes subtrees of an analysis tree involving
rules S3, S8, S10, S12, S15, S16 and constructs appropriate
branches from (let us say) the next higher node which involves
the rules that derive members of P_t and replaces the part of
the original string corresponding to the structure embedded
by an appropriate syntactic variable. Finally, labeled
brackets are added to the string in a way that is completely
determinate.

One difference between the two grammars lies in the
build-up of relative clauses. Although there will always be
a derivation from G of a sentence containing several relative

clauses in one common noun phrase that corresponds to the
'bottom-to-top' build-up of PTQ, the grammar will also allow
all permutations of the relative clauses to be derived for
the same translation (but because of the logical equivalence
of $p \& q$ and $q \& p$ the results will all be logically equivalent). If there is some semantic or implicative difference
between these different phrases (as I believe there is) then
this result must be considered a defect in G. I can think of
various brute-force solutions but no very good general
principle that might be adopted in the general theory. (E.g.,
we can build into the rule a condition to ensure embedding
from left to right.)

3.2. *Montague Grammars, KT-Grammars, C-Grammars, and I-Grammars.*

In this section I will make some general remarks about the
general frameworks illustrated by PTQ, G, and the two
'standard'-derived transformational grammars given in Cooper
and Parsons 1976.[3]

   (i) In common with other transformational frameworks, the
model explored here incorporates the hypothesis that significant generalizations about natural languages can best be
captured by describing an abstract language that is mapped
into the 'real' language by certain obligatory rules. This
feature has been exploited here, rather minimally, in the
treatment of tense and the use of late rules of a primarily
morphological nature. In Section 4.4 I will take up a suggestion for treating negation in a more abstract way.

   Montague's general theory as given in "Universal Grammar"
allows for this possibility (Partee forthcoming) and apparently
one could mimic G with a Montague grammar in which my M-rules
are part of the relation R and the language of T-markers is

the disambiguated language which is the domain of R. On the
other hand, the model violates the well-formedness constraint
of Partee (forthcoming), but in a fairly limited way. Motivation
for the particulars of the grammar must largely come from extending the grammar to accommodate richer fragments of English.
For example, the treatment of the Auxiliary in G (or the
fuller treatment traditional since Chomsky 1957) can be
motivated by the success with which it dovetails with a
treatment of questions and other sentences involving inversion.

However, the particularization of Montague's general theory
illustrated by PTQ has the feature that all morphological
details are built into the syntactic functions (and thus the
fragment meets Partee's constraint except for the presence
of the abstract forms he_i and him_i). One could motivate the
choice of objective base forms for pronouns on the basis of
predictive power even within PTQ. If one extended the
fragment to include double-object verbs like *give*, topi-
calized and clefted sentences, etc., the grammar would then
make the right predictions (*give it to her*; *give him it*;
Him, I saw yesterday, etc.), but the generalizations about
the form of English pronouns given in my M-rules would still
be splintered across six rules (S4 and the five functions
of S17). Additions of other tenses to PTQ would carry along
no predictions. Put another way, there would be no reason
even with this modified PTQ to expect that English should be
the way it is rather than, say, requiring the distribution
of pronouns in the following strings:

> he walks
> him will walk
> he will not walk
> he has walked

him has not walked

his does not walk

Questions of this sort have been discussed in the transformational linguistic literature largely under the heading 'explanatory adequacy.' They have not, so far, been treated in discussions of Montague grammar.[4]

(ii) Classical transformational grammar accorded special status to the sentence and implicitly carried with it the claim that a language could best be described as a system in which rules of a structure-dependent sort built up complicated structures from the structures underlying simple sentences. Many logicians and philosophers since Frege have accepted the idea that the logical structures of languages (artificial or natural) can best be understood by taking open sentences containing variable elements as well as closed sentences to be necessary building blocks. Transformational linguists (McCawley 1971; Bach 1968) originally incorporated Frege's insight at a time when the theory had developed the idea (not in the classical theory) that every sentence had some underlying 'deep structure' of a very abstract sort that was more or less directly related to a representation of the logical form of the sentence. More recently, Chomsky (1975; 1976) and others have been incorporating the insight by constructing rules which go from an enriched 'surface structure' to a representation of logical form (Cooper and Parson's C-grammar is like the former development, their I-grammar like the latter, but without 'traces'). Montague grammar and classical transformational grammar both incorporate the notion that part of how we represent the meaning of a sentence is by means of a representation of the order in which it is derived rather than by means of some structural configuration. Montague used this device in PTQ to represent quantificational

scope differences (this derives from Frege also; see Dummett
1973). Moreover, his treatment of term-phrases as representing
sets of properties allowed him to treat English sentences in
a way that did justice to the integrity of the noun-phrase as
a basic syntactic and semantic element in the construction
of sentences. But transformational theory did not use this
device to account for quantificational facts. The extension
of the classical theory illustrated here unites these two
historically quite different traditions, one derived from
Frege, the other ultimately from historical linguistics (see
Chomsky 1975a [1955]: Introduction).

The extension of classical theory made here singles out
noun-phrases and sentences as having a special status for
the purposes of building complex structures and for representing complex logical forms. Barbara Partee has pointed out to
me that these two categories correspond to the two categories
that Frege considered to be the only complete expressions of
a language: names and sentences. There are a number of respects in which these two categories seem to have a special
status. As far as I know, every natural language does have
these two syntactic categories, and it is hard to imagine a
natural language that would not. (An example of an unnatural
language that doesn't is given in Quine 1966: Ch. 23.) The
two categories are related in an intimate way to two necessary uses of language: to refer to objects and to make
statements that can be true or false. Moreover, I believe
that although native speakers of language do not in general
have very firm intuitions about the syntactic structure of
sentences in any very fine-grained way, they do have clear
intuitions about what pieces of sentences are noun-phrases
and what sentences and noun-phrases are well-formed, and this

is so because these are the two categories that can be used
alone in a relatively context-free way as complete utterances.

The use of sentence transforms to form VP-complements
(required by the general theory) represents an interesting
empirical hypothesis. Analyses like that of PTQ (with direct
recursion on VP) have been developed in post-*Aspects* versions
of transformational grammar (Brame 1976). Avery Andrews (1976)
has argued that in Icelandic, VP complements should be derived
from sentences and has suggested that general linguistic
theory should be constrained in such a way as to require this
result. It should be made clear that his hypothesis predicts
that no language will be found in which evidence can be
found against such an analysis and is quite consistent with
the fact (if it is a fact) that languages exist for which
there is no direct evidence *for* a derivation of VP's from
sentences (English may be such a language).

(iii) Standard transformational theories and their derivatives have made the assumption that the relation between
syntax and semantics is to be made via a set of rules relating
syntactic structures.at some level to representations of
semantic structure. Both of the grammars in Cooper and
Parson's paper use this configurational approach. The fragment given here shows that the older model can be used along
with a conception of the relation that is based on relationships between syntactic rules and translation rules instead.

(iv) Finally, it can be shown that the classical theory
is mathematically less powerful than the standard theory and
its derivatives. Thus there is some independent reason for
choosing to work within this framework rather than the more
recent versions of the theory. What I hope to have accomplished so far in this paper is to have shown that an
interesting and intuitively satisfying theory of syntax can

readily be extended to incorporate a rigorous and beautiful
semantic theory.

4. *Some Extensions of G*

4.1. *Variables.*

Suppose we add to G the rule (in the PST) (I'll give rules
schematically in this section):

   T105. *Pro-form desubscripting*

$$X \text{ pro-form}_i \ Y \text{ pro-form}_i \ Z \rightarrow X \text{ pro-form}_i \ Y \text{ pro-form } Z$$

where pro-form$_i$ stands for
$$\left\{ \begin{array}{l} \text{that}_i \\ \text{to}_i \\ \text{such}_i \\ _1 \text{ one}_i \end{array} \right\}_1$$

and *pro-form* stands for
$$\left\{ \begin{array}{l} \left\{ \begin{array}{ll} \text{that}_i & \text{if Y ends on} \\ & \textit{necessarily} \\ \text{it} & \text{otherwise} \end{array} \right\} \\ e \\ e \\ _1 \quad \text{one} \end{array} \right\}_1$$

and add to the M-rules the rule *a one → one*.

   Suppose further that we change the rules for *that*-embedding
and *to*-embedding to a more general form by adding X_1 and X_2
to the *if*-part of each rule inside the end brackets for the
matrix and changing [$_{Aux}$ Pres] to Aux. Now these rules will
be able to apply at any level of embedding. G will now
generate sentences like these:

   1. Mary asserts that Bill is a fish and John believes it.

2. Mary wants to date a unicorn or a fish and Bill

$$\left\{ \begin{array}{l} \text{does not} \\ \text{wants to} \\ \text{does not want to} \end{array} \right\}$$

3. Bill has seen a woman such that she walks and Mary has seen a man (= who walks).

4. John knows a woman such that she is a fish and Bill has seen one such that she walks.

(Actually, I'm cheating on the last example, since one_i is undefined for gender. If we let it be *any* gender, then the grammar will generate not only 4 but also a similar sentence with the second *she* replaced by *he* or *it*.)

We could also consider the possibility of letting the pro-form of $such_i$ be *such*, adding rules to get *such a CNP* from *a CNP such*, deleting it elsewhere and get sentences like (5):

5. John knows a man such that he walks and Bill knows such a woman.

(But Muffy Siegel and Greg Carlson have led me to be very suspicious of my treatment of *such*.)

I don't want to enter into an extended discussion of such examples in this paper (for some arguments *for* this treatment of VP's see Bach 1976). All I want to suggest, primarily to transformational linguists, is that the model used here shares with Montague grammar the possibility of treating various kinds of anaphora as direct reflexes of syntactic variables. Transformational grammarians have argued endlessly about whether such phenomena (of one or another kind) should be handled by deletion rules or interpretive rules. There are arguments against each position. Deletion rules have problems involving so-called sloppy identity. Interpretive rules have problems because various extra material gets left around (e.g., *Mary was seen by the police but Bill wasn't En by*). Maybe both positions are wrong.

4.2. *Gender*.

I'm not at all sure that the syntactic treatment of gender given in G or any syntactic treatment of gender in English can be defended (cf. Chapter 3 of Cooper 1975). The necessity to get gender straight in G requires an extremely cumbersome formulation of various rules (notably *to* embedding). I understand that Lauri Karttunen wants to treat English gender as part of conventional implicature. If this were done we could simplify our grammar greatly. The rules for *to*-embedding and relative clauses could look like this:

T6'. $\left.\begin{array}{l} X_1 \text{ to}_i \ Y \\ \\ \text{pro}_i \text{ Pres ViP} \end{array}\right\} \Rightarrow X_1 \text{ ViP } Y$ (where we understand the parentheses as linked)

T7'. $\left.\begin{array}{l} X_1 \text{ such}_i \ X_2 \\ \\ X_3 \text{ pro}_j \ X_4 \end{array}\right\} \Rightarrow X_1 \text{ such that } X_3 \text{ pro } X_2 \ X_4$

Then sentences like (6) would be syntactically and semantically O.K. but convey the wrong meaning:

6. The woman such that he walks runs.

If we take this approach, then we must face the question of what gets 'lambda'-ed in if we combine this treatment with the use of syntactic variables for VP's. Consider the sentence:

7. John wants to see himself but Mary doesn't want to.

There is certainly a reading of this sentence where we understand that Mary doesn't want to see *her*self. I don't

think that this sentence in any way implies that Mary is
a man.

4.3. *Extending Tenses.*

I have treated tenses the way I have mainly to show how
meaning-changing transformations can be used in the theory,
and I'm not at all sure that it's the right way to do the
Auxiliary. But to mimic the classical treatment of the
Auxiliary requires either dropping the rule-by-rule treatment of semantics (and using something like the configurational rules of Cooper and Parsons 1976) or removing the
Auxiliary from the main body of a sentence as in the UCLA
grammar adaptation of Fillmore's case grammar (Stockwell et
al. 1973).

We can, however, make fairly minimal changes to the
grammar to allow both *will* and *have* to occur in the same
sentence. If T1 is changed by adding a variable W (for
wflb's) after Pres in the Aux in parentheses (since *e* is not
a wflb) the grammar will generate for every sentence it used
to generate a sentence in which the Aux contains *will have*
and the translation for the sentence will be $W(H(\phi))$.
(A few changes are necessary in the M rules.) It is also
fairly easy to change the rules for *to*-embedding to get
things like *John wishes to have walked.*

4.4. *Negation.*

As pointed out in Bach 1976, it is possible to build into
the grammar an analysis of negation that was developed by
Klima (1964). Suppose we replace T3 by the rules:

Negation

NP Aux ViP $\Rightarrow$ Neg NP Aux ViP

Neg-placement (obligatory)

Neg NP Aux ViP ⇒ NP Aux not ViP

where NP ≠ [$_{NP}$ $\left\{ \begin{array}{c} a \\ every \end{array} \right\}$ CNP]

and add these M-rules:

Neg [$_{NP}$ a CNP] → [$_{NP}$ no CNP]

Neg → not

Now L(G) will include these sentences, with the order of Negation and quantification as indicated on the right:

1. A woman does not walk.   Vx ¬ φ

2. No woman walks.   ¬ Vx φ

3. Every woman does not walk.   ∧x ¬ φ

4. Not every woman walks.   ¬ ∧x φ

This follows because Neg-placement cannot apply if the subject of the sentence is *a woman* or *every woman*. Hence quantification must apply after Negation for those sentences in which the subject with *a* or *every* is followed by the negative.

APPENDIX A: Examples of Derivations from *G*

John seeks a unicorn is in L(G). This is shown by the following proof for a structural description given by our grammar.

(a) ⟨ [$_S$[$_{NP}$[$_N$ John]] [$_{Aux}$ Pres] [$_{ViP}$[$_{Vt}$ seek]
    [$_{NP}$ a [$_{CNP}$[$_{CN}$ unicorn]]]]], P̂ P{^j} (^seek' (P̂ Vx
    [unicorn'(x) & P {x}])))⟩ ∈ SD(G)

Proof

(i) $\langle [_{CNP}[_{CN}$ unicorn$]]$, unicorn'$\rangle \in SD_K(G)$

by Lexicon, KR0

(ii) $\langle [_{NP}$ a $[_{CNP}[_{CN}$ unicorn$]]]$, $\hat{P}$ $\vee x[$unicorn'(x) &

$P\{x\}]\rangle \in SD_K(G)$

by KR5(e)

(iii) $\langle [_{ViP}[_{Vt}$ seek$]$ $[_{NP}$ a $[_{CNP}[_{CN}$ unicorn$]]]]$,

seek'$(^\wedge\hat{P}$ $\vee x[$unicorn'(x) & $P\{x\})\rangle \in SD_K(G)$

by Lexicon, KR0, and KR3(c).

(iv) (a) $\in SD_K(G)$ and hence $\in SD(G)$

by Lexicon, KR0, KR2, KR5, and T0.

By M2 and M4(d) *seek* has the property ThirdPersonSingular Present, and by M8 Pres is deleted (and empty brackets erased), giving us in place of the first member of (a) the structure (after adding 's' to *seek*):

$[_S[_{NP}[_N$ John$]]$ $[_{ViP}[_{Vt}$ seeks$]$ $[_{NP}$ a $[_{CNP}[_{CN}$ unicorn$]]]]]$

The debracketization of this is the desired sentence.

As the reader can check, the following pairs are also in SD(G) all with the same first member as (a) (call it X):

(b) $\langle X$, $\hat{P}$ $\vee x[$unicorn(x) & $P\{x\}]$ $(\hat{x}_4$ [$j^*(^\wedge$seek$(^\wedge\hat{Q}$

$Q\{x_4\}))]\rangle$

(from *John Pres seek it*$_4$ + *a unicorn*)

(c) $\langle X$, $j^*(\hat{x}_2$ $[\hat{P}$ $P\{x_2\}$ $(^\wedge$seek $(^\wedge Q$ $\vee x[$unicorn'(x) &

$Q\{x\}]))]\rangle\rangle$

(he$_2$ Pres seek a unicorn + John)

(d) arising by quantifying in both NP's in either order.

(e) arising by quantifying in both NP's in either order.

(f) $\langle X, j^* (\hat{x}_2 [\hat{P} \lor y [unicorn'(y) \& P \{y\}] (\hat{x}_4 [\hat{Q} Q\{x_2$
$^\wedge seek' (^\wedge \hat{P}_1 P_1\{x_4\}))])])\rangle$

(actually a more complicated expression equivalent to this)

(John pres to$_1$ + (a unicorn + (he$_2$ Pres seek it$_4$)))

(g) a derivation similar to (f) but with *John* quantified in and a matrix *he$_8$ Pres to$_1$*

(h) our grammar gives a number of derivations not matched in PTQ (but with translations logically equivalent to ones given by PTQ, for example:

John Pres seek a one$_5$ $j^*(^\wedge seek' (^\wedge \hat{P} \lor x_2 [q_5\{x_2\}](x)$
$\& P \{x\}]))$

it$_4$ Pres be a unicorn $\hat{P} P \{x_4\}(^\wedge unicorn)$

(via KR3(f))

John seeks a unicorn (by *one*-embedding and M-rules)

λq_5 [the expression above] $(\hat{x}_4 (unicorn'(x_4))$

which gives by conversion

$j^*(^\wedge seek'(^\wedge P \lor x [\hat{x}_2 [\hat{x}_4 [unicorn(x_4)] (x_2)] (x) \& P \{x\}]$

which is logically equivalent to the second member of (a).

APPENDIX B: A T-grammar That Is Exactly Equivalent to PTQ and Almost Exactly Like It

By a T-grammar I mean a grammar of the same general form as a KT-grammar except that it defines directly a set of structural descriptions by a set of unordered rules of the If-then form and maps them by M-rules into sets of expressions (of all categories) of the language.

R0.   (= KR0)

R1.   XP → X for X = Vi, N, AvV, CN

R2.   NP → $\left\{ \begin{array}{l} \text{every} \\ \text{the} \\ \text{a} \end{array} \right\}$ CNP

R3. $\left. \begin{array}{l} \text{CNP} \\ [_S \ X_1 \ (\text{pro}_n) \ X_2] \end{array} \right\}$ → $[_{CNP}$ CNP such that $[_S \ X_1 \ X_2]]$

(CNP, pro_n agree in Gender)

R4.   S → NP $[_{Aux}$ Pres$]$ ViP

R5.   ViP → Vt NP

R6.   AvVP → Pres NP

R7.   ViP → Vthat that S

R8.   ViP → Vto to ViP

R9.   S → AvS S

R10.   ViP → ViP AvVp

R11.   S → S $\left\{ \begin{array}{l} \text{and} \\ \text{or} \end{array} \right\}$ S

R12.   ViP → ViP $\left\{ \begin{array}{l} \text{and} \\ \text{or} \end{array} \right\}$ ViP

R13. NP → NP or NP

R14.
$$\left. \begin{array}{l} [_S\ X_1\ (\text{pro}_n)\ X_2] \\ \\ NP \end{array} \right\} \Rightarrow [_S\ X_1\ (NP)\ X_2]$$

(NP, pro_n agree in Gender)

R15. same as (14) but with CNP and ViP for S

R16. same as (14) but with CNP and ViP for S

R17 - 20. = T1 - 4 in *G*

M1 - 10. T-terminal vocabulary to include *him_i, he_i*

The second member of each pair is gotten directly from
Montague's translation rules for R0 - 16.

Except for the results of R17 - 20, a T-marker from this
grammar will be an exact match for an analysis tree from PTQ
and the translations will be identical, including the results
of vacuous quantification and relative clause formation.
R3 and R14 - 16 are to be read as follows:

case (a): the rule with parentheses removed.

case (b): the rule with parenthesized material removed.

The mapping to and from M-trees is trivial.

Acknowledgments

My understanding of Montague's work has been aided immensely
by discussions with Robin Cooper, Muffy Siegel, and especially
Terry Parsons and Barbara Partee. An early version of the
paper was presented in a seminar conducted by Parsons and
Partee and I have benefited greatly from class discussions
and from personal communications. In particular, I'd like to
thank Barbara Partee for her generosity in letting me bug her
endlessly and helping me debug the paper. Naturally, all

remaining bugs are my own. I would also like to thank Mary
Tye for a difficult typing job well done. Completion of this
paper was made possible by the Center for Advanced Studies in
the Behavioral Sciences and a grant from the National Endow-
ment for the Humanities.

Notes

1. By 'local grammaticality' I mean the property of a
grammar such that every sentence-structure embedded into a
matrix must underlie some well-formed sentence of the language; cf. Bach, forthcoming, where I show that this property,
for classical grammars, makes them no more powerful than the
'local-filtering' transformational grammars of Peters and
Ritchie 1973b. For the 'well-formedness constraint' see
Partee, forthcoming.

2. The KR rules 1-7 are given in the form of phrase
structure rules, and partially similar rules are collapsed by
curly brackets. Except for KR7 they can be read 'backwards'
as parts of a recursive definition of the set of left members
of elements in the set of kernel structural descriptions. The
expressions on the right give the translation of the resul-
tant expression and 'A''' means 'the translation of $[_A X]$.' If
two categories of the same kind appear on the right of a rule
(KR5a) they are distinguished in an obvious way by subscripts.

3. I disclaim any competence about "Universal Grammar."

4. But see Partee, forthcoming, for some steps in this
direction.

References

Andrews, Avery. 1976. "The VP Complement Analysis in Modern
    Icelandic." *Recherches Linguistiques à Montréal* 6: 1-21
    (NELS 6).

Bach, Emmon. 1968. "Nouns and Noun Phrases." In E. Bach & R. T. Harms, eds., *Universals in Linguistic Theory*. New York.

———. 1976. "An Extension of Classical Transformational Grammar." In *Problems in Linguistic Metatheory*. Proceedings of the 1976 conference at Michigan State University.

———. Forthcoming. "'The Position of Embedding Transformations in a Grammar' Revisited." To appear in a volume of papers from the International Summer School of Computational Linguistics (Pisa), ed. A. Zampolli.

Bennett, Michael. 1974. "Some Extensions of a Montague Fragment of English." Ph.D. dissertation, UCLA; available from the Indiana University Linguistics Club.

Brame, Michael. 1976. *Conjectures and Refutations in Syntax and Semantics*. New York: Elsevier.

Chomsky, Noam. 1957. *Syntactic Structures*. The Hague: Mouton.

———. 1965. *Aspects of the Theory of Syntax*. Cambridge, Mass.: MIT Press.

———. 1975a [1955]. *The Logical Structure of Linguistic Theory*. New York: Plenum.

———. 1975b. *Reflections on Language*. New York: Pantheon.

———. 1976. "Conditions on Rules of Grammar." *Linguistic Analysis* 4: 303 - 351.

Cooper, Robin. 1975. "Montague's Semantic Theory and Transformational Syntax." Ph.D. dissertation, University of Massachusetts, Amherst.

Cooper, Robin, and Terence Parsons. 1976. "Montague Grammar, Generative Semantics, and Interpretive Semantics." In Barbara Partee, ed., *Montague Grammar*. New York: Academic Press.

Dummett, Michael. 1973. *Frege: Philosophy of Language*. London: Duckworth.

Fillmore, Charles J. 1963. "The Position of Embedding

Transformations in a Grammar." *Word* 19: 208 - 231.

Katz, Jerrold J., and Jerry A. Fodor. 1963. "The Structure
of a Semantic Theory." *Language* 39: 170 - 210.

Katz, Jerrold J., and Paul M. Postal. 1964. *An Integrated
Theory of Linguistic Descriptions*. Cambridge, Mass.: MIT
Press.

Klima, Edward S. 1964. "Negation in English." In Jerry A.
Fodor and Jerrold J. Katz, eds., *The Structure of Language*.
Englewood Cliffs, N.J.: Prentice-Hall.

Lee, Kiyong. 1974. "The Treatment of Some English Constructions in Montague Grammar." Ph.D. dissertation, University
of Texas, Austin.

McCawley, James D. 1971. "Where Do Noun Phrases Come From?"
In: Denny D. Steinberg and Leon A. Jakobovits, eds.,
Semantics. Cambridge: Cambridge University Press.

Montague, Richard. 1973. "The Proper Treatment of Quantification in Ordinary English." In Montague 1974.

————. 1974. *Formal Philosophy*. Ed. Richmond Thomason.
New Haven: Yale University Press.

Partee, Barbara H. 1975. "Montague Grammar and Transformational Grammar." *Linguistic Inquiry* 6: 203 - 300.

————. Forthcoming. "Montague Grammar and the Well-Formedness Constraint." To appear in Frank Heny and Helmut
Schnelle, eds., *Syntax and Semantics,* vol. 10: *Selections
from the Third Groningen Round Table*. New York: Academic
Press.

Peters, Stanley, and R. W. Ritchie. 1973a. "On the Generative
Power of Transformational Grammars." *Information Sciences*
6: 49 - 93.

————. 1973b. "Nonfiltering and Local-Filtering Transformational Grammars." In K. J. J. Hintikka et al., eds.,

Approaches to Natural Language, pp. 180 - 194. Dordrecht: D. Reidel Publishing Co.

Quine, W. W. 1966. *Selected Logic Papers*. New York.

Smullyan, Raymond M. 1961. *Theory of Formal Systems*. Annals of Mathematics Studies 47. Princeton, N.J.

Stockwell, Robert P., Paul Schachter, and Barbara Hall Partee. 1973. *The Major Syntactic Structures of English*. New York: Holt, Rinehart & Winston.

2

Constraining Transformational Montague Grammar: A Framework and a Fragment

Barbara H. Partee

1. *Introduction: Three Types of Constraints*

1.1. *The Need for Constraints*

Montague's theory of grammar[1] imposes strong constraints on
the correspondence between syntactic rules and semantic interpretation rules, but virtually no constraints on the form of
syntactic or semantic operations. His theory has been of
interest to linguists even without further constraints, I
think in large part because it provides an explicit and
rigorous semantic framework within which elegant solutions
have been provided to many classically difficult semantic
problems. Another point of particular interest to linguists
is the compositionality constraint, which is a strong and
interesting constraint whose soundness can to some degree be
confirmed or disconfirmed without formal constraints on the
operations, just by following some implicit standards for what
constitute reasonable rules. Nevertheless, I think linguists
are agreed that the task of imposing further constraints is
imperative if some form of Montague grammar is to be taken
seriously as a candidate for a theory of natural languages,
insofar as one of the linguist's chief goals in constructing
such a theory is to characterize the class of possible natural
languages as narrowly as possible.

This emphasis on the need for additional constraints is
not meant as a criticism of Montague's own work, since it
stems from goals not shared by Montague. On the one hand, he
clearly wanted a theory which would account equally well for
natural languages and the artificial languages constructed by
logicians.[2] On the other hand, he wanted a mathematically
elegant theory, and while a linguist would of course welcome
formal elegance if it is attainable within the limits set by
empirical constraints, the linguist is obligated to put higher
priority on the facts of natural languages. For example, if it
could be shown to hold universally that languages with
sentence-initial complementizers had only leftward unbounded
movement rules, and those with sentence-final complementizers
only rightward ones, the linguist would want to constrain the
theory so as to rule out the nonoccurring possibilities, even
though doing so would probably make the theory less elegant.
Considerations of elegance or simplicity do come in, of
course, particularly in trying to extrapolate from the
universal properties of the finite set of actual natural
languages to the universals of language that have a principled and not an accidental basis.

Insofar as constraints on grammars are hypotheses about
universals, it could be argued that it is premature to begin
proposing any for Montague grammar, and that many more "fragments" of many more languages should be written first. My
response would be that it is certainly too early to have much
confidence in any proposed constraints, but never too early
to start proposing and investigating potential constraints.
The fruitfulness of constraint-inspired research within
transformational grammar has been enormous, and it should be
neither surprising nor discouraging that there are nevertheless still fundamental disagreements about almost all the

constraints that have so far been proposed. So I will emphasize
at the outset that all the constraints suggested herein are
highly tentative; my hope is that they may stimulate others to
find better ones.

1.2. *The Compositionality Constraint*

The main constraint in Montague's theory, and the one that
makes it so interesting semantically, is the compositionality
constraint, i.e., the requirement that there be a semantic
interpretation rule corresponding to each syntactic formation
rule, so that the interpretation of each expression is determined by the interpretation of its syntactic subparts and
the rule by which they were combined. If we adopt the two-
stage semantics of Montague 1973 (henceforth PTQ), in which
the first stage consists of translation from the natural
language into a formalized language of intensional logic and
the second stage consists of a model-theoretic semantics for
that language, then the compositionality constraint can be
represented in part by the requirement that syntactic and
semantic rules come in pairs of the following form:

(1) Syntactic rule n: If $\alpha \in P_A$ and $\beta \in P_B$,
then $\gamma \in P_C$, where $\gamma = F_i(\alpha, \beta)$.

(2) Semantic rule n: If α, β translate into α', β',
respectively,
then $F_i(\alpha, \beta)$ translates into
$G_k(\alpha', \beta')$.

The parameters to be specified for the particular rules are
the following: (i) the categories A and B of the input expressions and the category C of the resulting expression, (ii) the
syntactic operation F_i, which may be as simple as concatenation or as complex as a transformational operation; and

(iii) the 'semantic' operation G_k, which is actually a
syntactic operation mapping two expressions of the intensional
logic onto an expression of the intensional logic; but I shall
continue to refer to it as a semantic operation to distinguish
it from the natural language syntactic operation F_i.

The compositionality constraint further requires that all
expressions of a given syntactic category be translated into
expressions of a single type, or semantic category, in the
intensional logic. It does not, however, require any correspondence between the form of the syntactic operation F_i and
the form of the semantic operation G_k of the corresponding
semantic rule, other than what is required by the correspondence between categories of expressions and the logical types
of their translations.

I said at the beginning that the compositionality constraint is a strong one; but in fact that assessment pre-
supposes some constraints on the syntactic operations F_i
and the semantic operations G_k. Otherwise, I believe it puts
virtually no constraint on either the syntactic or the
semantic analysis of a given possible language.[3] Hence an
additional reason to look for constraints on the form of the
rules is to give more substance to the compositionality
constraint. And with a more explicit statement of the permissible forms of rules, one could propose ways of tightening
the compositionality constraint itself, by imposing corres-
pondences between the form of the syntactic operation F_i for
a given syntactic rule and the semantic operation G_k of the
corresponding semantic rule.

1.3. *The Well-Formedness Constraint*

What I mean by the well-formedness constraint is given in
(3):

(3) *The well-formedness constraint.*   Each syntactic rule
    operates on well-formed expressions of specified
    categories to produce a well-formed expression of a
    specified category.

This constraint comes from Montague, but not in quite as
strong a form as I would like to propose. For any ambiguous
language, such as any natural language, Montague's general
theory as specified in Montague 1970b (henceforth UG) calls
for giving the syntax in two parts: a set of syntactic rules
of the form given in (1) above for a *disambiguated language,*
and the specification of an 'ambiguating relation' R which
pairs expressions of the disambiguated language with expressions of the actual ambiguous language. The well-formedness
constraint within Montague's theory holds only for the syntax
of the disambiguated language, which is in effect a construct
of the Montague grammarian, much as are the deep structures
of the transformational grammarian. The disambiguated language
L' 'underlying' a given natural language L could, if no
additional constraints are imposed, differ from the natural
language in quite arbitrary ways, which would rob the well-
formedness constraint of empirical content. If we could
eliminate the ambiguating relation completely, then the
well-formedness constraint would require that the inputs
and outputs of all syntactic rules be well-formed surface
expressions of the given language, which is presumably what
we have empirical data about.

    In an earlier paper,[4] I suggested that the following
limited differences between the disambiguated language L'
and the surface language L be tolerated, and no others:
(i) L' contains labeled brackets, L does not, and the
ambiguating relation simply deletes the brackets; (ii) L'
contains 'variables' like he_3, L does not, and the ambiguating

relation simply deletes the subscript; (iii) L' contains
morphological representations such as *see + Past* or   *she*
$$[+Acc]$$
which the ambiguating relation maps into the surface forms *saw*
and *her*. From the point of view of Montague's theory, these are
constraints on the form of the ambiguating relation R. From a
linguistic perspective, they might better be viewed as eliminating R completely but adding the specific devices of labeled
bracketing, indexed pronouns, and a morphological component to
the theory to take over some of the intended functions of R.
Taken either way, my aim is to make the well-formedness constraint empirically as strong as possible without giving up
descriptive adequacy.

The strength of the well-formedness constraint can be
illustrated best by showing some of the sorts of analyses it
disallows. For example, Siegel (1976b) presents syntactic
and semantic arguments in favor of a dual categorization of
adjectives in English (and in Russian), with some adjectives
classified as applying directly to common nouns (CN/CN in
PTQ terminology) and others classified as one-place predicates
(t///e). If the well-formedness constraint is taken seriously
as part of the syntax, the analysis of at least some adjectives as common noun modifiers is independently selected
on purely syntactic grounds over the classic transformational derivation of all pronominal adjectives from predicate
adjectives in relative clauses, since the classic analysis
requires the generation of ill-formed expressions as part of
the derivation of well-formed ones, as in (4):

(4) *a convert who is recent → a recent convert

Although the analysis of all adjectives as common noun
modifiers as in Montague 1970a (EFL) cannot be completely
ruled out by the well-formedness constraint,[5] the constraint

does rule out any analysis which would syntactically generate such expressions as (5a) as part of the derivation of (5b).

(5) a. *be an asleep entity
    b. be asleep

As this example illustrates, one effect of the well-formedness constraint is to automatically disallow obligatory rules.

I will briefly mention some further examples of analyses ruled out by the well-formedness constraint; these are discussed further in Partee, forthcoming.

(i) Analyses of the *easy-to-please* construction like that of Lasnik and Fiengo (1974) would be ruled out because of the ill-formedness of the source structure as exemplified in (6), and those like that of Chomsky (1978) would be ruled out by the ill-formedness of the source as shown in (7).

(6) *John is easy to please John. → John is easy to please.

(7) *John is easy whom to please. → John is easy to please.

Chomsky's classical analysis of the *easy-to-please* construction, illustrated in (8), does not violate the well-formedness constraint; an analogous rule in a Montague framework was proposed in Partee 1973.

(8) To please John is easy. → John is easy to please.

(ii) There have been many analyses proposed in the transformational literature for pseudo-cleft sentences like (9); of the hypothesized sources listed below as (10a - e), only (10a) and (10b) satisfy the well-formedness constraint.

(9) What John ate was the meat.
(10) a. S[John ate the meat]
     b. NP[what John ate] was NP[the meat]
     c. NP[S[John ate the meat]] was NP[the meat]

> d. $_{NP}[_S[$John ate wh-something$]]$ was $_{NP}[_S[$John ate the meat$]$
>
> e. $_{NP}[_S[$John ate the meat$]]$ was $_{NP}[\,\Delta\,]$

(iii) The constraint would also rule out all cases of lexically governed obligatory extraposition, as illustrated by the widely accepted transformational derivation of (11b) from (11a).

> (11) a. *That Susan is asleep appears.
>
> b. It appears that Susan is asleep.

It may be that the well-formedness constraint is too strong and needs to be weakened somewhat; I believe that its effects are good ones in the cases cited, but I do not want to try to argue for that here. The examples were included primarily to illustrate that the constraint does indeed have quite strong effects on the class of grammars compatible with given data about the well-formed surface expressions of a given natural language. If it is correct, it could have important effects for theories of first-language acquisition, since it places rather severe limitations on the abstractness of the relation between surface forms and the structures that need to be posited for their derivation.

1.4. *The Need for Constraints on the Form of Rules*

The compositionality constraint limits the possible pairings of syntactic and semantic rules, and the well-formedness constraint indirectly limits the class of syntactic rules for a given language by constraining their outputs to be well-formed expressions of that language. But neither of these kinds of constraints puts any limits on the syntactic operations F_i or the semantic operations G_i that occur in the

rules, and without some constraints on these as well, the
class of grammars available within a Montague framework still
includes infinitely many grammars that are incompatible with
strongly supported linguistic universals. Consider, for
example, a hypothetical rule that formed the conjunction
of two sentences by a syntactic operation F_i that inter-
leaved the successive words of the first sentence with the
successive words of the second sentence, so that F_i *(John
went to the store, Mary raked the leaves*) would yield 'John
Mary went raked to the leaves store'. Compositionality does
not rule out any particular choice of F_i; as long as the rule
is uniformly interpreted, say as conjunction, the compositionality requirement is met. The well-formedness constraint
can eliminate such a rule from English, or any other known
natural language, since its output is clearly ill-formed, but
the well-formedness constraint does not furnish us with a
basis for predicting that no possible human language could
have such a rule. Clearly the potential of Montague grammar
as a theory of human linguistic competence would be streng-
thened by the inclusion of constraints on the form of the
rules in addition to compositionality and the well-formedness
constraint. In the remainder of the paper I will consider a
number of possible constraints of this sort on the syntactic
rules and suggest ways of incorporating them into a tightened
format for writing syntactic rules in a (modified) Montague
framework.

2. *Constraints on the Form of Rules*

2.1. *The Nature of Montague Syntax*

Since a Montague syntax consists of rules which work
'bottom-up', combining well-formed expressions to produce

new well-formed expressions, many of Montague's rules have
the effect of what would normally be expressed as two or
more rules in a transformational grammar. Montague's PTQ has
many examples of such rules: S4, the simple subject-predicate
rule, for instance, is analogous to a phrase-structure rule
(t → T IV) plus a transformation of subject-verb number
agreement. One immediate concern to the linguist is whether
it will be possible to find a constrained form of syntactic
rules when one rule may have to incorporate a number of
diverse operations into a single operation F_i. I will propose
that each syntactic operation F_i must be statable as a
composition of subfunctions,[6] where each subfunction is itself
a composition of certain primitive operations (to be specified below, section 3.1). The intuitive idea is that the
factors that should make one grammar preferable to another
in this framework should be reflected in the simplicity of
the definition of each subfunction together with the simplicity of expressing each full syntactic operation F_i as a
composition of subfunctions.

The fact that Montague syntax works 'bottom-up' also has
certain effects on the possible form of rules. Suppose we
want the rules to operate on and produce labeled bracketed
structures[7] as in transformational grammar (TG). One
plausible constraint in TG is that no 'structure-building'
be allowed: transformations must operate on the tree structure[8] of the input expression but not create new labeled
nodes except by operations such as copying or Chomsky-
adjunction which do so uniformly. This prohibition would
rule out, for instance, the 'extraction analysis' of pseudo-
clefts which derives sentence (9) from (10a) (repeated
below), building a number of new nodes in the process.

(9)   What John ate was the meat.

(10a) John ate the meat.

In a Montague syntax with labeled bracketing, some structure-
building is inevitable because of the absence of a separate
phrase structure component. Consider a syntactic rule of the
form (1) above, in which F_i is simple concatenation. The
interpretation of such a rule in a labeled bracketed system
is that it operates on a pair of inputs as shown in (12) and
produces an output as shown in (13): concatenation then
amounts to sister-adjunction plus creation of a parent node.

(12) $_A[\,\alpha\,]$, $_B[\,\beta\,]$

(13) $_C[_A[\,\alpha\,]\ _B[\,\beta\,]]$

While one cannot absolutely prohibit structure-building
in a bottom-up system, a comparable effect would be achieved
by adopting the following:

(C1) *No internal structure building.* The only new node
     that can be added by a rule is a single parent node
     labeled to indicate the category of the resulting
     expression. (The pair of brackets labeled C in (13)
     represent such a node.)

(As in TG, certain primitive operations may be defined to
create duplicates of existing nodes; the constraint in effect
prohibits node-addition from being a separate primitive
operation.) I am in favor of this constraint in part because
it can help to tighten the notion of syntactic category and
strengthen the degree to which surface structure facts
provide evidence for deeper structure. The free insertion
of new labeled nodes into derived structures would seem to
weaken the empirical import of the labeled nodes in both
these respects.

A second constraint which is built into the Montague
syntax is that there is no extrinsic rule ordering.

(C2) *No extrinsic rule ordering.*

There is a high degree of intrinsic rule ordering because
every category is recursively defined, so that the domains
of the rules are sets of n-tuples of categories and not just
the single category S.[9] So one cannot, for example, apply the
relative clause rule until one has built up a common noun
phrase and a sentence to apply it to, and one cannot apply
that rule *after* a determiner has been added to the common
noun phrase to produce a term phrase.

2.2. *Consequences of the Well-Formedness Constraint*

Suppose we adopt the well-formedness constraint in the form
proposed in section 1.3 above, where the only exceptions to
surface well-formedness to be tolerated are (i) the inclusion
of labeled brackets, (ii) the inclusion of indexed variables,
and (iii) the inclusion of abstract morphological representations that can be mapped into actual phonological forms
by morphological and morphophonemic rules. Then two immediate
constraints follow, both of which I want to accept.

(C3) *No obligatory rules.*

(C4) *No purely abstract morphemes.*

The first of these is clear enough; note that what standardly
happens to rules considered obligatory in TG is that they get
incorporated as subfunctions in rules that do more besides,
in the way that number-agreement is incorporated into subject-
predicate rules. Not everyone working in the MG framework
has accepted this constraint; my own reflexive rule in Partee
1973 violates it, as do several of the rules involved in

Rodman's analysis of relative clauses (Rodman 1976). My
proposal that late obligatory morphological rules should be
permitted reflects the judgment that the complexity of doing
all the morphology as one builds expressions up (with the
concomitant need to 'undo' some of it at later stages) is so
great as to outweigh the appeal of the well-formedness
constraint in such cases; advocacy of a larger class of
obligatory rules would presumably involve similar considerations for other cases.

The class of elements that (C4) is intended to prohibit
are those which *never* have a phonological realization. This
would permit a present tense morpheme which is sometimes
phonologically null, but rule out such elements as Bennett's
$ and # (Bennett 1974), or morphemes such as Q and IMP which
are sometimes used in TG to 'trigger' certain rules before
being obligatorily deleted.

2.3. *Transformational Modifications of Montague Syntax*

Since Montague himself put no constraints on the syntactic
operations F_i, not even that they be limited to recursive
functions (a minimal constraint if the grammar is to be
learnable), his rules already have at least as much power as
transformational rules. So although the introduction of
labeled brackets is in one sense an extension rather than a
restriction of his system, my motivation in adding the
brackets to the generated expressions is to make it possible
to restrict the class of rules by making the labeled
bracketing (which represents the derived constituent structure) one of a limited set of properties of expressions to
which the rules may refer, and in particular to disallow
reference to previous stages of the derivational history.

(C5) *No appeal to derivational history.*

Labeled bracketing will not be the only property of expressions to which rules may be sensitive, however; see the discussion of recursively defined properties in section 2.4 below.

Another modification I am introducing into Montague's system, one which does represent an extension rather than a restriction, is to allow the syntactic operations to be partial functions. This corresponds to the inclusion of 'structural analysis' statements in transformations, and requires a modification in the basic form of the syntactic rules:

(14) Syntactic rule n: If $\alpha \in P_A$ and $\beta \in P_B$ and α, β are of the form SA_n, then $\gamma \in P_C$, where $\gamma = F_i(\alpha, \beta)$.

The addition of the structural analysis clause means that a given syntactic rule will not necessarily apply to all expressions of the input categories. The requirement that the functions always be total functions is linguistically unnatural, and its abandonment does not, as far as I am aware, have any undesirable consequences for the rest of the system.[10] Restrictions on the allowable form of the structural analysis statement will be specified in later sections, and will be in part borrowed from transformational theory. It may be noted that transformational rules in the framework of Chomsky 1957 have the form of (14), with the restriction that the category of both input(s) and output is always S.

2.4. *Features as Recursively Defined Properties*

In Partee (forthcoming) it is proposed that Montague's bottom-up form of syntax, in which the syntactic rules take the form

of a recursive definition of the set of expressions of each
category, provides a natural way to unify the linguists' use
of features on lexical items and features on nonterminal
nodes if both kinds of features are viewed as properties of
expressions.[11] Consider syntactic gender, for example, in
languages like those of the Romance family.[12] Each lexical
common or proper noun has a specified gender, and for each
syntactic rule which creates a common noun phrase or a term
phrase, one can write a rule specifying the gender of the
resulting phrase, given the gender of each constituent CN or
T phrase. For endocentric constructions, such a recursive
property specification rule will simply state that the gender
of the resulting phrase is the gender of one of the constituent phrases (the head); this corresponds to the notion of
'feature-climbing' in the linguistic literature. For non-
endocentric constructions, the rules will be less uniform.
The gender of a term phrase formed from a sentence, such as
a *that*-clause, will always be a certain fixed gender, such
as neuter or masculine, and the gender of a conjoined term
phrase will be a specifiable function of the genders of the
constituent term phrases. What I propose, then, is a set of
property specification rules that accompany the formation
rules, recursively defining properties to which syntactic
rules may refer, starting with lexically specified properties
and specifying properties of derived expressions on the basis
of the properties of the constituents and the rule that is
combining them.

In addition, it appears to be necessary to allow some of
the syntactic formation rules themselves to add or change
property specifications, either by copying, as in the case
of agreement rules, or by stipulation, as in the case of
government rules, e.g., the addition of case marking when a

verb is combined with its object. This last case represents something of a problem for this approach for languages in which there is a rich case morphology, since addition of a case specification to a full term phrase would seem to require top-down rather than bottom-up transmission of the case specification to the appropriate subconstituents of the term phrase. (The problem is not so great for English, where only pronouns show case, so I have been able to make do with an ad hoc treatment of case in this fragment. But I do not see any way to give a satisfactory treatment for the general case within this framework, so further modification seems inevitable.)

One must of course seek constraints on the set of permissible properties in this framework, just as one must constrain the use of features in a transformational framework, if one wishes to forbid the encoding of arbitrary aspects of derivational history.[13] Although I do not have specific constraints to offer at this point, I will list here the properties used in the fragment of section 4 below, which can be grouped into four types. Further work will be needed to see whether these types can be narrowly defined by some formal means, whether some can be eliminated, and whether others need to be added.

Type 1: *Morphological Properties*

(i) GENDER (α) is defined recursively for term phrases and common noun phrases, and is copied by rules onto pronouns. The values for this property are Masc(uline), Fem(inine), Neut(er), and Com(mon). Common gender is the gender assigned to conjoined terms whose constituents differ in gender; in various dialects it is realized as *he, he or she,* or *they* (the latter creating problems for the treatment of number which are ignored here).

(ii) PERSON (α), a feature whose values are 1, 2, and 3, is defined recursively for term phrases, copied by rules onto pronouns, and referred to in the subject-verb agreement operation (subfunction AGR in the fragment). The PTQ fragment has only third-person term phrases, but the person property is included here to illustrate the more general case.

(iii) NUMBER (α), with values Sg and Pl, is also defined recursively for term phrases and referred to in the subject-verb agreement rule as well as in the rules of quantification and relativization. In this fragment, all term phrases are singular; in an extended fragment, a treatment of plural along the lines of Bennett 1974 could be given by referring to the property specification 'NUMBER (α) = Pl' where Bennett has 'α is of the form $ β'.

(iv) CASE (α) is a property whose values are Nom and Acc; it is not an inherent property of expressions in this fragment, but is assigned to term phrases by the subfunction ACC (α), which occurs in the rules combining term phrases with transitive verbs and prepositions.

Type 2: Categorial Properties

There is just one property of the sort I am calling categorial in this fragment, namely VERB (α), whose values are + and -. This property is not a particularly attractive one, since it is simply a reflection of the absence of the grammatical category 'verb' in the PTQ fragment. However, recent work on cross-categorial generalizations within the X-bar theory has led to a number of suggestions for decomposing even the more traditional categories like Verb into complexes of features (e.g., Verb as [+V, -N], Adjective as [+V, +N], etc.),[14] so there may be independent justification for features of this sort. At any rate, such properties do not significantly increase overall expressive power, since they are (at worst) replaceable by finite disjunctions of category membership statements.

Type 3: Relational Properties

Following a suggestion of Friedman (1974),[15] we introduce two recursively defined relational properties: MAINVERB (α, β) ('α is a main verb of β') and MAINTERM (α, β) ('α is a main term of β'), each of which has the values + and -. The principal need for such relational properties is the existence of rules which apply to full term phrases or verb phrases in ways that require identifying the head (or heads in the case of conjoined phrases), such as the attachment of the present tense morpheme to the head verb(s) of a verb phrase in sentence-formation. It is well known that PTQ incorrectly generates (15a) instead of (15b) because Montague's rule S4 changes only the leftmost basic verb of the verb phrase to its present tense form.

(15) a. *John walks and talk.
     b. John walks and talks.

The introduction of the relational property MAINVERB (α, β) represents a choice of one among four possible ways of solving this and related problems. The other three are (i) appeal to derivational history, which we wish to exclude generally; (ii) the introduction of abstract morphemes like Bennett's #, which we also wish to exclude generally; and (iii) defining the tense-attachment operation in terms of the labeled bracketing of the verb phrase. The first two of these are in a sense notational variants of the relational property solution,[16] since both the relational property and the introduction of Bennett's # can be viewed as encoding

the relevant aspects of the derivational history (as a
property of the derived string in one case and as an overt
marker in the derived string in the other). My preference for
the recursively defined property solution derives largely
from the expectation that only a small set of such relational
properties like MAINVERB will be needed and that they will
be universally definable. Thus, even if the three solutions —
Friedman's, (i), and (ii) — are equivalent with respect to
the PTQ fragment, I would expect to find evidence that they
are not equivalent in terms of predictions about the class of
possible grammars of natural language. (The remaining approach,
(iii), was one I advocated in introducing labeled bracketing
into the Montague framework in Partee 1973 and 1975, but I
have not found any way of implementing it without defining
the attachment subfunction itself recursively, which in
effect is just another form of the derivational-history
solution.)

Type 4: Indexed Pro-Form Properties

The two properties PRO (α) and INDEX (α) are of a somewhat
special kind, and perhaps would better be treated in an
entirely separate component of the grammar.[17] The PRO property
value is + for both subscripted and unsubscripted pronouns
(and - for all other basic terms and term phrases) and is
used to identify term phrases to be put into the accusative
as well as in the operations affecting subscripted pronouns.
The INDEX property is the only property with infinitely many
values: - , 0, 1, 2, ... The substitution of a 'real pronoun'
for an indexed one is viewed, partly following Bach (1976;
Chapter 1 of this volume) as just 'desubscripting' the
indexed pronoun (changing a numerical value of the INDEX
property to -), with accompanying addition of gender and

number features as specified in the particular rule. This
treatment fits in with the constraint suggested in Partee,
forthcoming, that indexed elements be permitted in the syntax
only as indexed forms of actually occurring pro-forms (such
as pronouns, *there, then, do so,* etc.).

One respect in which the PRO and INDEX properties differ
from the other properties is that they are lexically determined and not modified recursively in the way that properties
like GENDER, MAINVERB, etc., are (except in the trivial
respect that the value of PRO is specified as — for all
recursively built-up, nonbasic term phrases).

2.5. *Bound Variables and 'Everywhere Substitution'*

Both the relative clause rule and the quantification rules in
PTQ include the operation of substituting an appropriate pronoun for every occurrence of he_i in a certain domain. This
operation, because of the 'every occurrence' clause, cannot
be defined in any natural way as a transformational rule,
since the structural description of a transformation must
partition the input structure into a fixed finite number of
factors. Attempts to reproduce such rules as transformations
(e.g., in the Cooper-grammar of Cooper and Parsons 1976)
involve innovations such as allowing 'iterable' factors such
as (16):

(16) $(X\ he_i\ Y)^*$

The introduction of such terms into transformations not only
makes the structural description nonfinite but raises questions about the interpretation of the structural description,
since what is intended is to allow for multiple occurrences
of the *same* he_i surrounded by *different* X's and Y's. Allowing
iterated application of a single finitely stated transformation

won't work either, unless some way could be found to insure
that the same *he$_i$* is chosen for each successive application.[18]

Rather than make the primitive operations powerful enough
so that such an operation of 'everywhere substitution' could
be defined in terms of them, I have chosen to make 'everywhere substitution' itself one of the primitive operations,
with constraints on its use designed to limit its application
to cases where the elements substituted for are interpreted
as bound variables. I believe that an operation of this sort
is needed in some component of the grammar in any framework.
An explicit statement of the generative semanticists' rule
of quantifier-lowering requires such an operation, and an
analogous operation is needed in the interpretive rules if
it is not included in the syntactic rules.[19]

2.6. *Functions, Subfunctions, and Primitive Operations*

The fact that the output of each rule must be a syntactically
well-formed expression appears to require a loss of generalization with respect to what in a transformational grammar
would be treated as obligatory transformations. For example,
in PTQ, person and number agreement of the tensed verb with
the subject is stated separately for each tense as it is
introduced; accusative marking must be stated separately
as part of each rule that combines a verb or preposition
with a term-phrase object. If reflexivization is not to be a
single obligatory rule (which it cannot be if the well-
formedness constraint is correct), reflexivization must be
built into the subject-predicate rule(s) and additionally
into one or more verb-phrase creating rules (to handle cases
where the antecedent of a reflexive is in the verb phrase).
The significance of this loss of generalization is that we
then have no basis for predicting that, say, reflexivization

should operate in the same way in each rule in which it is
introduced.

To remedy this shortcoming, I will follow a suggestion
made by Emmon Bach and require that each syntactic operation
F_i be specifiable as a composition of 'subfunctions', where
each subfunction is itself defined as a composition of certain
primitive operations (to be specified below). A frequently
recurring operation, specific to a particular language, that
is smaller than a whole rule but bigger than a primitive
operation will be defined just once in the grammar, given a
name, and then simply referred to by that name in the statement of each rule in which it is used. For example, one
useful subfunction for PTQ is the subfunction PROFORM (α),
which defines the pronoun agreeing in gender and number with
the common noun or term phrase.

(17) If $\alpha \in P_{CN} \cup P_T$, PROFORM (α) = $_T$[$\quad$ *he* $\quad$]
$$\begin{bmatrix} \text{GENDER } (\alpha) \\ \text{NUMBER } (\alpha) \\ \text{PRO: +} \\ \text{INDEX: ---} \end{bmatrix}$$

(The bracketed feature specifications represent the composition of four primitive operations of property specification.)

Using this subfunction, we can define further a subfunction
PROSUB (α, ι, δ) which substitutes for every occurrence of
he$_i$ or *him*$_i$ in δ a pronoun which is the appropriate pro-form
of α (see the fragment in section 4). This subfunction
shows up in the relativization and quantification rules of
PTQ, and would show up in other rules as well in extensions
of PTQ.

'Capturing generalizations' depends not only on the form
of grammars but on the evaluation metric as well. It is
intended here that the evaluation metric should count a

defined subfunction as a single operation within a large
function definition, but should also take into account for
the grammar as a whole the number and complexity of the
defined subfunctions. Intuitively, this use of subfunctions
is analogous to the use of subroutines in complicated computer
programs. There is no advantage to separately defining a
subroutine if it will be used only once; there may be if it
recurs at several different points in the program. A sharper
definition of the evaluation metric, incorporating appropriate
tradeoff values among complexities in different parts of the
grammar, is eventually needed but is probably not within
reach in the near future.

The initial motivation for defining the rule-size operations F_i in terms of intermediate-level subfunctions was to
capture a kind of generalization that is normally captured
in transformational grammar by a single transformation; in
this respect it may appear simply to be a 'patch' on MG to
enable it to reach a level of adequacy already attained by
TG. Recent work by Bach (ms. a; ms. b) suggests, however,
that the subfunction notion may have fruitful application
to cases not representable as single transformations;[20] it
may turn out, for instance, to provide a helpful tool for
expressing some of the kinds of typological generalizations
about families of rules that tend to cluster together in
languages (e.g., Greenberg 1963).

The particular primitive operations to be taken as basic
will be specified in section 3.1 below; some of them have
already been discussed above (e.g., 'everywhere substitution'). The choices are quite tentative at this point, since
the primitives should be universal (unlike the language-
particular functions and subfunctions), and there has not

been very much work done so far in the MG framework on
languages other than English.[21]

2.7. *Conjunction and 'Across-the-Board' Rules*

Several of the errors in PTQ involve failure of rules to apply
correctly when one of the input expressions is a conjoined
phrase (Friedman 1974). For example, as Friedman notes, PTQ
generates all of the following:

(18) Bill seeks John and find he or Mary.

(19) John has talked and walk.

(20) Mary or John finds a fish and she eats it.

The last example has both a reasonable derivation, on which
she is coreferential with *Mary*, and an inappropriate derivation, on which *she* is coreferential with *Mary or John*. The
error responsible for the second derivation is that the
pronoun corresponding to a given term phrase is determined
by considering just the gender of the *first* basic term or
common noun in the term phrase. In PTQ, the first basic term
or common noun phrase is the head of the term phrase in all
cases except conjoined term phrases.

Sentence (18) illustrates two errors: present tense marking
applies only to the first verb of the verb phrase (again
appropriate for all cases except conjoined verb phrases), and
accusative marking applies only when the term phrase to be
marked is a single pronoun. Sentence (19) illustrates another
tense-marking failure: a verb phrase is put into the present
perfect by prefixing *has* and putting the first verb of the
verb phrase into the past participle form.

In the fragment below, these errors are corrected by a
means similar to that employed by Friedman. The device of

recursive property specification described in section 2.4 is
used to define the notions 'main verb of a verb phrase' and
'main term of a term phrase'; whenever conjunction is involved,
there will be more than one main verb or main term, and subfunctions such as tense-attachment and accusative marking are
defined to apply to all main verbs or main terms of the
affected phrases. The recursive definition of the gender
property provides for the appropriate specification of the
gender of conjoined phrases, so that a pronoun whose antecedent is *Mary or John* will be given common gender (*he or she*
or *they,* depending on dialect[22]).

These corrections solve most of the problems connected
with conjunction in PTQ (some remaining ones are discussed in
section 5), and the devices employed are for the most part
independently justifiable. But there seems to be a higher-
order generalization that is not reflected in the rules, since
it is probably universal that rules like accusative marking
should apply to all conjuncts of a conjoined phrase. A similar
problem exists in transformational grammar, where the notion
of 'across-the board rules' (first proposed by Ross 1967)
has been suggested as a solution, though never completely or
adequately formalized, as far as I am aware. What is needed,
in either framework, is a way of predicting, from the form
of a rule as stated for simple nonconjoined input structures,
exactly how the rule will apply when one or more of the
input structures is or contains a conjoined phrase. I do
not have such a formulation to offer; the treatment in
section 4 should therefore be regarded as something of a
'brute force' solution.

2.8. *The Separation of Morphology and Syntax*

The fragment presented in section 4 below incorporates certain
working assumptions about the separation of morphology and
syntax. I have nothing to offer here about the basis for a
principled distinction; this is an area much in need of
further research. I assume that the rule for the alternation
of *a/an* does not belong in the syntax (where Montague had it
in PTQ), and I generate such terminal strings as (21)
(brackets omitted), leaving it to later components to turn
this into (22).

(21)   Mary   believe   Pres   that   He
    [CASE: NOM]   [NUM: Sg] $\begin{bmatrix} \text{GENDER: Fem} \\ \text{NUM: Sg} \\ \text{PRO: +} \\ \text{INDEX: -} \end{bmatrix}$

        have   Pres   walk en.
           [NUM: Sg]

(22) Mary believes that she has walked.

How much power the morphological rules have can of course
make a difference to the demands placed on the syntax. I
assume that morphological rules must follow all syntactic
rules and may not operate across the board or across
variables. Hence I assume, for instance, that the problem
of across the board case marking noted in the previous section
must be solved within the syntax, and that the morphological
component can only tell us what the actual case forms of
various lexical items are.

3. *A Formal Framework*

The framework proposed here is tentative; I am sure that
neither the form nor the content is optimal. In this framework, the specification of the syntax of a natural language

has four parts: (i) a lexicon, (ii) a defined set of
syntactic subfunctions, (iii) a set of syntactic rules, and
(iv) a set of property-specification rules. The framework
specifies the form of all of these as well as the primitive
syntactic operations from which the functions and subfunctions
are built. Perhaps the framework should also specify the
set of properties and property values that may be used in
the property-specification rules (and operated on in the
other rules), but it seems premature to try to specify such
a set universally at this point.

3.1. *Primitive Operations*

The primitive operations are all operations on labeled
bracketed strings (or trees), although the inputs may also
include strings without labeled bracketing. There are five
primitive operations: concatenation/adjunction, simple substitution, everywhere substitution, property specification, and
property copying.

(i) *Concatenation/adjunction.* The concatenation/adjunction
operation applies to any number of arguments, concatenates
them, and provides a new outermost pair of labeled brackets
(in tree terms, it provides a parent node). The label on the
added brackets can be specified in one of two ways: (a) by
stipulating it to be a particular category symbol; (b) by
requiring it to be identical to the category of one of the
arguments. For illustration of type (a), see all of the
syntactic rules of section 4 except S14 and S15. For illustration of type (b), see the definition of the subfunction
ATTACH, whose outputs include such expressions as (23) and
(24).

(23) $_{IV}[_{IV/t}[_{IV/t}[believe]\ en]\ _t[that\ ...]]$

(24) $_{IV}[_{TV}[_{TV}[\text{find}]$ en] $_T[\text{Mary}]]$

Since the operation takes any finite number of arguments
and includes the addition of outer brackets with a specified
label, it is really a family of operations. We could write a
given one of these operations as, e.g., $\text{CONCAT}_{n,A}$, where n
is the number of arguments and A the category label to be
added, as illustrated in (25):

(25) $\text{CONCAT}_{2,t}$ $(\alpha, \delta) = {}_t[\alpha\ \delta]$

For perspicuity, however, I have used in the fragment below
a notation which more nearly displays the form of the output,
as in (26):

(26) $_t[\alpha\ \delta]$

The composition of concatenation operations is illustrated
in rule S7 of the fragment; F_6 could be written in the notation of (25) above as (27):

(27) F_6 $(\delta, \beta) = \text{CONCAT}_{2,IV}$ $(\delta, \text{CONCAT}_{2,t}$ $(that, \beta))$

(ii) *Simple substitution.* This operation, which is written
as SUB (α, β, δ), substitutes α for β in δ. We require that
α and β be constituents of the same category. (The require-
ment is independent and could be dropped if it turns out to
be too strong.) Any properties that have been specified for
β that do not conflict with properties of α are preserved as
properties of α in the result (e.g., case, if α is unmarked
for case). Deletion results if α is the null string e; we
assume that the null string counts as a member of any category, so that by fiat deletion does not violate the category-
preserving requirement. Additional constraints on deletion
should be added; there is no deletion at all in the fragment
below.

There is not much use of SUB in the fragment below; it
occurs only in the definition of three subfunctions, NOM (α),
ACC (α), and ATTACH (β, δ), all of which are slightly atypical
in that they are designed as across-the-board rules. Consider
ACC (α), given in (28).

(28) ACC (α) = SUB (β , β, α)
                    [CASE: ACC]

     for all β such that MAINTERM (β, α) = +.

The effect of this subfunction is to add the property specification indicating accusative case to α or to each conjunct
of α if α is a conjoined term phrase. The prose quantification
in the statement of the subfunction should probably not be
permitted; I have used it in the absence of a good general
scheme for across-the-board operations.

One place in the grammar where SUB would be expected to
turn up is in the quantification rules S14 and S15; the
reason it does not is discussed in section 5.

(iii) *Everywhere substitution*. This operation, discussed
in section 2.5 above, is represented as ESUB (α, β, δ). Its
effect is to substitute α for every occurrence of β in δ,
retaining any properties of β that do not conflict with
properties already specified for α. As in simple substitution,
α and β must be of the same category. Further, β must be an
indexed pro-form; these are always *he$_i$* in the fragment, but
an extended fragment might have pro-forms for additional
categories. This restriction reflects the hypothesis that
ESUB is always associated with variable building.

In the fragment below, ESUB is used in the definition of
the subfunction PROSUB: PROSUB (α, i, δ) substitutes the
pronominal form of α for every occurrence of *he$_i$* in δ.
(In an interpretive variant of Montague grammar such as that

in Cooper and Parsons 1976, in which no indexed pro-forms occur in the syntax, ESUB would be eliminated from the syntax completely.) The retention of nonconflicting properties has the effect that whatever case properties have been assigned to the various occurrences of he_i will be carried over to the pronouns that are substituted for them. Without this convention, it is hard to see how one could write a uniform rule that has the same effect as Montague's complex condition involving '... for he_i or him_i respectively' in his rules S3, S14 - 16.

(iv) *Property specification*. In addition to the property specification rules themselves, to be discussed below, the syntactic operations can include the addition of properties with particular values. Properties can be added to individual lexical items or to constituents, but not to strings which are not constituents. Property specification is illustrated in the definition of the subfunction ACC, given above in (28). The notation adopted here is much like standard feature notation: property names and specified values are put in brackets under the constituent to which the property is added.

(v) *Property copying*. This operation is similar to property specification, except that instead of specifying a particular value for the added property, we write, e.g., [GENDER (α)] to mean that the gender value to be assigned is whatever the gender value of α is. This operation is used for agreement rules, and is illustrated in the fragment in the definition of the subfunction AGR. Both kinds of property operations are illustrated in the subfunction PROFORM. Both property specification and property addition are to be understood as overriding any previously specified values for the mentioned properties, but leaving intact the values of any properties not mentioned in the rule.

This completes the inventory of the primitive operations.

3.2. *Syntactic Rules*

Each syntactic rule is to be of the form given in (29).

(29) If $\alpha_1 \in P_{A1}, \ldots, \alpha_n \in P_{An}$, and $\alpha_1, \ldots, \alpha_n$

are of the form SA,

then $F_i (\alpha_1, \ldots, \alpha_n) \in P_B$,

where $F_i (\alpha_1, \ldots, \alpha_n) = \ldots$

What is further required is a specification of the form of
the 'structural analysis' conditions SA, and of the form of
the syntactic operations F_i. With respect to the former I
do not have a clear set of criteria, and there is more prose
in that part of the rules of the fragment than I would like.
I permit reference to labeled bracketings much as in standard
transformational grammar, reference to specified properties,
reference to lexical items, and both quantification and
negation (see S14 and S15).

The operations F_i are more tightly constrained: these must
be definable as a composition of primitive operations and
subfunctions, where the subfunctions themselves are language-
specific operations defined as compositions of primitive
operations. The only violations of the requirement in the
fragment occur in the definitions of the subfunctions NOM,
ACC, and ATTACH, which have been complicated to make them
operate across the board in conjunctions.

One important respect in which the framework is still
deficient is in the connection between the specification of
the structural analysis SA and the specification of the
operands of the subfunctions used in F_i. In standard
transformational grammar, the SA of a transformation is

always a specification of a finite partition of a tree, and
the rule operates on the pieces of tree determined by the
partition. But as noted above, the operation ESUB cannot be
formulated in this way, because there may be no fixed limit
on the number of occurrences of the form to be substituted
for in the string. I have not found any fully satisfactory
formalism for integrating ESUB with the other operations
(see section 4.2 for some particular problems); this may
eventually lead to an argument for leaving all ESUB operations
out of the syntax and following an interpretive variant of
Montague grammar, such as Cooper 1975. The problem may be
only in devising a suitable notation; there is no difficulty
that I can see in stating rules involving ESUB as well as
other operations explicitly in prose while obeying all the
constraints on operations suggested in the previous sections.

3.3. *Rules of Property Specification*

For each syntactic formation rule S_n, there are zero or more
associated rules of property specification (PS_n). If S_n
combines α and β to form a new expression γ, the rules of PS_n
will specify values for properties of γ in terms of values
for properties of α and β. A typical set of property specifications can be seen in PS2. A more problematic use of the
property-specification mechanism is its use to specify the
'MAINVERB' of a verb phrase (the lexical item(s) to which
tense or other affixes should be attached): when two verb
phrases are conjoined, each of their main verbs becomes a
main verb of the result (PS12), and since an adverb may be
applied to conjoined as well as simple verb phrases, the
property-specification rule PS10 must have a quantifier in
it to guarantee that *all* of the main verbs of the input verb
phrase become main verbs of the resulting verb phrase.

(Bennett's device of using # to mark main verbs does not need
any additional stipulation when adverbs are added; the main
verbs are automatically still main verbs unless some rule
deletes the #.)

   Because of this and related problems, I suspect it may be
a mistake to permit 'binary properties' like MAINVERB (of)
to be treated in the same way as ordinary properties like
gender. The binary properties used in this fragment are all
devices for identifying heads of phrases, and that task
should probably have a separate device of its own, with
universal principles for such predictable cases as the fact
that the addition of adverbs and adjectives does not affect
what is the main verb or main noun of a phrase. This in
turn relates to larger questions of the representation of
categories (since IV/IV adverbs are 'modifiers', while IV/IV
verbs like *try to* do become new heads of verb phrases; hence
the relevant universals are not directly statable in PTQ
terms).

3.4. *The Lexicon*

A full theory of the lexicon is beyond the scope of this
paper; see Dowty 1976 and 1978 for interesting and extensive
treatment of the lexicon and its relation to syntax within a
Montague framework. The only addition I propose here is the
addition of certain property specifications to lexical items,
to serve as initial inputs to the property-specification
rules. I have used an abbreviated feature-like notation in
the lexicon of the fragment; an entry such as (30) is to be
understood as an abbreviation for (31).

(30)   John
$$\begin{bmatrix} \text{Masc} \\ \text{PRO: } - \end{bmatrix}$$

(31) GENDER (*John*) = Masc

PRO (*John*) = –

I have also specified in the fragment that all members of B_{IV}, B_{TV}, $B_{IV/t}$, and $B_{IV//IV}$ have the value + for the feature V; this is a makeshift device for recapturing the lexical category 'verb', which I believe should rather be accomplished by a modification of the categorial notation (see, e.g., Bach (ms. a)).

This completes the presentation of the framework. The main innovations are the decomposition of syntactic operations into subfunctions, the proposals for particular primitives, and the inclusion of property-specification rules. The main deficiency, in my opinion, is that prose has not been more fully eliminated from the writing of the rules.

4. *A Fragment*

4.0. *Introductory Remarks*

The fragment of English treated here is almost identical to that generated by PTQ, and the rules are virtually identical in effect with exceptions as noted below. The semantics is unchanged and has been omitted. Property-specification rules have been added.

The fragment differs from that of PTQ in the following ways:

(1) Conjunction errors noted in section 2.7 above have been corrected.

(2) Relative clause formation requires at least one occurrence of the variable being relativized on, so vacuous relativization (*unicorn such that John loves Mary,* etc.) is eliminated.

(3) Montague's S15 CN-scope quantification rule is
eliminated; (see Partee 1975; the marginal evidence cited there
in favor of such a rule now appears to be spurious).[23]

(4) In the sentence-scope and IV-scope quantification
rules, vacuous quantification is eliminated (see Cooper and
Parsons 1976 for discussion), and the term phrase quantified
in may not be a subscripted pronoun or a disjunction
including a subscripted pronoun.

Some discussion of the rules follows in section 5.

4.1. *The Fragment*

Lexicon

B_{IV} = {run, walk, talk, rise, change} all [V: +]

B_T = { John , Mary , Bill , ninety ,
$\begin{bmatrix} \text{Masc} \\ \text{PRO: } - \end{bmatrix}$ $\begin{bmatrix} \text{Fem} \\ \text{PRO:} \end{bmatrix}$ $\begin{bmatrix} \text{Masc} \\ \text{PRO: } - \end{bmatrix}$ $\begin{bmatrix} \text{Ncut} \\ \text{PRO: } - \end{bmatrix}$

he_0 , he_1 , ...} all [Number: Sg]
$\begin{bmatrix} \text{PRO: } + \\ \text{INDEX: } 0 \end{bmatrix}$ $\begin{bmatrix} \text{PRO: } + \\ \text{INDEX: } 1 \end{bmatrix}$

B_{TV} = {find, lose, eat, love, date, be, seek, conceive}

all [V: +]

B_{IAV} = {rapidly, slowly, voluntarily, willingly}

B_{CN} = { Man , woman, park , fish , pen , unicorn,
[Masc] [Fem] [Neut] [Neut] [Neut] [Neut]

price , temperature}   all [Number: Sg]
[Neut]   [Neut]

$B_{t/t}$ = {necessarily, allegedly}

$B_{IAV/T}$ = {in, about}

$B_{IV/t}$ = {believe, assert}
[V: +]   [V: +]

$B_{IV//IV}$ = { try , wish }
          [V: +] [V: +]

$B_{T/CN}$ = {every, the, a}

Defined Subfunctions

1. PROFORM (α) = $_T[$ HE $]$ (for $\alpha \in P_{CN} \cup P_T$)
$$\begin{bmatrix} \text{GENDER } (\alpha) \\ \text{NUMBER } (\alpha) \\ \text{PRO: +} \\ \text{INDEX: -} \end{bmatrix}$$

2. PROSUB (α, i, δ) = ESUB (PROFORM (α), he_i, δ)

   for $\alpha \in P_{CN} \cup P_T$, any δ)

3. AGR (α, β) = β (for $\alpha \in P_T$, β = Pres)
                    [NUMBER (α)]

4. NOM (α) = SUB (β , β, α)
                  [CASE: NOM]

   for all β such that MAINTERM (β, α) = +

5. ACC (α) = SUB (β , β, α)
                  [CASE: ACC]

   for all β such that MAINTERM (β, α) = +

6. ATTACH (β, δ) = SUB (CAT γ [β γ], γ, δ)

   for all γ such that MAINVERB (γ, δ) = +

   (for β an 'affix', $\delta \in P_{IV}$)

Syntactic Rules and Property-Specification Rules

S1. If $\alpha \in B_A$, then F_0 $(\alpha) \in P_A$,

   where F_0 (α) = $_A[\alpha]$, for every category A.

PS1. (Property-specification 1).

    (i) For all properties P which are defined for lexical items, $P(F_0(\alpha)) = P(\alpha)$.

   (ii) If $V(\alpha) = +$, then $\text{MAINVERB}(\alpha, F_0(\alpha)) = +$

  (iii) If $\alpha \in B_T$, then $\text{MAINTERM}(\alpha, F_0(\alpha)) = +$

S2. If $\alpha \in P_{T/CN}$ and $\beta \in P_{CN}$, and $\text{NUMBER}(\beta) = Sg$, then $F_1(\alpha, \beta) \in P_T$, where $F_1(\alpha, \beta) = {}_T[\alpha\ \beta]$

PS2.   (i) $\text{GENDER}(F_1(\alpha, \beta)) = \text{GENDER}(\beta)$

   (ii) $\text{NUMBER}(F_1(\alpha, \beta)) = Sg$

  (iii) $\text{MAINTERM}(F_1(\alpha, \beta), F_1(\alpha, \beta)) = +$

  (iv) $\text{PRO}(F_1(\alpha, \beta)) = -$

S3. If $\alpha \in P_{CN}$ and $\phi \in P_t$ and ϕ is of the form ${}_t[\beta\ he_n\ \gamma]$, then $F_{2,n}(\alpha, \phi) \in P_{CN}$, where $F_{2,n}(\alpha, \phi) =$ ${}_{CN}[\alpha\ such\ that\ \text{PROSUB}(\alpha, n, \psi)]$

PS3.   (i) $\text{GENDER}(F_{2,n}(\alpha, \phi)) = \text{GENDER}(\alpha)$

   (ii) $\text{NUMBER}(F_{2,n}(\alpha, \phi)) = \text{NUMBER}(\alpha)$

S4. If $\alpha \in P_T$, $\delta \in P_{IV}$, then $F_4(\alpha, \delta) = {}_t[\text{NOM}(\alpha)\ \text{ATTACH}$ $(\text{AGR}(\alpha, Pres), \delta)]$

PS4. $\text{MAINVERB}(\gamma, \text{ATTACH}(\text{AGR}(\alpha, Pres), \delta)) = +$ for all γ such that $\text{MAINVERB}(\gamma, \delta) = +$.

S5. If $\alpha \in P_{TV}$ and $\beta \in P_T$, then $F_4(\delta, \beta) \in P_{IV}$, where $F_4(\delta, \beta) = {}_{IV}[\delta\ \text{ACC}(\beta)]$

PS5. $\text{MAINVERB}(\gamma, F_4(\delta, \beta)) = +$ for all γ such that $\text{MAINVERB}(\gamma, \delta) = +$

S6. If $\delta \in P_{IAV/T}$ and $\beta \in P_T$, then $F_5(\delta, \beta) \in P_{IAV}$, where F_5 $(\delta, \beta) = {}_{IAV}[\delta\ ACC\ (\beta)]$

PS6. (none)

S7. If $\delta \in P_{IV/t}$ and $\beta \in P_t$, then F_6 $(\delta, \beta) \in P_{IV}$,

where F_6 $(\delta, \beta) = {}_{IV}[\delta\ {}_t[that\ \beta]]$

PS7. MAINVERB $(\gamma,\ F_6\ (\delta,\ \beta)) = +$

for all γ such that MAINVERB $(\gamma,\ \delta) = +$

S8. If $\delta \in P_{IV//IV}$ and $\beta \in P_{IV}$, then F_7 $(\delta, \beta) \in P_{IV}$,

where F_7 $(\delta, \beta) = {}_{IV}[\delta\ {}_{IV}[to\ \beta]]$

PS8. MAINVERB $(\gamma,\ F_7\ (\delta,\ \beta)) = +$

for all γ such that MAINVERB $(\gamma,\ \delta) = +$

S9. If $\delta \in P_{t/t}$ and $\beta \in P_t$, then F_8 $(\delta, \beta) \in P_t$,

where F_8 $(\delta, \beta) = {}_t[\delta\ \beta]$

PS9. (none)

S10. If $\delta \in P_{IV/IV}$ and $\beta \in P_{IV}$, then F_9 $(\delta, \beta) \in P_{IV}$,

where F_9 $(\delta, \beta) = {}_{IV}[\beta\ \delta]$

PS10. MAINVERB $(\gamma,\ F_9\ (\delta,\ \beta)) = +$

for all γ such that MAINVERB $(\gamma,\ \delta) = +$

S11. If $\phi,\ \Psi \in P_t$, then F_{10} $(\phi,\ \Psi)$, F_{11} $(\phi,\ \Psi) \in P_t$,

where F_{10} $(\phi,\ \Psi) = {}_t[\phi\ and\ \Psi]$

where F_{11} $(\phi,\ \Psi) = {}_t[\phi\ or\ \Psi]$

PS11. (none)

S12. If $\gamma,\ \delta \in P_{IV}$, then F_{12} $(\gamma,\ \delta)$, F_{13} $(\gamma,\ \delta) \in P_{IV}$,

where F_{12} $(\gamma,\ \delta) = {}_{IV}[\gamma\ and\ \delta]$

where F_{13} $(\gamma,\ \delta) = {}_{IV}[\gamma\ or\ \delta]$

PS12. MAINVERB $(\beta, F_{12} (\gamma, \delta)) = +$ for all β such that

MAINVERB $(\beta, \gamma) = +$ or MAINVERB $(\beta, \delta) = +$. (Same for F_{13})

S13. If $\alpha, \beta \in P_T$, then $F_{14} (\alpha, \beta) \in P_T$,

where $F_{14} (\alpha, \beta)) = {}_T[\alpha$ *or* $\beta]$

PS13.   (i) MAINTERM $(\gamma, F_{14} (\alpha, \beta)) = +$ for all γ such that

MAINTERM $(\gamma, \alpha) = +$ or MAINTERM $(\gamma, \beta) = +$

(ii)

$$\text{GENDER } (F_{14} (\alpha, \beta)) = \begin{cases} \text{GENDER } (\alpha) \text{ if} \\ \text{GENDER } (\alpha) = \text{GENDER } (\beta) \\ \\ \text{COM if} \\ \text{GENDER } (\alpha) \neq \text{GENDER } (\beta) \end{cases}$$

(iii) NUMBER $(F_{14} (\alpha, \beta)) = $ NUMBER (α)

[grammar book dialect]

S14. If $\alpha \in P_T$ and $\phi \in P_t$ and (i) PRO $(\beta) = -$

for all β such that MAINTERM $(\beta, \alpha) = +$

and (ii) $\phi = {}_t[\gamma \, \delta \, \xi]$, where $\delta = he_n$ and γ

does not contain he_n, then

$F_{15,n} (\alpha, \phi) \in P_t$, where $F_{15,n} (\alpha, \phi) =$

${}_t[\gamma \, \alpha \text{ PROSUB } (\alpha, n, \xi)]$

PS14. (none)

S16. If $\alpha \in P_T$ and $\delta \in P_{IV}$ and (i) PRO $(\beta) = -$ for all

such that MAINTERM $(\beta, \alpha) = +$ and (ii) $\delta = {}_{IV}[\gamma \, \xi \, \theta]$,

where $\xi = he_n$ and γ does not contain he_n, then

$F_{16,n} (\alpha, \delta) \in P_{IV}$, where $F_{16,n} (\alpha, \delta) =$

${}_{IV}[\gamma \, \alpha \text{ PROSUB } (\alpha, n, \theta)]$.

PS16. MAINVERB $(\gamma, F_{16,n} (\alpha, \delta)) = +$ for all γ such that

MAINVERB $(\gamma, \delta) = +$.

S17.1. If $\alpha \in P_T$ and $\delta \in P_{IV}$, then F_{17} $(\alpha,\ \delta) \in P_t$,

where F_{17} $(\alpha,\ \delta) = {}_t[\text{NOM}\ (\alpha)\ {}_{\text{AUX}}[do\ \text{AGR}\ (\alpha,\ \text{Pres})]$

$not\ \delta]$

PS17.1. (none)

S17.2. If $\alpha \in P_T$ and $\delta \in P_{IV}$, then F_{18} $(\alpha,\ \delta) \in P_t$,

where F_{18} $(\alpha,\ \delta) = {}_t[\text{NOM}\ (\alpha)\ {}_{\text{AUX}}[will\ \delta]$

PS17.2. (none)

S17.3. If $\alpha \in P_T$ and $\delta \in P_{IV}$, then F_{19} $(\alpha,\ \delta) \in P_t$,

where F_{19} $(\alpha,\ \delta) = {}_t[\text{NOM}\ (\alpha)\ {}_{\text{AUX}}[\text{will}]\ not\ \delta]$

PS17.3. (none)

S17.4. If $\alpha \in P_T$ and $\delta \in P_{IV}$, then F_{20} $(\alpha,\ \delta) \in P_t$,

where F_{20} $(\alpha,\ \delta) = {}_t[\text{NOM}\ (\alpha)\ {}_{\text{AUX}}[have\ \text{AGR}\ (\alpha,\ \text{Pres})]$

$\text{ATTACH}\ (en,\ \delta)]$

PS17.4. (none)

S17.5. If $\alpha \in P_T$ and $\delta \in P_{IV}$, then F_{21} $(\alpha,\ \delta) \in P_t$,

where F_{21} $(\alpha,\ \delta) = {}_t[\text{NOM}\ (\alpha)\ {}_{\text{AUX}}[have\ \text{AGR}\ (\alpha,\ \text{Pres})]$

$not\ \text{ATTACH}\ (en,\ \delta)]$

PS17.5. (none)

5. *Problems and Alternatives*

5.1. *Gender*

No gender is assigned to he_i; as a result, the property-
specification rule for gender of conjoined term phrases
(PS13) is undefined when either conjunct is an indexed pro-
form. This should not cause a problem in this fragment
because of the prohibition against quantifying in pro-forms

(S14, S16) (which extends to pro-forms as conjuncts as term phrases), but it could cause a problem for languages in which predicate adjectives agree in gender with subjects. Perhaps languages in which gender is clearly syntactic (which might not include English) should have separate pro-forms for each gender. Lauri Karttunen (personal communication) has suggested that gender in English might best be treated entirely as a matter of conventional implicature, and not handled in the syntax at all.

5.2. *Case*

As mentioned in section 2.4, there is an asymmetry between the treatment of number and gender on the one hand and case on the other; the former are specified by the recursive property-specification rules, the latter assigned by a syntactic rule when a verb or preposition combines with an object. For languages with a rich inflectional morphology, this would seem to imply that number and gender are specified bottom-up, while case is imposed top-down. Given that the same elements (determiners, adjectives) often show agreement in all three features, something seems wrong. The only uniform treatment I can think of is to define case bottom-up as well, generating term phrases of each case separately, and having verbs and prepositions select term phrases of a particular case to combine with rather than combining with un-case-marked term phrases and assigning case to them. The unattractiveness of generating all the cases separately could be lessened by providing a single schema with a variable ranging over the values of the case property. One interesting consequence of such an approach is that it would render impossible rules like Passive or Raising which entail the reassignment of case.

(Dowty 1978 and Bresnan 1978 argue independently that such rules should be eliminated in favor of lexical rules.)

5.3. *Problems with the Quantification Rules*

Rules S14 and S16 do not quite work as they are stated, and what may seem at first like a trivial problem with them is probably a serious one. The crucial part of S14 is repeated below (the problem with S16 is identical).

(32) $F_{15,n} (\alpha, \phi) = {}_t[\gamma \ \alpha \ \text{PROSUB} \ (\alpha, \ n, \ \xi)]$

The SA part of the rule specifies that δ is the first occurrence of *he$_n$* in ϕ; $\phi = {}_t[\gamma \ \delta \ \xi]$. The problem is that in many cases, neither γ nor ξ will be a constituent, yet the concatenation operation is defined only on constituents. My intention is that α should simply substitute for δ without affecting the rest of the structure, and that the PROSUB function should make appropriate substitutions in ξ without affecting the rest of *its* structure. If PROSUB were applying to the entire string ϕ, there would be no such difficulty (as there is no comparable difficulty with the relative clause rule S3). But there is no way within the proposed framework to apply PROSUB (or any ESUB operation) to a part of an expression which is not a constituent. I have written the rule almost as if it were a transformation; the substitution of δ for α would be easily expressible in transformational terms (leaving surrounding tree structure intact). But as mentioned earlier, ESUB cannot be a transformation. The problem seems to be that I haven't found any way to have operations apply to specific parts of strings without having either (i) a factorization of the TG sort of SA statement or (ii) a reconcatenation of the affected parts, violating constituenthood requirements.

An earlier formulation of the quantification rules avoided
the concatenation problem but ran into a different one
(Stanley Peters, Jr., personal communication). The earlier
formulation of S14 was as follows:

(33) If $\alpha \in P_T$ and $\phi \in P_t$ and (i) PRO (β) = - for all
$\beta \in$ MAINTERM (α) and (ii) $\phi = {}_t[\gamma \; \delta \; \xi]$, where $\delta = he_n$
and γ does not contain he_n, then $F_{15,n}$ (α, ϕ) $\in P_t$,
where $F_{15,n}$ (α, ϕ) = PROSUB (α, n, $F_{16,n}$ (α, ϕ)) and
$F_{16,n}$ (α, ϕ) = SUB (α, δ, ϕ)

In effect, this rule first quantifies the term phrase in for
the first occurrence of he_n (by $F_{16,n}$), and then uses PROSUB
to substitute the appropriate pronoun for all remaining occurrences of he_n. Since each operation has the whole string ϕ as
an argument, there is no need to break the string apart and
reconcatenate it. This version also conforms more closely to
the spirit of the proposal to build up rules by composition
of subfunctions than does the final version. The problem,
however, is that the quantified-in term phrase, δ, may itself
contain occurrences of he_n, and these would incorrectly be
changed to pronouns by $F_{15,n}$ (they would not be bound semantically, since the semantics is exactly as in PTQ). So in
fact I cannot see any way to write the quantification rule
within this framework; unless there is a solution I have
overlooked, it seems that I must change the framework in some
fundamental way, either by changing the way the rules work
or by removing indexed pro-forms (and ESUB) from the syntax.

5.4. *The Auxiliary System*

I had originally hoped to give a more uniform treatment than
Montague did to the auxiliary system; the main obstacle turned
out to be the problem of conjoined verb phrases. The need

for a better treatment of across-the-board phenomena was
discussed in section 2.7. I will add here only one particular
problem that so far as I know has not been solved in any
extensions of PTQ, and perhaps not in any other framework
either. There are conjoined verb phrases such as 'be in the
park and walk'; what should happen when such a verb phrase
is put into the present tense negative form? PTQ gives (34);
Friedman (1974) gives (35); there seems to be no possible
form at all.

(34) *John is not in the park and walk.

(35) * John doesn't be in the park and walk.

(For reasons noted by Friedman (1974), (36) would be a
semantically incorrect form for this rule to produce, though
syntactically acceptable.)

(36) John is not in the park and doesn't walk.

The behavior of copular *be* greatly complicates the treatment
of verb phrase conjunction, since it originates in the verb
phrase but behaves like an auxiliary if there are no other
auxiliaries present. (This presents problems for many frameworks, not just this one.)

It would be possible to list a number of further problems,
but the ones cited include the most serious problems for this
framework that I am aware of. Some of them present problems
for other frameworks as well; I cannot be sure at this point
to what extent the phenomena in question are not yet well
enough understood.

Let me add a personal note by way of conclusion. It can
be very frustrating to try to specify frameworks and fragments
explicitly; this project has not been entirely rewarding.
I would not recommend that one always work with the constraint

of full explicitness. But I feel strongly that it is
important to do so periodically, because otherwise it is
extremely easy to think that you have a solution to a problem
when in fact you don't. If the failure of this attempt to
provide a framework both constrained and descriptively adequate can help to lead toward the construction of a better
one, I won't regret the headaches.

Acknowledgments

I am grateful first of all to my husband, Emmon Bach, for
ideas, discussion, criticism, support, and encouragement.
Also to Marianne Mithun and Steven Davis for organizing the
stimulating conference at which this paper was presented and
for their patience and encouragement through the delays of
completion of the manuscript. Also, for particularly helpful
comments and suggestions, to Stanley Peters, Lauri Karttunen,
William Ladusaw, Joyce Friedman, Ewan Klein, and Terence
Parsons.

The preparation of this paper was supported in part by a
fellowship at the Center for Advanced Study in the Behavioral
Sciences (1976 - 1977), for which I am most grateful.

Notes

1. See Montague 1970b; 1973.

2. Once, when Montague was told about linguists' aim of
constructing a theory of language to characterize all and
only possible *human* languages, his response was to ask why
linguists wished to disqualify themselves from fieldwork on
other inhabited planets.

3. This has been pointed out by a number of writers;
discussion together with a vivid illustration can be found
in Bach and Cooper 1978.

4. Partee, forthcoming. In PTQ, it is the analysis trees that play the role of disambiguated language. Cooper (1975) suggests a way of dispensing entirely with the level of disambiguated language.

5. It would be possible to treat all adjectives as common noun modifiers by introducing a syntactic category CN//CN for those Siegel treats as t///e; a meaning postulate could be written to 'reduce' them in effect to the type $\langle\langle s, e\rangle, t\rangle$.

6. The introduction of these 'subfunctions' was suggested to me by Emmon Bach. The notion bears some resemblance to the introduction of subroutines in computer programming.

7. See Partee 1973; 1975. Friedman (1974) suggests that unlabeled bracketing may be all that is required for the resolution of the particular difficulties with PTQ conjunction.

8. I refer interchangeably to tree structures and labeled bracketings, since either is easily convertible into the other. (Labeled bracketings are typographically more convenient than trees, but structural relations such as 'sister node' and 'parent node' are easiest to express in tree terms.)

9. Within transformational grammar, an increase in the number of cyclic categories similarly leads to a decrease in the need for extrinsic rule ordering. See, for example, Williams 1975.

10. Linguistically unnatural features of PTQ that appear to be consequences of the requirement of total functions include vacuous relativization (where the clause to be relativized contains no occurrence of the relevant he_n), vacuous quantification, and the quantifying in of subscripted pronouns.

11. The treatment of 'features' as recursively defined predicates was suggested to me by Terry Parsons.

12. In the fragment presented here I treat gender as syntactic in English to illustrate the idea of recursively defined properties. Such a treatment would be appropriate for a language like French or Russian, but it is likely that English gender should not be treated in the syntax at all (Lauri Karttunen, personal communication).

13. Ewan Klein pointed out to me the possibility that recursively defined properties potentially have all the power of reference to derivational history; he has shown (unpublished notes) how Thomason's (1976) use of derivational history in the statement of reflexivization can be replaced by a recursively defined property of expressions. Nothing I say here rules out his example; the property he uses bears some resemblance to the 'Type 3' properties discussed below.

14. Jackendoff, Bresnan, and others have made various suggestions of this sort.

15. A similar device was employed by Montague (1970a) to identify main verb occurrences in verb phrases.

16. That (i) may be equivalent was pointed out to me by Ewan Klein (see note 13); that (ii) may be was suggested by David Lewis at the conference where this paper was presented.

17. See, for instance, the I-Grammar variant of PTQ in Cooper and Parsons 1976.

18. This effect is achieved by Bach (1976; Chapter 1 of this volume) by eliminating syntactic gender agreement rules, having all of he_i, she_j, it_k separate from the start and with disjoint subscripts.

19. In the I-grammar of Cooper and Parsons 1976, the selection of an index for a term phrase (and its consequent 'quantified-in' interpretation) is followed by the selection all at once of whatever pronouns are to be interpreted as co-indexed to it.

Variable binding is evidently the only thing that makes the syntax of the set of closed formulas of the predicate calculus non-context-free (personal communication from both Herbert Bohnert and William Marsh, independently).

20. See the discussion of passive, complex transitive verbs, and the 'right-wrap' subfunction in Bach (ms. a; ms. b).

21. At the time this paper was begun, the only published work in Montague grammar on languages other than English that I knew of was that of Siegel (1976a; 1976b) on Russian and that of Cooper (1975) on Hittite. There were two such papers presented at this conference, one by Thomason and Thomason on Serbo-Croatian and one by Thomason and Mithun on Mohawk. There is also now a dissertation by Marion Johnson on Kikuyu (Ohio State), one by James McCloskey on Irish (University of Texas at Austin), and one in progress in part on Sanskrit by Dave Davis (University of Massachusetts at Amherst). There are probably others that I am unaware of or have forgotten to mention.

22. *She or he* might be better here, but that would require a more complicated device with the power of the 'respectively' transformation.

23. Evidence *for* the rule came from Joan Bresnan (personal communication), whose example was a noun phrase of the following form:

(i) every man who loses a pen who finds it

Subsequent discussion with Emmon Bach has persuaded me that such examples do not involve genuine bound-variable anaphora and are probably better grouped with the problematical 'donkey-sentences' like (ii), however these are best treated.

(ii) Every man who owns a donkey beats it.

References

Bach, Emmon. 1976. "An Extension of Classical Transformational Grammar." In *Problems in Linguistic Metatheory*. Proceedings of the 1976 Conference at Michigan State University, East Lansing, Mich.

————. Ms. a. "Control in Montague Grammar." University of Massachusetts, Amherst.

————. Ms. b. "In Defense of Passive." University of Massachusetts, Amherst.

Bach, Emmon, and Robin Cooper. 1978. "The NP-S Analysis of Relative Clauses and Compositional Semantics." *Linguistics and Philosophy* 2(1): 145 - 150.

Bennett, Michael. 1974. "Some Extensions of a Montague Fragment of English." Ph.D. dissertation, UCLA; available from the Indiana University Linguistics Club.

Bresnan, Joan. 1978. "A Realistic Transformational Grammar." In M. Halle et al., eds., *Linguistic Theory and Psychological Reality*. Cambridge, Mass.: MIT Press.

Chomsky, Noam. 1957. *Syntactic Structures*. The Hague: Mouton.

————. 1978. "On Wh-Movement." In *Formal Syntax*, ed. P. Culicover et al. New York: Academic Press.

Cooper, Robin. 1975. "Montague's Semantic Theory and Transformational Syntax." Ph.D. dissertation, University of Massachusetts, Amherst.

Cooper, Robin, and Terence Parsons. 1976. "Montague Grammar, Generative Semantics, and Interpretive Semantics." In Partee, ed. 1976.

Dowty, David. 1976. "Montague Grammar and the Lexical Decomposition of Causative Verbs." In Partee, ed. 1976.

————. 1978. "Governed Transformations as Lexical Rules in a Montague Grammar." *Linguistic Inquiry* 9(3) (Summer 1978): 393 - 426.

Friedman, Joyce. 1974. "Conjoined Phrases in Montague Grammar."
Draft ms., University of Michigan.

Greenberg, Joseph H. 1963. "Some Universals of Grammar with
Particular Reference to the Order of Meaningful Elements."
In Joseph Greenberg, ed., *Universals of Language*. Cambridge,
Mass.: MIT Press.

Lasnik, Howard, and Robert Fiengo. 1974. "Complement Object
Deletion." *Linguistic Inquiry* 5: 535 - 571.

Montague, Richard. 1970a. "English as a Formal Language."
In *Linguaggi nella società e nella tecnica*, by B. Visentini
et al. Milan: Edizioni di Comunità. Reprinted in Montague
1974.

———. 1970b. "Universal Grammar." *Theoria* 36: 373 - 398.
Reprinted in Montague 1974.

———. 1973. "The Proper Treatment of Quantification in
Ordinary English." In K. J. J. Hintikka et al., eds.,
Approaches to Natural Language, pp. 221 - 242. Dordrecht:
D. Reidel Publishing Co. Reprinted in Montague 1974.

———. 1974. *Formal Philosophy: Selected Papers of Richard
Montague*, ed. Richard Thomason. New Haven: Yale University
Press.

Partee, Barbara. 1973. "Some Transformational Extensions of
Montague Grammar." *Journal of Philosophical Logic* 2:
509 - 534. Reprinted in Partee, ed. 1976.

———. 1975. "Montague Grammar and Transformational Grammar."
Linguistic Inquiry 6: 203 - 300.

———. Forthcoming. "Montague Grammar and the Well-Formedness
Constraint." To appear in Frank Heny and Helmut Schnelle,
eds., *Syntax and Semantics*, Vol. 10: *Selections from the
Third Groningen Round Table*. New York: Academic Press.

———, ed. 1976. *Montague Grammar*. New York: Academic
Press.

Rodman, R. 1976. "Scope Phenomena, 'Movement Transformations',
    and Relative Clauses." In Partee, ed. 1976.

Ross, John Robert. 1967. "Constraints on Variables in Syntax."
    Ph.D. dissertation, MIT.

Siegel, Muffy E. A. 1976a. "Capturing the Russian Adjective."
    In Partee, ed. 1976, pp. 293 - 309.

―――. 1976b. "Capturing the Adjective." Ph.D. dissertation,
    University of Massachusetts, Amherst.

Thomason, Richmond. 1976. "Some Extensions of Montague
    Grammar." In Partee, ed. 1976.

Williams, Edwin. 1975. "Small Clauses in English." In
    J. Kimball, ed., *Syntax and Semantics,* Vol. 4. New York:
    Academic Press.

3

Helpful Hints to the Ordinary Working Montague Grammarian

James D. McCawley

In alluding to Fillmore's phrase 'the ordinary working
grammarian', it is my intention to emphasize that the remarks
that follow are directed more at those who are using Montague
grammar as a framework for the detailed description of specific languages than at pure theoreticians. I propose to
provide some perspective on various details of the current
analytical tradition in Montague grammar and the extent to
which different details deserve to be taken seriously, to
comment on the respects in which Montague grammar is commen-
surable with transformational grammar in some version or
other, and to discuss certain transformational analyses for
which Montague analogues could be developed which could
provide viable alternatives to not fully satisfactory Montague
analyses that have been proposed or suggested. It is important
for the ordinary working Montague grammarian to have a clear
idea not only of what the similarities and differences are
between Montague grammar and transformational grammar, but
also of how significant or insignificant the various differences are, that is, of how much of a deviation it would
be from the standard claims and policies of Montague grammar
to adopt direct analogues of given transformational analyses,
and for the grammarian to be able to recognize when an
existing transformational analysis is not far removed from a

possible Montague analysis. I propose to demonstrate below
that various 'abstract' syntactic analyses are not as irrecon-
cilable with the 'surfac-y' syntax of Montague grammar as
might at first be thought, a point that is worth emphasizing,
since it expands the range of linguistic word that the
ordinary working Montague grammarian can draw on as a source
of relevant insight.

Drawing on both Partee 1975 and McCawley 1977a, I will
begin with a rough sketch of Montague syntax and transformational syntax, stated in terms that will facilitate comparison.
Montague syntax does not accord to the category 'sentence'
the privileged role that it has in transformational syntax.
Whereas a transformational grammar is 'officially' taken to
be a specification of what are the sentences of a given language, a Montague syntax is supposed to provide a recursive
specification of the membership of all syntactic categories,
with the category 'sentence' being at most a first among
equals. This difference correlates with a difference as to
the domains to which syntactic rules apply: transformations
are generally taken as applying only to sentences, or only to
sentences and NP's, whereas every syntactic category is the
domain of application of some Montague syntactic rule or
other. Transformational grammar keeps separate two types of
rules: phrase structure rules, which specify how elements may
combine with one another in deep structures, and transformations, which specify how underlying structures of sentences
are related to more superficial levels of structure. A syntactic rule in Montague grammar will typically be a combination
of a phrase structure rule and what amounts to one or more
transformations, as in rule S4 of "The Proper Treatment of
Quantification in English" (PTQ), which in effect combines
the phrase structure rule S → NP VP (i.e., a sentence

consists of an NP followed by a VP) and an agreement transformation that makes the verb of the VP agree in person and number with its subject.

The reason that Montague syntactic rules lump phrase structure rules and transformations into what often take on the appearance of paragraphs of the internal revenue code is that Montague grammar makes no provision for obligatory transformations. A Montague syntactic rule is stated in terms of the surface membership of syntactic categories, i.e., it tells one how to get surface members of category B from surface members of categories $A_1, \ldots, A_n$:

(1) If $\alpha_1 \in P_{A_1}$, $\alpha_2 \in P_{A_2}$, $\ldots$ and $\alpha_n \in P_{A_n}$,

then $f(\alpha_1, \alpha_2, \ldots, \alpha_n) \in P_B$.

What one derives by such a rule is a surface member of the category B regardless of whether one applies any subsequent rules to it. Thus, classical Montague grammar does not allow one to separate Montague's S4 into the phrase structure rule $S \rightarrow NP\ VP$ and a separate rule of agreement, since the result of applying the one rule but not the other would be ill-formed sentences such as *He like me, and the rule corresponding to $S \rightarrow NP\ VP$ would then be failing as a recursive characterization of the (surface) category S.

Note that the exclusion of obligatory transformations is really a restriction on the individuation of syntactic rules rather than on their content. An orthodox Montague grammarian can have as many obligatory transformations as desired simply by formulating them as riders on other rules. One can relax the exclusion of obligatory rules without thereby changing the descriptive power of Montague grammars if one compensates by adopting a certain principle of rule interaction, namely an extra strict principle of 'strict cyclicity'. I maintain

that a Montague syntax can be recast in the following transformational form, in which the rules are individuated
differently, but the expressive capabilities are the same:
(a) the grammar consists of a system of phrase structure
rules, which generate deep structures, and a system of
transformations, which convert deep structures by steps into
surface structures; (b) transformations can be either optional
or obligatory; (c) every constituent of the deep structure
is a cyclic domain; (d) a syntactic rule can apply only at
the point of the derivation at which the constituent that
it affects is being processed; and (e) *cyclic outputs* are
required to be well-formed surface representations of their
respective categories, i.e., the transformations must convert
each deep-structure constituent into a well-formed surface
member of its category before the processing of higher
constituents can begin, though the intermediate stages in
this processing need not be well-formed. Note that (c) makes
(e) a much more stringent restriction on grammars than it at
first sight might seem to be.

The correspondence between classical Montague grammar and
the Montaguish transformational syntax (MTS) just sketched
can be illustrated by the following pair of derivations:

(2) a.

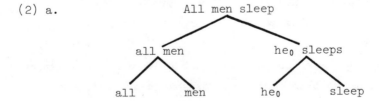

b.[1] Deep structure

Derivational steps

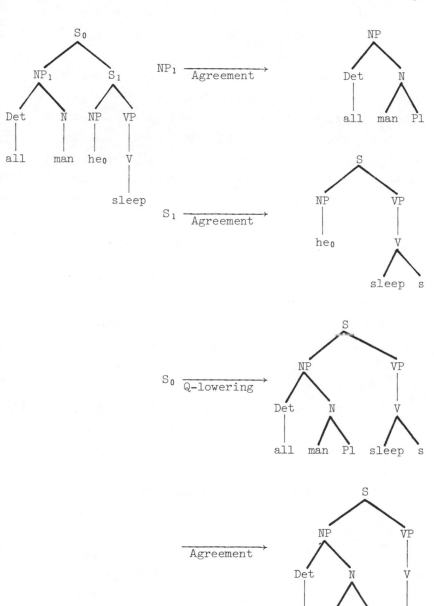

In this brief sketch, I have glossed over three important
issues which I will now take up: (i) in classical Montague
grammar, there is one semantic rule for every syntactic rule;
can the revised individuation of syntactic rules proposed here
be matched by an appropriate reindividuation of semantic
rules? (ii) What is the nature of the objects that figure as
inputs and outputs of the rules? Are they strings? trees?
dependency structures? Are their ultimate units words?
morphemes? strings of phonemes? (iii) What exactly is the
nature of the 'local well-formedness condition' (the constraint
that the items generated by the syntactic rules be well-formed
surface representatives of the category in question) that
Montague grammarians have generally abided by — what sorts of
things are required to have what sorts of well-formedness?

Regarding (i), I can only report that an appropriate reindividuation is available in the cases where I have looked
for one. For example, when Montague's S4 is broken up into
S → NP VP and an agreement rule, the semantic rule corresponding to S4 can be assigned to S → NP VP and a vacuous
semantic rule to the agreement rule, i.e., the agreement rule
is 'meaning-preserving'.[2] Note that in MTS, even phrase
structure rules need not be meaning-preserving: the semantic
rule corresponding to a particular phrase structure rule
might do more than just concatenate the semantic interpretations of the constituents. The semantic rule corresponding to
Montague's quantification rule can be divided in two to
conform to (2b) provided one is willing to tolerate a semantically incoherent formula as an intermediate stage in the
semantic derivation. Specifically, the effect of Montague's
semantic rule, which is to yield $\alpha'\ ^\wedge(\lambda\ x_n)\ \beta'$, where α'
is the translation of the quantified NP, β' that of the sen-
tence in which the NP is to be inserted, and $\underset{\sim\sim}{he}_n$ the variable

that it replaces, can be achieved through a semantic rule
corresponding to the phrase structure rule, yielding α β,
and one corresponding to the transformation, converting
α β into α' $^\wedge$(λx$_n$) β'. Note that an incoherent formula such
as α β (or α $^\wedge$β) is forced on one because the deep structure
in (2b) does not indicate what pronoun the NP is to be
substituted for; an alternative analysis is of course available
in which the sentence is derived from three constituents (the
NP, the 'host' S, and he$_n$) rather than two and the quantifier-
lowering transformation is meaning-preserving.

I turn now to question (ii) — the nature of syntactic
objects. The work of both Montague and Chomsky is heavily
influenced by an arbitrary decision to take strings rather
than some more structured kind of object as the items that
the grammar provides derivations of and associates semantic
interpretations to. In both cases the decision is not surprising, in that their work developed out of traditions (that
of Carnap in logic and that of Harris in linguistics) that
operated exclusively in string terms; indeed, explicit statements of formation rules in logic are almost invariably given
in string terms.[3] The decision remains arbitrary, however:
one could as well have implemented Montague's program in
tree terms rather than string terms, i.e., each syntactic
rule could be formulated as a function with a sequence of
trees as arguments and a tree as value. (I note parintheti-
cally that most transformational grammar has in effect been
done in tree terms, despite frequent pronouncements to the
effect that strings were the relevant units.)

The most obvious way in which Montague's decision to
operate in string terms has affected the Montague analytic
tradition is in the way that it has rendered various analyses
more easily or less easily accessible to the investigator.

Consider, for example, Montague's formulation of his
quantification rule:

(3) ... $F_{10,n}$ (α, ϕ) comes from ϕ by replacing the *first*
occurrence of he_n/him_n by α and all other occurrences
of he_n/him_n by he/she/it or him/her/it respectively,
according as the gender of the *first* B_{CN} or B_T in α is
masc/fem/neuter. (Emphasis added)

The reference to 'first member of B_{CN}' amounts to an algorithm,
stated in string terms, for finding the head noun of the NP.
Montague's intention in the rule was presumably to have the
pronoun chosen on the basis of features of the head noun.
The algorithm in fact will not work in general: it fails in
the case of compound nouns or of common noun expressions
that have a preposed modifier, as in the following examples,
where it would incorrectly pick out the underlined noun as
the head and choose the pronoun accordingly:[4]

(4) every bricklayer such that it is happy

a tailor's thimble such that he can be bought for
under 15 cents

The algorithm could of course be fixed up so that it would
pick out bricklayer or tailor's thimble as the head noun,
while still operating in string terms. The point is that
Montague's string-based framework makes conditions like
'first basic noun' more easily available to the grammarian
than conditions like 'head of a CN expression' or 'T-expres-
sion$_1$ does not command T-expression$_2$',[5] and it is the
latter types of condition that are relevant to the formulation of syntactic rules.

    A less trivial instance of the way in which the string-
based character of Montague's system affects the accessibility

of alternative analyses is presented by Bennett (1976). In
order to avoid derivations like

(5)   *That no man walks is believed by him

```
           /\
     no man    that he_0 walks is believed by him_0
```

which Montague's quantifier rule would allow if combined with
an analysis of subject complement clauses as simply 'subjects',
Bennett adopted a Montague analogue of Emonds' (1970, 1975)
treatment of complements: subject complements are not NP's
and they are derived not by the usual S → NP VP but by a
special rule combining S with VP, and that rule has a
condition rendering it inapplicable if the sentence to be
embedded contains any free variables. By imposing that last
condition, Bennett rules out the step that would give That
he_0 walks bothers him_0 in (5) and thus rules out the derivation (5) entirely. Why did Bennett not adopt the (to me)
more obvious solution of revising Montague's quantifier rule
so that the T-phrase is substituted not for the *first* occurrence of he_i but rather for an occurrence of he_i that commands
all other occurrences of it? (Under that condition, no man
would have to be substituted for him_0 rather than for he_0 in
(5), thus yielding the acceptable That he is sick bothers
no man.) I leave it to Bennett to answer this question
himself, though I conjecture that one reason for his choice
is simply that his solution conforms to Montague's string-
based framework, in which the alternative solution just suggested is not available to the analyst.

   Montague's decision to do string-based grammar has also
affected point (iii) of this digression. Note that the local
well-formedness condition plus Montague's policy of taking
the entities generated by the syntax to be strings of words

forced Montague to build morphophonemic rules into syntactic
rules, e.g.,

(6) F_2 (ζ) is a̰ ζ or a̰ṉ ζ, according as the first word
in ζ takes a̰ or a̰ṉ. (PTQ, p. 251)

Since a̰ a̰p̰p̰l̰ḛ is not a well-formed string of words (of
Montague's category T), Montague's syntax had to be prevented
from generating it, and thus the rule choosing between a̰ and
a̰ṉ had to be built into the rule for combining determiners
with CN-expressions to form T-expressions (NP's). But the
fact that the string of words a̰ a̰p̰p̰l̰ḛ is ill-formed does not
imply that a constituent consisting of an indefinite article
indeterminate as to form (a̰, a̰ṉ, or zero) and a CN must be
regarded as ill-formed: to call it ill-formed is to make the
mistake of identifying the morpheme in question with its
'standard' realization. Whether an object is ill-formed
depends on what sort of object it is viewed as. The same
physical object may be equally well regarded as a well-
formed scissor-blade or as a pair of scissors that is ill-
formed by virtue of its lacking one blade. The local well-
formedness condition will have different implications
depending on how completely specified one requires the various
objects to be. It makes a difference, for example, whether
one is talking about structures that are specific as to what
morphemes occur and in what order they occur but is indeterminate as to what the exact pronunciation or graphic form of
each morpheme is (in which case 'a apple' is well-formed) or
whether one is talking about structures that *are* determinate
as the pronunciation or graphic form of each morpheme (in
which case 'a apple' is ill-formed).

A problem of this type arises in connection with the
description of German word order. In German, main clauses have

the finite verb in second position, subordinate clauses
have it in final position. Partee (forthcoming: §3.6.4)
states that 'The well-formedness condition would seem to
require that verb-second be the basic structure of German
clauses.' Whether this conclusion follows depends on what the
relevant constituents are viewed *as*. Der Hauptmann seine
Frau tötete is ill-formed as an independent utterance, but
it is not clear that that fact is of any relevance as to the
choice between the analyses at issue:

(7) a. basic V-second order

    der Hauptmann tötete seine Frau

        in subordinate clause

  b. basic V-final order

    der Hauptmann seine Frau tötete

        in main clause

A large proportion of the constituents that figure in
Montague analyses cannot be used as independent utterances
(e.g., the or put on the table); the local well-formedness
condition should not be interpreted as excluding such
constituents from syntactic analyses. The problem presented
by German word order is in essence the same as that relating
to an orthographic detail that has hitherto been ignored in
Montague grammar, namely capitalization. Suppose, for the
moment, that one is doing a Montague analysis in which the
syntactic constituents are to be in orthographic form. The
question then arises whether items such as every man and
kiss John should be treated as basically beginning with a
capital letter or with a lower-case letter. A direct analogue
to Partee's argument would call for each constituent of the

analysis tree to begin with a capital letter, and thus for
all syntactic rules to decapitalize words that they put in
non-initial position (other than proper names, which would
have to be exempted from decapitalization): the various
expressions require an initial capital letter when used as
independent orthographic 'utterances'. The more reasonable
interpretation of the local well-formedness condition would
throw this argument out, demanding only well-formedness as
surface constituents, not as independent utterances, and
would thus leave the question of basic German word order open:
both orders occur as surface constituents of German sentences.

I turn now to the final area that I promised to touch on
in this paper, namely, some transformational analyses that
could in an interesting way be reworked into Montague analyses.
Analyses in which some verbs obligatorily trigger Raising
can be accommodated in a Montaguish treatment: either one
accepts obligatory transformations under the revision of
Montague syntax outlined above, or one tacks Raising onto
S → NP VP as an additional rider. The latter alternative
would give rise to a very messy rule, but those who would
object to the former alternative aren't likely to hold the
messiness of rules against them. An analysis with Raising for
sentences like (8) has strong semantic points in its favor in
that it readily yields a semantic interpretation in which
seem has higher scope than most, i.e., an interpretation
paraphrasable as 'It seems as if most of the students have
failed the exam':

(8) Most of the students seem to have failed the exam.

Without 'Most of the students failed the exam' as a syntactic
constituent, it is hard to see how the semantics could be
compositional.

Consider now auxiliary verbs. Most English auxiliary verbs can be analyzed as taking sentential subjects with obligatory Raising, i.e., as behaving syntactically like seem except that they lack the option of Extraposition that seem allows:[6]

(9) It seems that most of the students failed the exam.

   *It has that John seen/saw the committee report.

Otherwise, seem and auxiliary have would simply be intransitive verbs with underlying sentential subject which undergoes Raising:

(10)

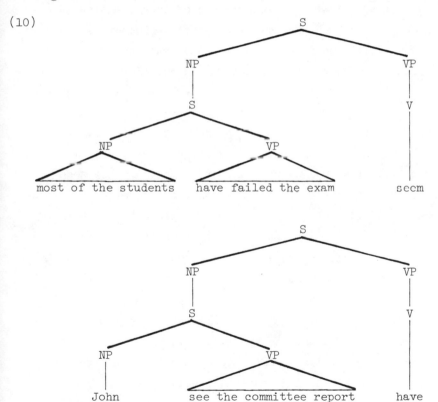

Whether this analysis can be incorporated into the Montaguish
syntactic scheme sketched above depends on a detail of the
interpretation of the local well-formedness condition, namely
that of whether it rules out the tenseless embedded sentences
that the auxiliary-as-main-verb analysis requires.[7] There is
in fact a surface clause type that is arguably tenseless:

(11) The Director ordered that Schwartz kill
     the Zambian ambassador.

On the basis of sentences like (11) one could argue that P_t
(the set of well-formed expressions of type t = 'sentence')
includes tenseless surface representatives and thus that
tenseless clauses do not violate the local well-formedness
condition. A proper treatment of this question will have to
get into two important questions that I have glossed over:
(i) how can one tell that two items are of the same syntactic
category (i.e., why is the complement clause in (11) of the
same syntactic category as the proposed tenseless complements
of auxiliaries and not of a different category and thus
irrelevant to the question of whether the local well-formedness condition rules out tenseless complements of auxiliaries?),[8] and (ii) accepting the claim that (11) involves a
tenseless complement, how can one account in a Montaguish
framework for the distribution of tensed and tenseless
clauses? Answering those questions currently goes beyond my
ability to impersonate a revisionist Montague grammarian.
Let me assume for the remainder of this paper that I have
been able to justify allowing tenseless complements without
in the process reducing the local well-formedness condition
to vacuity. Let us now see what the implications of this
proposal are for the analysis of passive clauses.

Partee (forthcoming, n. 24) states that 'If Passive is a
sentence-to-sentence rule, then either Affix-Hopping has
to be undone and redone in going from an active sentence to
its passive, or else sentences in which Affix-Hopping has
not been done at all should be counted as well-formed.' Partee
was here assuming that, as in *Syntactic Structures* and the
bulk of the transformational literature, any Passive transformation would be applying to structures containing a tense
marker and whatever auxiliary verbs are to co-occur with the
passive be. However, under the analysis proposed here, that
assumption would not hold. Passive would have to apply to the
tenseless clause below any auxiliaries. It could not apply
to one of the higher clauses that are headed by auxiliaries,
for the same reason that seem and other subject-complements
cannot be passivized (though their complements can):

(12) a. Deep structure

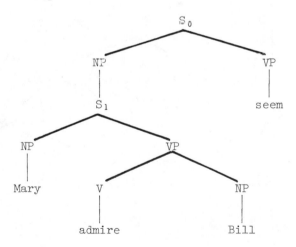

b. Possible derivation

Passive on S_1:

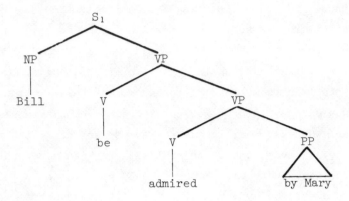

Raising on S_0:

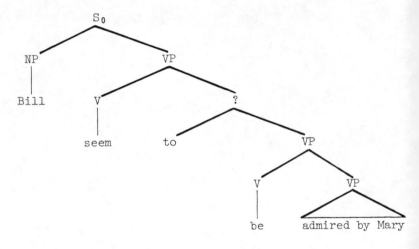

c. Impossible derivation

Raising on S_0:

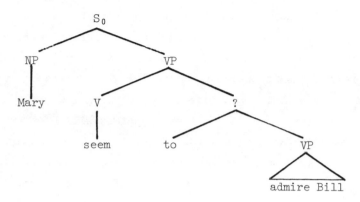

Passive on S_0:

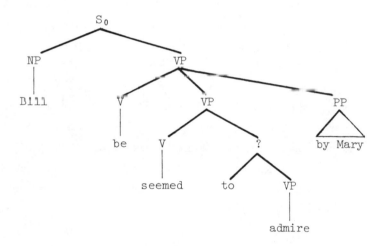

Thus, if auxiliary have is the main verb of its own clause
in deep structure, as in (10), Passive on the embedded tenseless clause will yield (13a), just as (12b) yields the
grammatical Bill seems to be admired by Mary, and Passive on
the upper clause will yield the ungrammatical (13b), just
as (12c) yields the ungrammatical *Bill is seemed to admire
by Mary:

(13) a. The committee report has been seen by John.

    b. *The committee report is had seen by John.

Thus, if passive is applied to anything but the tenseless 'core' of a clause, a general restriction on Passive will be violated (presumably, that the NP that is moved into subject position has to be in the same 'simplex VP' as the verb of the clause being processed, and not in a lower VP). Hence, the structure to which Passive applies will have not undergone Affix-Hopping and thus it will not be necessary to undo any Affix-Hopping to have all cyclic outputs be well-formed.

    The local well-formedness condition indeed provides grounds for choosing between the Affix-Hopping analysis of have -en, be -ing, and passive be -en and an alternative that has competed with it in an argumentative vacuum: to my knowledge, no arguments have hitherto been adduced by anyone for preferring either alternative to the other.[9] In the Affix-Hopping analysis, first popularized in *Syntactic Structures*, the auxiliary verbs originate alongside of their associated affixes (i.e., there are deep-structure constituents have -en and be -ing), and the affix is attached to the following verb by a transformation (Affix-Hopping). In the alternative proposal that figures in Ross 1969, the affixes are not present as such in deep structure and are directly attached to the complement verb by a minor transformation that inserts -en, -ing, or no affix at all, depending on what the (auxiliary) verb is. Only the latter alternative is consistent with anything but a very relaxed version of the local well-formedness condition.

    The present and past tense markers still remain to be integrated into this analysis. Chomsky's original Affix-Hopping analysis affected tense markers as well as -en and -ing. Ross's (1969) treatment leaves it unclear how tense

markers fit in (he represents them as features of the
relevant verbs but leaves unclear how the alternation between
tensed do and tensed main verb, e.g., Does he live here? vs.
He lives here, will then work). My revision (McCawley 1971)
of Ross's analysis treats tenses as main verbs, with Affix-
Hopping moving them to their ultimate positions. Even if one
accepts my arguments given there for identifying the past
tense marker with auxiliary have, the local well-formedness
condition could hardly be stretched so as to accommodate an
analysis with the present tense marker as a verb: it is not
a variant of any item that occurs in a surface 'verb position'.
The one way that I can see to accommodate tense markers in
the analysis sketched here while still conforming to the local
well-formedness condition would be to smuggle tense markers
into underlying structures as adjuncts of the do that bears
them when there is no other immediately available bearer, as
in Does he live here? or He doesn't live here. This do would
then be treated as triggering an obligatory transformation
that replaces the do with the next verb down, retaining the
tense of the do. I leave to others the problem of working
out a treatment of questions, negatives, and elliptical
sentences, in which the do ceases to be adjacent to the lower
verb and is not replaced by it. Working out those details
may require weakening the principle of 'strict cyclicity'
discussed above, in that for it to be possible to derive
such sentences as John left and Mary did too via a rule of
deletion of repeated VP's, either that rule would have to
reintroduce a do that had been replaced by a lower verb in
an earlier step of the derivation or one would have to make
the replacement of do by the lower verb to be 'postcyclic'
in order to postpone it until after any application of VP-
deletion and other relevant rules.

I am not particularly happy with the analysis with deep
structure do's, since it makes too much hinge on whether the
language has a semantically empty verb to hang tense markers
on, and since it treats tense markers on auxiliary do as
derived differently from tense markers on other verbs. Also,
such an analysis would not be available for German, and
German would thus require that tenses get into syntactic
structures in a different way, which I find makes English and
German look more different than they really are.

My purpose in sketching this last analysis is not to
seriously advocate it in all its details but to demonstrate
that 'abstract' syntactic analyses need not require gross
deviation from the more basic tenets of Montague grammar. The
deviation in this case was expository more than anything
else: a new policy on the individuation of rules, coupled
with a policy on rule interaction (the strict cycle principle)
and an associated relaxation of the local well-formedness
condition that add up to no change at all in the descriptive
power of the framework. However, expository changes are
rarely unimportant: they change the units in terms of which
the investigator constructs the analysis and accordingly
the investigator's perceptions of what are large or small
differences among alternative analyses. They may have no
effect on what the theory can do, but they have an enormous
effect on what can be done to the theory, which is to say
that they profoundly influence what progeny the theory will
have, if any.

Notes

1. One detail of this derivation is suspicious: that
subject-verb agreement applies twice to what really is 'the
same sentence'.

2. See McCawley 1977a for discussion of the notion of 'meaning preservation' in Montague grammar.

3. See McCawley 1972 for criticism of this standard policy and arguments that the operands of rules of inference must be subtrees of trees rather than substrings of strings.

4. The semantic interpretation assigned by Montague's rules would still relate to happiness on the part of the bricklayers rather than the bricks and cheapness of the thimble rather than of a tailor.

5. A node of a syntactic structure commands those nodes that are in the clause of which it is an immediate constituent or in a clause subordinate to that clause. The notion of command is introduced and discussed in detail in Langacker 1969.

6. See McCawley 1971 for a demonstration that an analysis of auxiliary verbs as auxiliary verbs with sentential complements provides the basis of an explanation of why English auxiliary verbs appear in the order in which they do: modal before have before progressive be, with no more than one of each.

7. Or at least, even if that analysis does not strictly speaking *require* tenseless embedded sentences, tenses on the embedded sentences would be there only to get wiped out, both syntactically and semantically, thus making an analysis without them both more 'natural' and easier to reconcile with compositional semantics.

8. See McCawley 1977b for discussion of the abysmal state of argumentation about syntactic categories in transformational grammar. Montague grammar can boast having something closer to a real theory of syntactic categories than is provided in any version of transformational grammar, in view

of the tight relationship between syntactic categories and
semantic types that Montague grammar demands.

9. I emphasize that I am separating the question of how
-ing and -en get into their surface position from the corresponding question about the present and past tense markers.
See Akmajian and Wasow 1975 for arguments that attachment of
tense markers is a distinct syntactic process from attachment
of participial morphemes.

References

Akmajian, Adrian, and Tom Wasow. 1975. "The Constituent
    Structure of VP and Aux and the Position of the Verb *Be*."
    Linguistic Analysis 1: 205 - 245.

Bennett, Michael. 1976. "A Variation and Extension of a
    Montague Fragment of English." In Partee, ed. 1976,
    pp. 119 - 163.

Chomsky, Noam A. 1957. *Syntactic Structures*. The Hague: Mouton.

Emonds, Joseph. 1970. "Root and Structure-Preserving Transfor-
    mations." Ph.D. dissertation, MIT.

————. 1975. *A Transformational Approach to Syntax*. New York:
    Academic Press.

Langacker, Ronald. 1969. "On Pronominalization and the Chain
    of Command." In D. Reibel and S. Schane, eds., *Modern
    Studies in English,* pp. 160 - 186. Englewood Cliffs, N.J.:
    Prentice-Hall.

McCawley, James D. 1971. "Tense and Time Reference in English."
    In C. J. Fillmore and D. T. Langendoen, eds., *Studies on
    Linguistic Semantics,* pp. 96 - 113. New York: Holt,
    Rinehart, and Winston. Also in McCawley 1973, pp. 257 -
    272.

————. 1972. "A Program for Logic." In D. Davidson and
    G. Harman, eds., *Semantics of Natural Language,* pp.

498 - 544. Dordrecht: Reidel Publishing Co. Also in
McCawley 1973, pp. 285 - 319.

———. 1973. *Grammar and Meaning*. Tokyo: Taishukan.

———. 1977a. "Evolutionary Parallels between Montague
Grammar and Transformational Grammar." NELS VII, pp. 219 -
232. Cambridge, Mass.: MIT Department of Linguistics and
Philosophy.

———. 1977b. "The Nonexistence of Syntactic Categories."
In *Proceedings of the 1977 Michigan State Conference on
Linguistic Metatheory*.

Montague, Richard. 1974. "The Proper Treatment of Quantifica-
tion in English." In *Formal Philosophy: Selected Papers of
Richard Montague*, ed. Richard Thomason, pp. 247 - 270.
New Haven: Yale University Press.

Partee, Barbara H. 1975. "Montague Grammar and Transformational Grammar." *Linguistic Inquiry* 6: 203 - 300.

———. 1976. *Montague Grammar*. New York: Academic Press.

———. Forthcoming. "Montague Grammar and the Well-Formed-
ness Constraint." In Frank Heny and Helmut Schnelle, eds.,
Syntax and Semantics, Vol. 10: *Selections from the Third
Groningen Round Table*. New York: Academic Press.

Ross, John Robert. 1969. "Auxiliaries as Main Verbs."
Journal of Philosophical Logic 1: 77 - 102.

4

Type Theory and Ordinary Language
Terence Parsons

1. *Introduction*

The so-called logical paradoxes have had a profound impact on
the foundations of mathematics and of formal work in the
semantics of artificial languages. One such paradox is this:
All sorts of things have properties, including properties
themselves. The property of being a unicorn has the property
of being nowhere exemplified in reality; the property of
being a material object has the property of having been much
discussed by philosophers. Some properties even appear to
have (or 'exemplify') themselves; e.g., the property of being
a property seems to have the property of being a property;
it has itself. But most properties do not have themselves;
e.g., the property of being red is not itself red.

Now consider the property of not having itself. This seems
to be a property which most properties have. Does *it* have
itself? Either answer seems incorrect. If it does have itself,
this means that it has the property of not having itself;
i.e., it doesn't have itself. But, on the other hand, if it
doesn't have itself then it seems to have the property of not
having itself; i.e., it has itself. (This argument will be
discussed in more detail in section 4 below).

By far the most popular solution to this and similar
paradoxes in logic and mathematics is to invoke some sort of

type theory. Properties are divided (in some manner) into
types, and attribution of one property to another is possible
only if their types are appropriately related.[1] In particular,
a property is never attributable to another of the *same* type,
and so there is no such thing as 'the property of not having
itself'. Languages which do not accord with some such theory
of types are often regarded as meaningless, inconsistent, or
at least deeply defective.

Ordinary English is often cited as a language that does
not obey a theory of types, and which is thereby defective.
But it is not at all obvious that *ordinary* English, as opposed,
say, to technical extensions of ordinary English, does *not*
obey a theory of types; debates on this issue soon run afoul
of the vagueness of the question of what does and does not
count as ordinary English. For example, native speakers
typically regard the phrase 'the property of not having
itself' as highly suspicious, but it's not clear whether this
is because of its conceptual complexity or because it just
isn't good English.

The task of this paper is to explore the question: what
would English be like if it *did* obey a theory of types? My
procedure will be to articulate a fragment of English which
is rich enough to include talk about properties and the
having of properties by properties, and to do so by means
of a type-theoretic syntax and semantics. It will be an
extension of the type-theoretic grammar of Richard Montague's
"The Proper Treatment of Quantification in Ordinary English"
(hereafter PTQ).[2] My approach will be indirect, because I am
going to begin by addressing myself to a different problem,
a problem that has arisen in the tradition commonly called
Montague grammar. It's this:

There seems to be a need in Montague grammar to proliferate the syntactic categories of English far beyond those of PTQ.[3] This is in order to accommodate mass terms, factives, gerundives, plurals, etc. Also, we eventually want to add common nouns such as event, action, property, proposition, ... , and (if we follow Montague's ideas in "On the Nature of Certain Philosophical Entities")[4] these must be of categories different from the category of ordinary common nouns like woman, unicorn, ... But every time we add a new category of one sort (say for a new kind of common noun) we generate other new categories. For example, if proposition is added and given a new category, t/t_n, then we also need a new category of term phrases, so that we can have pronouns of the appropriate sort (e.g., in proposition such that John believes it the it must come from a pronoun of the type $t/(t_m/t_n)$). But then we need new categories of transitive verbs and prepositions to take the new term-phrases as objects, and we need new categories of adverbs to modify the new verbs, etc.

The trouble with this approach is that the multiplicity of new categories seems unreal, or at least highly inelegant. It would be one thing if these new categories had recognizably different members, but instead they seem to largely duplicate the old categories. For example, whatever new kind of term-phrase (NP) is added, a new word it will have to be added to pronominalize the new terms (NP's). But the new it is spelled and pronounced just like the old one. Another case: there will have to be a new word, about, for every new type of term-phrase; the word about becomes (potentially) infinitely ambiguous.

This bothers some people. Why should about be ambiguous, simply because it occurs in both of:

> John talked about a woman, and
>
> John talked about a proposition?

It seems to me that there are two objections to this ambiguity:

(A) In *just* multiplying categories we miss a syntactic uniformity — that about is a *preposition* in both sentences. The category system of PTQ does not reflect this fact.

(B) In some sense, the same word, about, ought to occur in both of these sentences, having the same meaning in each. One could argue in terms of language learning here — having learned about for some types we freely use it with respect to new ones, without having to learn a new meaning. Perhaps in some sense the meaning of about does change with the type of its object, but if so it has a more basic meaning from which these others are predictable.

One way to answer objection (A) is to refuse to complicate the syntactical categories when the semantic types seem to proliferate. This is Thomason's approach (in "Some Extensions of Montague Grammar").[5] For example, he freely generates sentences like:

> a proposition dates Mary, and
>
> that John loves Mary gives Bill a fish.

and then he leaves it to the semantics to explain their bizarreness.

I want to explore a different approach here. The main idea is to utilize a fixed stock of familiar syntactic categories — categories such as S, NP, VP, ... — but each category will be indexed with respect to semantic type. Extensions of the system will typically employ old familiar categories, with

new type indices when the semantics demands it. For example,
woman will be in category CN^e; and if we add proposition it
will be in category $CN^{\langle s,t \rangle}$. Extensions which do not affect
the semantic types but which do affect the syntax will be
handled by means of familiar syntactic features. E.g., if we
add gold to CN^e it will have the feature [-count].[6]

The system comes in two parts: PTQA is designed to partly
answer objection (A); it is then extended to PTQB, which
purports to answer both (A) and (B). Both systems use the
semantic type system of PTQ, namely:

e is a type (the type of entities)

t is a type (the type of truth-values)

If a and b are types, so is ⟨a, b⟩ (the type of
   functions from entities of type a to entities of type b)

If a is a type so is ⟨s, a⟩ (the type of senses of words
   that denote entities of type a)

I will use greek letters τ, τ_1, τ_2, ... to stand for arbitrary
semantic types.

2. *PTQA*

The syntax of PTQA deals entirely with what I will call
fixed types. Roughly speaking, a fixed type is a syntactic
category supplemented by an index which indicates the corresponding semantic type. These fixed types replace the syntactic
category system of PTQ. If X is a fixed type, then f(X) is
its corresponding semantic type. The function f is defined
by the table on the following page. I've added double-object
verbs to relieve somewhat the monotony of PTQ. Notice that if
τ, τ_1, τ_2, τ_3 are all given the value e, then the system
yields a notational variant of the category system of PTQ,
except that some of Montague's systematic appeal to senses

The Fixed Types	Corresponding Semantic Types
S	t
CN^τ	$\langle \tau, t \rangle$
VP^τ	$\langle \tau, t \rangle$
NP^τ	$\langle f(VP^\tau), t \rangle$
$\tau_1 V^{\tau_2}$	$\langle \langle s, f(NP^{\tau_2}) \rangle, f(VP^{\tau_1}) \rangle$
$\tau_1 V^{\tau_2, \tau_3}$	$\langle \langle s, f(NP^{\tau_2}) \rangle, \langle \langle s, f(NP^{\tau_3}) \rangle, f(VP^{\tau_1}) \rangle \rangle$
ADV^τ	$\langle \langle s, f(VP^\tau) \rangle, f(VP^\tau) \rangle$
ADF	$\langle \langle s, t \rangle, t \rangle$
$\tau_1 PREP^{\tau_2}$	$\langle \langle s, f(NP^{\tau_2}) \rangle, f(ADV^{\tau_1}) \rangle$

has been eliminated for the sake of simplicity.[7] Replacing τ, τ_1, τ_2, τ_3 by types other than e produces categories not already manifested in PTQ. Basically, words of type CN^τ will denote properties of things of type τ, proper names of type NP^τ will denote property-sets of things of type τ, etc.

There is no syntactic type of Montague's believe-that because I feel that believe ought to be treated as a transitive verb in its own right, and that-clauses ought to be treated as NP's. The verb believe occurs without an associated that in sentences with obvious NP's, sentences like: 'Mary believes everything Agatha tells her,' and that-clauses occur as subjects of ordinary copula + adjective sentences, such as 'That John loves Mary is amazing.'

I have omitted treatment of try-to and wish-to because I am not sure how to handle them, and because it would be distracting to discuss them.

A *word of fixed type* is a sign (typically resembling a word of English) with a type superscript or superscripts.

Here are the words of fixed type of PTQA.

Words of Fixed Type of PTQA	*Type*
man^e, woman^e, park^e, fish^e, pen^e, unicorn^e, -body^e	CN^e
fact$^{\langle s,t\rangle}$, proposition$^{\langle s,t\rangle}$, answer$^{\langle s,t\rangle}$	CN$^{\langle s,t\rangle}$
run^e, walk^e, talk^e, rise^e, change^e	VP^e
obtain$^{\langle s,t\rangle}$ (in the sense of 'be true')	VP$^{\langle s,t\rangle}$
John^e, Mary^e, it$^e_0$, it$^e_1$, it$^e_2$, ...	NP^e
The Pythagorean Theorem$^{\langle s,t\rangle}$, it$^{\langle s,t\rangle}_0$, it$^{\langle s,t\rangle}_1$, it$^{\langle s,t\rangle}_2$, ...	NP$^{\langle s,t\rangle}$
^{e}eat^e, ^{e}date^e	^{e}V^e
^{e}believe$^{\langle s,t\rangle}$, ^{e}assert$^{\langle s,t\rangle}$	^{e}V$^{\langle s,t\rangle}$
$^{\langle s,t\rangle}$amaze^e	$^{\langle s,t\rangle}$V^e
^{e}buy^{e,e}	^{e}V^{e,e}
^{e}tell$^{e,\langle s,t\rangle}$	^{e}V$^{e,\langle s,t\rangle}$
rapidly^e, slowly^e, voluntarily^e	ADV^e
necessarily	ADF
^{e}in^e (in the sense of spatial location)	^{e}PREP^e

The syntactic rules of PTQA are essentially those of PTQ, except that the rule Montague uses to handle try to and wish to, S8, is omitted, and there is an added proviso that type superscripts must match. For example, you can combine every woman^e with run^e to get every woman runs, but you can't combine every proposition$^{\langle s,t\rangle}$ with run^e to get every proposition runs, because the types don't match. The rules are:

Syntactic Rules of PTQA

S1. The words listed above are members of the categories listed to their right.

S2. If $\alpha \in CN^T$ then F_0 (α), F_1 (α), F_2 (α) $\in NP^T$ where F_0 (α) = every α, F_1 (α) = the α, and F_2 (α) = a(n) α, except that F_0 (-body) = everybody, F_1(-body) = somebody, and F_2 (-body) is undefined.

S3. If $\alpha \in CN^T$ and $\phi \in S$ then $F_{3,n,\tau}$ (α, ϕ) $\in CN^T$ where $F_{3,n,\tau}$ (α, ϕ) = α such that ϕ', and ϕ' comes from ϕ by replacing every occurrence of it_n^τ in ϕ by a pronoun of appropriate gender and case.

S4. If $\alpha \in NP^T$ and $\beta \in VP^T$ then F_4 (α, β) $\in S$, where F_4 (α, β) = α β' and β' comes from β by making the first basic verb in β agree with α in number.

S5. If $\alpha \in {}^{\tau_1}V^{\tau_2}$ and $\beta \in NP^{\tau_2}$ then F_5 (α, β) $\in VP^{\tau_1}$ where F_5 (α β) = α β if β isn't a pronoun; otherwise F_5 (α, β) = α it_n^τ [+acc].[8]

S5'. If $\alpha \in {}^{\tau_1}V^{\tau_2, \tau_3}$ and $\beta \in NP^{\tau_2}$ then F_5 (α, β) $\in {}^{\tau_1}V^{\tau_3}$.

S6. If $\alpha \in {}^{\tau_1}PREP^{\tau_2}$ and $\beta \in NP^{\tau_2}$ then F_5 (α, β) $\in ADV^{\tau_1}$.

S7. If $\phi \in S$ then that $\phi \in NP^{\langle s,t \rangle}$.

S9. If $\alpha \in ADF$ and $\phi \in S$ then α $\phi \in S$.

S10. If $\alpha \in ADV^T$ and $\beta \in VP^T$ then β $\alpha \in VP^T$.

S11. If ϕ, $\psi \in S$ then ϕ and ψ, ϕ or $\psi \in S$.

S12. If α, $\beta \in VP^T$ then α and β, α or $\beta \in VP^T$.

S13. If α, $\beta \in NP^T$ then α or $\beta \in NP^T$.

S14. If $\alpha \in NP^T$ and $\phi \in S$ then $F_{10,n,\tau}$ (α, ϕ) $\in S$ where $F_{10,n,\tau}$ (α, ϕ) comes from ϕ by replacing the first occurrence of it_n^τ by α and all other such occurrences by pronouns of the appropriate case and gender.

S15. Similar to S14.

S16. Similar to S14.

S17. Similar to S4.

Here are some sample analysis trees from PTQA:

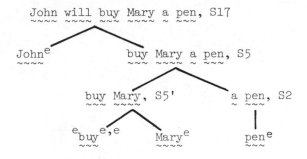

John will buy Mary a pen, S17

John^e　　　buy Mary a pen, S5

buy Mary, S5'　　　a pen, S2

$e_{buy}^{e,e}$　Mary^e　　pen^e

Somebody believes that Mary loves him, S14

somebody, S2　　it_0^e believes that Mary loves it_0^e [+acc], S4

$-\text{body}^e$　　it_0^e　believes that Mary loves it_0^e [+acc], S5

$e_{believe}^{\langle s,t \rangle}$　　that Mary loves it_0^e [+acc], S7

Mary loves it_0^e [+acc], S4

Mary^e　　love it_0^e [+acc], S5

e_{love}^e　　it_0^e

(The notation to the right of each node indicates the syntactic rule which produces that node from those immediately below it.)

The type system allows the generation of:

that John runs or that he walks amazes Mary

that John runs or he walks amazes Mary

that John runs or walks amazes Mary

but disallows:

Bill or that John runs ...

... walks or obtains

That John walks runs

Bill obtains

The translation of the sentences of PTQA is just like that of PTQ except that types other than e replace e at certain places, and we have the following rule for that:

$$(\text{that } \phi)' = \hat{\P} \; \P \; (\hat{} \; \phi')$$

where $\P$ is a variable of type $\langle \langle s, t \rangle, t \rangle$.

3. *PTQB*

The theory underlying PTQA allows for an infinite number of fixed types corresponding to each syntactic category of English; e.g., it allows for the types NP^e, $NP^{\langle s,e \rangle}$, $NP^{\langle s,t \rangle}$, $NP^{\langle \langle s,e \rangle, \langle s,t \rangle \rangle}$, ... But PTQA uses very little of these resources. That's partly because PTQA is a very restricted fragment of English — certainly we'll eventually need to use more fixed types. Also we have not yet faced the problem of one word having more than one fixed type. For example, consider:

John eats something that Bill eats

John believes something that Bill believes

Assuming that something comes from a determiner plus a CN, thing, we will need at least two words thing, one for each of the above sentences (namely words of type CN^e, $CN^{\langle s,t \rangle}$). Also, it isn't just individuals that have properties; properties themselves have properties. Consider this sequence of sentences:

Every property has a property.

Every property which some property has has a property.

Every property which some property which some property has has has a property.

etc.

If the first word property of the first sentence is a property of individuals, then it will be of type $CN^{\langle s, \langle e,t \rangle \rangle}$. But then the second word property in the first sentence must be of type $CN^{\langle s, \langle \langle s, \langle e,t \rangle \rangle, t \rangle \rangle}$. The second sentence requires a higher type than this (for the last word property), and the third sentence a still higher type, and so on. The types of the various occurrences of has must go up too.

We're inclined to say that certain words — words like thing, property, has, somehow float freely through the various levels of types — whereas the words of PTQA — words like woman, unicorn, walk, believe, stay fixed at a given type. The point of PTQB is to accommodate the type-floaters in a natural way, without giving up the background system of semantic types.

Notice that these words cannot take on just any old type. Whereas thing seems to be able to occupy any category CN^τ for

any τ, property is restricted to categories of the form
$CN^{\langle s, \langle \tau, t \rangle \rangle}$ for any τ. And has can only occupy category
$\tau_1 V^{\tau_2}$ when τ_1 and τ_2 are related in a certain manner — namely
when $\tau_2 = \langle s, \langle \tau_1, t \rangle \rangle$. We accommodate these constraints as
follows:

A *word of floating type* is a function of a certain sort.
It takes semantic types as arguments, and yields words of
fixed type as values. Furthermore, it must do so by means of
a certain pattern. An example of such a word will be thing$^\zeta$.
This will be a function which for any given semantic type τ
yields the word of fixed type: thing$^\tau$.

I'll make this precise in two stages. First I'll give a
list of floating types; then I'll give particular examples
of words of these types. In doing this I'll follow Frege's
custom of using ζ to indicate the argument-places of the
functions I'm talking about. (I'll also use ζ_1, ζ_2, ζ_3, $\cdots$).
And I'll use the notation $\pi(\tau)$ to stand for a (typically)
complex semantic type which contains τ in zero, one, or many
specified places.

The floating types are given on the following page. Words
of a given floating type must be functions, as specified.
In addition, I'll require that all the values of any such
function be words which look the same except for their superscripts. So I will specify words of floating type by giving
a sign — typically one that resembles a word of English —
and a superscript. *Any* result of filling in ζ, or ζ_1, ζ_2
with semantic types will be a word of fixed syntactic type.

The words of floating type of PTQB are given on p. 140.

Floating Types	*A Word of This Type Will Be:*
	A one-place function whose value for any given τ will be a word whose fixed type is:
$CN^{\pi(\zeta)}$	$CN^{\pi(\tau)}$
$VP^{\pi(\zeta)}$	$VP^{\pi(\tau)}$
$NP^{\pi(\zeta)}$	$NP^{\pi(\tau)}$
$\pi_1 (\zeta)_V \pi_2 (\zeta)$	$\pi_1 (\tau)_V \pi_2 (\tau)$
$\pi_1 (\zeta)_V \pi_2 (\zeta), \pi_3 (\zeta)$	$\pi_1 (\tau)_V \pi_2 (\tau), \pi_3 (\tau)$
$ADV^{\pi(\zeta)}$	$ADV^{\pi(\tau)}$
$\pi_1 (\zeta)_{PREP} \pi_2 (\zeta)$	$\pi_1 (\tau)_{PREP} \pi_2 (\tau)$
	A two-place function whose value for any given ι_1, ι_1 will be a word whose fixed type is:
$\pi_1 (\zeta_1)_V \pi_2 (\zeta_2)$	$\pi_1 (\tau_1)_V \pi_2 (\tau_2)$
$\pi_1 (\zeta_1)_V \pi_2 (\zeta_1), \pi_3 (\zeta_2)$	$\pi_1 (\tau_1)_V \pi_2 (\tau_1), \pi_3 (\tau_2)$
$\pi_1 (\zeta_1)_{PREP} \pi_2 (\zeta_2)$	$\pi_1 (\tau_1)_{PREP} \pi_2 (\tau_2)$

Words of Floating Type	Type
$\underset{\sim\sim\sim\sim\sim}{\text{-thing}}{}^{\zeta}$	CN^{ζ}
$\underset{\sim\sim\sim}{\text{set}}{}^{\langle \zeta,\ t \rangle}$	$CN^{\langle \zeta,\ t \rangle}$
$\underset{\sim\sim\sim\sim\sim\sim\sim\sim}{\text{property}}{}^{\langle s,\ \langle \zeta,\ t \rangle \rangle}$	$CN^{\langle s,\ \langle \zeta,\ t \rangle \rangle}$
$\underset{\sim\sim\sim\sim\sim}{\text{exist}}{}^{\zeta}$	VP^{ζ}
$\underset{\sim\sim_0}{\text{it}}{}^{\zeta},\ \underset{\sim\sim_1}{\text{it}}{}^{\zeta},\ \underset{\sim\sim_2}{\text{it}}{}^{\zeta},\ \ldots$	NP^{ζ}
$^{e}\underset{\sim\sim\sim\sim}{\text{find}}{}^{\zeta},\ ^{e}\underset{\sim\sim\sim\sim}{\text{lose}}{}^{\zeta},\ ^{e}\underset{\sim\sim\sim\sim}{\text{love}}{}^{\zeta},\ ^{e}\underset{\sim\sim\sim\sim}{\text{hate}}{}^{\zeta},$	
$\qquad ^{e}\underset{\sim\sim\sim\sim}{\text{seek}}{}^{\zeta},\ ^{e}\underset{\sim\sim\sim\sim\sim\sim\sim\sim}{\text{conceive}}{}^{\zeta}$	$e_{V}{}^{\zeta}$
$^{\zeta}\underset{\sim\sim\sim\sim}{\text{have}}{}^{\langle s,\ \langle \zeta,\ t \rangle \rangle},\ ^{\zeta}\underset{\sim\sim\sim\sim\sim\sim\sim\sim}{\text{exemplify}}{}^{\langle s,\ \langle \zeta,\ t \rangle \rangle}$	$\zeta_{V}{}^{\langle s,\ \langle \zeta,\ t \rangle \rangle}$
$^{e}\underset{\sim\sim\sim\sim}{\text{give}}{}^{e,\zeta}$	$e_{V}{}^{e,\zeta}$
$\underset{\sim\sim\sim\sim\sim\sim\sim\sim\sim}{\text{allegedly}}{}^{\zeta}$	ADV^{ζ}
$^{e}\underset{\sim\sim\sim\sim\sim}{\text{about}}{}^{\zeta}$	$^{e}PREP^{\zeta}$
$^{\zeta_1}\underset{\sim\sim}{\text{be}}{}^{\zeta_2}$	$\zeta_{1V}{}^{\zeta_2}$
$^{\langle \zeta_1,\ t \rangle}\underset{\sim\sim\sim\sim}{\text{elect}}{}^{\zeta_2}$	$^{\langle \zeta,\ t \rangle}{}_{V}{}^{\zeta_2}$

The syntactic rules of PTQB are just those of PTQA; the only difference is that we now have a much larger stock of words of fixed type to work with — namely, all those which come from applying words of floating type to given types. To go back to our earlier example, we now have an infinite number of about's, one for each fixed type. The analysis tree on the following page illustrates the use of the version of about that is appropriate to properties of individuals. (The dotted lines indicate the sources for each word of fixed type which is not already a word of PTQA.)

John talks about a property such that Mary has it, S4

John^e talk about a property such that Mary has it, S5

talk^e about a property such that Mary has it, S10

about$^{\langle s,\langle e,t\rangle\rangle}$ a property such that Mary has it, S2

$\langle s, \langle e, t\rangle\rangle$ about$^\zeta$ property such that Mary has it, S3

property$^{\langle s,\langle e,t\rangle\rangle}$ Mary has it$_0$, S4

e   property$^{\langle s,\langle \zeta,t\rangle\rangle}$ Mary^e have it$_0$, S5

e$_{have}$$^{\langle s,\langle e,t\rangle\rangle}$ it$_0$$^{\langle s,\langle e,t\rangle\rangle}$

e $^\zeta_{have}$$^{\langle s,\langle \zeta,t\rangle\rangle}$ $\langle s, \langle e, t\rangle\rangle$ it$_0^\zeta$

===

Certain of the words of floating type are of special metaphysical interest which should be reflected by their translations. The following translations indicate that -thing, set, property, and exist are the most general words of their types, and that be and exemplify (have) have the right meanings:

For each τ, τ_1, τ_2:

-thing translates as $\lambda V_{0,\tau} [V_{0,\tau} = V_{0,\tau}]$

set$^{\langle \tau,t\rangle}$ translates as $\lambda V_{0,\langle \tau,t\rangle}[V_{0,\langle \tau,t\rangle} = V_{0,\langle \tau,t\rangle}]$

property$^{\langle s,\langle \tau,t\rangle\rangle}$ translates as

$$\lambda V_{0,\langle s,\langle \tau,t\rangle\rangle} [V_{0,\langle s,\langle \tau,t\rangle\rangle} = V_{0,\langle s,\langle \tau,t\rangle\rangle}]$$

exist$^\tau$ translates as $\lambda V_{0,\tau}$ $[V_{0,\tau} = V_{0,\tau}]$

$^{\tau_1}$be$^{\tau_2}$ translates as $\lambda V_{1,\tau_1}$ $\lambda V_{2,\tau_2}$ $[V_{1,\tau_1} = V_{2,\tau_2}]$[9]

$^\tau$exemplify$^{\langle s,\langle \tau,t\rangle\rangle}$ translates as

$$\lambda V_{0,\tau} \ \lambda V_{0,\langle s,\langle \tau,t\rangle\rangle} \ [V_{0,\langle s,\langle \tau,t\rangle\rangle}\{V_{0,\tau}\}]$$

Now let's look at some sample sentences and nonsentences of PTQB.

First, some sentences are generated in exactly one way:[10]

(1) every woman runs   [only one source per word]

(2) something runs   [thing has lots of sources, but only its CN^e version will combine with run]

(3) a property runs*   [lots of sources for property, but none of them will combine with run^e]

Second, some sentences have many sources:

(4) John hates everything   [infinite number of sources; each has a different meaning; one meaning per type of what is hated]

(5) everything has a property   [infinite number of sources; one meaning per type of thing] AUTOMATICALLY TRUE

(6) every property has a property   [like (5)] AUTOMATICALLY TRUE

(7) a property has it(self)*   [type of has rules this out]

(8) a property is a proposition   [infinite number of sources; one meaning per type of property] AUTOMATICALLY FALSE

4. *Paradoxes and Properties*

PTQA and PTQB come from PTQ essentially by expanding the type-
system which is already in PTQ. This type-system is quite
complex, and a reasonably skeptical person will want to know
whether the complexity can be avoided without paying too
great a price. To understand this, we have to know why the
type system is there in the first place.

One answer that some people have given is that it naturally
reflects a datum about language. The claim here is that we
naturally talk in types, although this typically goes un-
noticed. For example, suppose that the following sentence is
uttered in the course of a normal conversation:

> Agatha hates everything.

Usually it would be quite inappropriate to express surprise
at Agatha's dislike of the proposition that some proposition
has some property. Usually when we say everything we aren't
talking about propositions, properties, etc., but rather
about the sorts of entities that would count as individuals
in the system of PTQ. Here it's appropriate to suppose that
the utterance expresses the proposition yielded by words
typed as:

> Agatha^e ^{e}hates^e everything^e.

On the other hand, if we are discussing propositions, and
the notion of truth, someone might thoughtlessly utter:

> Everything is true.

Here it would be inappropriate to cite an individual (say,
the Eiffel Tower) as a counterexample. In this utterance
everything should be typed as:

> Everything$^{\langle s,t \rangle}$ (is true)$^{\langle s,t \rangle}$

(I'm supposing here that we have added adjectives to the fragment.)

All this may be true, and even insightful, but it doesn't mean that type theory is correct. For there are *other* occasions on which we seem to speak in such a way as to violate any restriction to types. For example, having reflected on the type system we can now say something like:

Some things are not classifiable into types.

The point isn't that this utterance has to be true, but rather that in order for it to say what we mean to say by it, it seems that the word thing cannot be assigned to any definite type. Another example may make this clearer. Suppose we endorse type-theory by saying:

Everything has exactly one type.

Then, if our utterance obeys type theory, it seems that we *haven't* endorsed type theory. For according to type theory we have said:

Everything$^\tau$ has exactly one type

for some τ — i.e., we have asserted that everything of type τ has exactly one type, which is uncontroversial, and not what is in question. What we *want* to say is that *every*thing has a type, where our everything is not restricted to a type.

So there is a conflict between what type theory says we can meaningfully say and what we want to say (and believe we do say). Which is right ... it or us?

Well, what would we have to give up if type theory were correct? We would have to give up any enterprise which requires for its success the ability to discuss absolutely everything. There seem to be three such enterprises:

Religion

Philosophy

Linguistics

Religion would have to give up its universality. You couldn't say, for example, that God created *every*thing. Philosophy would go, at least major parts of semantics and metaphysics. And Linguistics would probably have to give up semantics. I should perhaps add Psychology to the list, insofar as it takes itself to study *thought* in complete generality; for if anything can address itself to *every*thing, without restriction, it seems that thought can. (Exercise for the reader: try thinking to yourself everything has some property without restricting the everything to a given type. Can you?)

Now some people if given a choice would choose type theory over Philosophy, Religion, Linguistics, and Psychology — indeed they might naturally maintain that type theory makes clear what reasonable people have suspected all along — that these fields contain a large ingredient of nonsense. But probably most people would forego type theory, no matter how plausible it might seem at first glance. But now comes the crunch. For there are powerful reasons for accepting type theory that aren't apparent at first glance. These reasons spring from the presence of paradoxes in our normal manner of reasoning about semantical matters. Type theory is not the only response to these paradoxes, but it is one of the most natural ones. Let me illustrate this by discussing a paradox about properties which resembles the famous Russell paradox.

Consider the sentence:

The property of not exemplifying

itself exemplifies itself.

If we abbreviate 'the property of not exemplifying itself' by *P*, this has the simple form:

> *P exemplifies itself*

Now is this sentence true or not? Let us suppose it is true. Then:

(1) P exemplifies itself.

I.e.:

(2) P exemplifies the property of not exemplifying itself.

But *any*thing which exemplifies the property of not exemplifying itself must not exemplify itself. So:

(3) P doesn't exemplify itself,

contradicting the assumption that the original sentence is true. Presumably, then, it isn't true. I.e.,

(4) P doesn't exemplify itself.

This seems to say that P has the property of not exemplifying itself:

(5) P exemplifies the property of not exemplifying itself.

I.e.,

(6) P exemplifies P.

I.e.,

(7) P exemplifies itself.

So the original sentence is true after all. But we proved that it isn't true. A paradox.

We *could* conclude from this that talk of properties and exemplification is never meaningful, but this seems too extreme. Type theory legitimizes a great deal of such talk, while also ruling out the paradox. Here is how it works:

First, we need some way of generating constructions like the property of not being a dog. Let us add to PTQB a new formation rule:

S18. If $\alpha \in VP^{\tau}$ then the property of (not)ing (have en) $\alpha \in NP^{\langle s, \langle \tau, t \rangle \rangle}$.

The intent here is that the morphemes ing and en combine with the following word to form present and past participles respectively, as in transformational grammar, and that items in parentheses are optional. Thus the rule generates:

$$\left.\begin{array}{l} \text{the property of being a unicorn} \\ \text{the property of not being a unicorn} \\ \text{the property of having been a unicorn} \\ \text{the property of not having been a unicorn} \end{array}\right\} NP^{\langle s, \langle e, t \rangle \rangle}$$

the property of hating something $\in NP^{\langle s, \langle e, t \rangle \rangle}$

[lots of sources]

the property of being something $\subset NP^{\langle s, \langle \tau, t \rangle \rangle}$ for any τ

the property of exemplifying the property

of not being a unicorn $\in NP^{\langle s, \langle e, t \rangle \rangle}$

The translation for such an NP is:

the property of ing α translates as
$$\hat{\P} \; \P \; (^{\wedge}\alpha')$$

the property of not ing α translates as
$$\hat{\P} \; \P \; (\hat{v}_0 \; \neg \; \alpha' \; (v_0))$$

the property of having en α translates as
$$\hat{\P} \; \P \; (\hat{v}_0 \; H \; \alpha' \; (v_0))$$

the property of not having en α translates as
$$\hat{\P} \; \P \; (v_0 \; \neg \; H \; \alpha' \; (v_0))$$

where α' is the translation of α, and variables are chosen to be of the appropriate type.

Lastly we need some way to form reflexives. A simple treatment that will suit our purposes is:

S19. If $\alpha \in {}^{\tau}V^{\tau}$ then α itself $\in VP^{\tau}$

where we must also supplement rule S4 so as to make itself agree in gender with the subject of the sentence. The translation would be:

$$\alpha \text{ itself translates as } \lambda V_{0,\tau}\,[\alpha'\,(V_{0,\tau},\,V_{0,\tau})].$$

We now have the standard type-theoretic solution to the paradox sketched above; the sentence:

> The property of not exemplifying itself
> exemplifies itself

is not a meaningful sentence. It cannot even be generated by the syntax because exemplify itself cannot be generated. This is so because every fixed type version of exemplify has different types at its subject and object ends, and so S19 cannot apply to it. (These reasons are paraphrases of normal accounts of how type theory 'solves' the paradox).

This so-called 'solution' is a bit strange, for the paradoxical sentence does look meaningful. But perhaps this intuition can be captured by the following: we call a sentence *grammatical* if it is generable by our rules, and *quasi-grammatical* if it could be generated by our rules if we were to ignore the type superscripts. Quasi-grammatical sentences bear strong resemblances to grammatical ones. Here are some examples:

> Some proposition dates Mary.
> John believes a pen.
> That John loves Mary gives Bill a fish.

The paradoxical sentence is also quasi-grammatical. Perhaps this is what accounts for our intuition that it is grammatical.

There is another standard 'solution' to the paradox, which differs slightly from the above, and which can also be formulated within PTQB. Suppose we revise our treatment of the type-floating exemplify so as to get its surface realizations from $\zeta_1$exemplifyζ_2. This allows us to meaningfully say of any thing that it exemplifies any other thing, regardless of type. But we still hold that such an assertion is true only if true in the first version of PTQB. Then exemplify itself will be meaningful and generable, but it will always be a property which necessarily applies to nothing. On this account our derivation of the paradox consists entirely of meaningful sentences, but there is a fallacy in going from line (4) to line (5).

5. *An Evaluation*

If type theory is correct, we can't meaningfully say all that we might want to say. For example, we can't say:

> Everything has a property

and thereby assert a proposition that talks about things of all types. This seems unacceptable. But that may not be an objection. The paradoxes, after all, are paradoxical. They reach absurd conclusions using only deeply believed principles, and they thereby show that at least one deeply believed principle must be rejected. Thus we can expect that any systematic attempt to deal with them will have some unacceptable consequences!

Bertrand Russell indicated a way in which the above consequence need not be as bad as it appears. [11] The idea is to supplement our grammar with a theory of pragmatics

according to which when one utters the above sentence one
automatically asserts *all* of its meanings — i.e., for each
τ, one asserts that everything of type τ has a property.
Roughly speaking, instead of asserting a universal generalization, one asserts all of its instances. These aren't the
same thing, but they're interchangeable for many purposes.
E.g., in each case one commits oneself to:

John has a property.

This technique will probably not furnish a good general
account, but it may be the best we can do.

The type-theoretic grammar discussed in this paper at
least has the following virtues — it adequately treats the
logical paradoxes (in one or more ways) without having too
much effect on ordinary discourse. Indeed, for everyday talk
about automobiles, politics, sex, and the weather, the type-
theoretic structure remains hidden in the background. And
for more intellectual, and generally more suspect, discourse
it surfaces only in the occasional ill-formedness of a quasi-
sentence that looks like a sentence. Perhaps for the most
part we speak in types as we speak in prose — without really
noticing.

Acknowledgments

Much of this material was developed for or during a seminar
at the University of Massachusetts in Spring 1976. I am
especially indebted to Emmon Bach and Barbara Partee for
support and criticism.

Notes

1. I am being purposely vague here. Saying of a property
of one type that it has a property of an inappropriate type

is meaningless according to some theories, and meaningful but automatically false according to others. These two different approaches are discussed in section 4.

2. In *Formal Philosophy: Selected Papers of Richard Montague,* ed. Richard Thomason (New Haven: Yale University Press, 1974).

3. See Michael Bennett, "Some Extensions of a Montague Fragment of English," Ph.D. dissertation, UCLA, 1974.

4. In Montague, *Formal Philosophy*.

5. In Barbara Partee, ed., *Montague Grammar* (New York: Academic Press, 1976).

6. For simplicity, features are omitted in the fragments discussed.

7. As in Bennett, "Some Extensions."

8. I am supposing here that a feature gets added to a pronoun to indicate *case* in the appropriate environments; these features are then exploited in rules such as S14.

9. The translations of *he* and *exemplify* are actually somewhat more complex than this; I have given the translations of the 'reduced forms' as in PTQ, p. 265, first full paragraph. In the translation of *be* I am supposing that we expand the intensional logic to allow variables of different type to flank =; I assume however that this always produces a false formula.

10. I use an asterisk in accordance with the custom in linguistics to mark a string of words which is not syntactically well-formed; for example, phrase (3) is *not* generated by the rules of PTQB.

11. In "Mathematical Logic as Based on the Theory of Syntax," reprinted in R. Marsh, ed., *Logic and Knowledge* (London: Allen & Unwin, 1956).

5

Dative 'Movement' and Thomason's Extensions of Montague Grammar

David R. Dowty

In his paper "Some Extensions of Montague Grammar" (Thomason 1976) and in recent unpublished papers (ms. May 1976, ms. July 1976), Richmond Thomason has proposed several analyses of active/passive sentence pairs which eschew the familiar Passive Transformation of transformational grammar in favor of a treatment that relates such pairs of sentences entirely by semantic rules. That is, a passive sentence such as (1) is not derived from the corresponding active sentence, but instead is produced as in the analysis tree (2) (cf. Thomason 1976: 104 - 107):

(1) *A fish is stolen by John.*

(2)

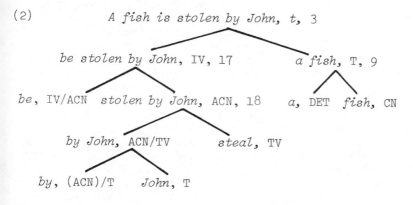

Here, a syntactic operation on the transitive verb *steal* converts this verb directly into its passive form *stolen*

(by John) before it is combined with its subject *a fish*.
Nevertheless, the sentence (1) can be shown to be logically
equivalent to the active sentence (3) in Thomason's extension:

(3) *John steals a fish*.

Though there is still some linguistic evidence for the Passive
Transformation that Thomason has not yet contended with in
a completely successful way in his system (namely, *'there-*
Insertion' sentences), it seems, surprisingly, that most
linguistic arguments for a Passive Transformation are
satisfied by Thomason's treatment as well. In particular, his
latest version (ms. May 1976) gives an example such as (4) all
readings in common with (5), (including specifically, the
reading in which *a unicorn* has narrower scope than *expect*):

(4) *A unicorn is believed by Bill to be expected by John
    to be found by Mary*.

(5) *Bill believes that John expects Mary to find a unicorn*.

The theoretical interest in this approach to passive
sentences is, according to Thomason, the following:

> Montague grammar is the first grammatical theory to have
> a separate semantic component capable of bearing its share
> of the explanatory burden. It is an interesting project
> to see how far the strategy can be pushed of using this
> component to explain as much as possible, with the aim of
> keeping the syntactic component simple. This represents
> an extreme position on the relation of syntax and seman-
> tics, and at present I don't want to claim more than that
> it is worth exploring. We know what types of theories we
> will get if we use the syntactic component as much as
> possible; the generative semanticists have done this. From
> the work of Barbara Partee and others we have an idea of
> what intermediate theories will look like. But the other
> alternative [i.e., 'to make the syntax of Montague grammar
> "surfacy"' — DRD] hasn't been worked out, and so we have
> no very clear idea of what difficulties such theories are
> likely to encounter, of what the price would be of
> adopting them. (Thomason ms. May 1976, pp. 1-2)

Thomason's nontransformational method of dealing with
passive sentences can be extended to cases related by the
transformations Raising to Subject and Raising to Object.
That is, a 'raised' sentence such as *A Republican seems
certain to win* would not be derived transformationally from
It seems that it is certain that a Republican will win, but
would rather be produced independently and related to this
second sentence only by semantic rules. The same comment
applies to (4) and (5), where both Passive and Raising (to
Object) are involved in the usual transformational analysis.
Since the Passive and Raising transformations are crucially
involved in arguments about some very basic assumptions about
transformational theory (e.g., the transformational cycle),
a theory of syntax which could get along without these transformations might be strikingly different from the familiar
transformational one. (I will argue later in this paper that
Thomason's approach also affords a superior treatment of
lexical exceptions to syntactic rules.)

Unfortunately, the usual transformational analysis of
Dative Movement, or *Dative Shift,* as a transformation converting (6) to (7), turns out to be incompatible with Thomason's
analysis of passive.

(6) *John gave a book to Mary.*

(7) *John gave Mary a book.*

This is because there is not one passive sentence corresponding to (6) and (7), but two — the *regular passive* (8) and
the *dative passive* (9).

(8) *A book was given to Mary.*

(9) *Mary was given a book.*

As long as (6) and (7) are related by a transformation (and by 'transformation' in this context I mean a syntactic rule taking a full sentence as input and giving a syntactically altered sentence as output), then only one of the two sentences (8) and (9) can be produced by Thomason's passive rule, not both of them.

The first task of this paper is to try to rescue Thomason's approach by giving an account of the 'dative-movement' sentences (8) and (9) that is compatible with Thomason's rules for passive sentences — compatible in the sense that both (8) and (9) can be produced automatically by Thomason's passive rule. This task will be discharged rather quickly (Sections 1-2). This is only the beginning of the story, however. Dative Movement is a notoriously ill-behaved transformation. It is well known that some three-place verbs (e.g., *donate*) forbid this transformation to take place, other verbs (e.g., *refuse*) require that it take place obligatorily. When the interaction of Dative Movement with the various kinds of passive sentences is considered (Section 3), even more complicated types of exceptions arise, and it has been observed by Georgia Green (1974) that a theory of syntactic exceptionality as powerful as Lakoff's (1967) is required to describe the data in transformational grammar.[1] When the interaction of Dative Movement with the transformation of *Unspecified Object Deletion* is considered, new kinds of exceptions arise (Section 4) which cannot even be treated within Lakoff's theory.

The upshot of this depressing catalog of syntactic irregularity is to suggest (in section 6) that 'Dative Movement' is not a syntactic rule of English at all in the usual sense, but rather the kind of rule called a *lexical rule* in the Extended Standard Theory and akin to the *word formation*

rule of traditional grammar. Under the proposal for a theory
of lexical rules for a Montague grammar I have proposed
earlier (Dowty 1975), Dative 'Movement' when recast as a
lexical rule would have exactly the same form and method of
semantic interpretation as that given it in the first part of
this paper, differing from a syntactic rule only in the role
it is claimed to play in the overall grammar of English. (For
this reason, it will be simpler for me to initially describe
the treatment of dative sentences as if the dative 'movement'
rule were a syntactic rule, in order to clarify its interaction with the other, syntactic rules of the grammar.) I conclude by discussing briefly *for*-datives and their passives
(section 7), the 'ordering predictions' made by this lexical
treatment of Dative Shift and Object Deletion (Section 8),
and the history of Dative Shift and Passive in English
(Section 9).

1. *Rules for Thomason's Treatment of Passive Sentences*

The rules for passive sentences I present here are not
literally those given by Thomason but are rather a simplified
version of them; my version more closely resembles the
grammar of Montague's PTQ (Montague 1973) and will hopefully
be easier for the reader to apprehend at first glance.
However, the rules I will shortly give for Dative Movement
sentences can easily be modified to fit into Thomason's more
complex version as well.[2] The new syntactic categories to be
added to those of PTQ are given on the following page. The
new category ADJ_p will include both basic adjectives that
can appear in predicate position and past participle phrases
like *stolen by John*; both types of phrases are interpreted
semantically as one-place predicates of individuals and are
thus distinguished from adjectives like *former* which are

	New Categories:	*Basic Expressions:*
ADJ_p	(the category of *predicative adjectives*, defined as $t///e)^2$	{*blue, awake,* etc.}
COP	(the category of *copulas*, defined as IV/ADJ_p)	{*be*}
PP	(the category of *past participle formers*, defined as ADJ_p/TV)	{*-en*}
PP/T	(a category of 'transitive' past participle formers)	{*by*}

---

classified as CN/CN and interpreted as predicate modifiers. The verb *be* appearing here in COP is a 'dummy' copula making no semantic contribution of its own and is distinct from $be \in P_{TV}$, the '*be* of identity.' The new syntactic rules (numbered in accord with Thomason 1972) are the following:

S19. If $\alpha \in P_{PP/T}$, $\beta \in P_T$, then $F_{19}(\alpha, \beta) \in P_{PP}$, where

$F_{19}(\alpha, \beta) = \alpha \beta$ if β is not a variable,

$\alpha \ him_n$ if β is he_n.

Translation:[3] $\alpha' \ (^\wedge\beta')$

Examples: $F_{19}(by, John) = by \ John$; $F_{19}(by, he_4) = by \ him_4$

S18. If $\alpha \in P_{PP}$, $\beta \in P_{TV}$, then $F_{18}(\alpha, \beta) \in P_{ADJ_p}$, where

(i) if α is *-en*, then $F_{18}(\alpha, \beta) = \beta'$, and β' is the result of replacing the first basic term in β by its past participle form, and (ii) if α is *by* γ, then $F_{18}(\alpha, \beta) = \beta''$, and β'' is the result of replacing the basic verb in β by its past participle form and inserting *by* γ

immediately after this past participle.

Translation: α' (^β')

Examples: F_{18} (*-en, steal*) = *stolen*

F_{18} (*by John, steal*) = *stolen by John*

S17. If α ∈ P_{COP}, β ∈ P_{ADJ_p}, then F_{17} (α, β) ∈ P_{IV},
where F_{17} (α, β) = α β.

Translation: α' (^β')

Examples: F_{17} (*be, blue*) = *be blue*; F_{17} (*be, stolen*)

= *be stolen*

F_{17} (*be, stolen by John*) = *be stolen by John*

These rules will generate both 'full passives', as in (10),
and the so-called 'truncated passives' as in (11):

(10)

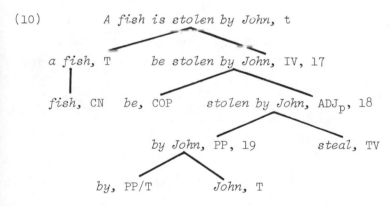

(11)

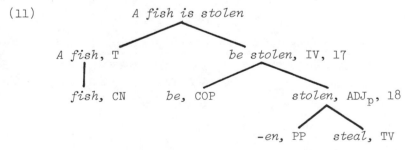

This system requires the following meaning postulates for *-en'*, *by'* and *be'*, which are the translations of the 'past participle formers' *-en* and *by* respectively; *be'* translates the 'dummy' copula *be*. In these postulates and elsewhere below, I indicate the type of the variables appearing in the formula by a subscript on the first occurrence of each variable.[4]

MP8.1. $\wedge \mathcal{R}_{\langle s,f(TV)\rangle} \wedge x_{\langle s,e\rangle} \Box \, [en' \, (\mathcal{R}) \, (x) \leftrightarrow$
$\qquad \vee y_{\langle s,e\rangle} [^{\vee}\mathcal{R} \, (P[\hat{P}\{x\}]) \, (y)]]$

MP8.2. $\wedge \mathcal{R}_{\langle s,f(TV)\rangle} \wedge \mathcal{P}_{\langle s,f(T)\rangle} \wedge x_{\langle s,e\rangle} \Box \, [by' \, (\mathcal{P}) \, (\mathcal{R}) \, (x) \leftrightarrow$
$\qquad \mathcal{P}\{\hat{y}_{\langle s,e\rangle}\} \, [^{\vee}\mathcal{R} \, (\hat{P} \, [P \, \{x\}]) \, (y)]\}]$

MP9. $\wedge P_{\langle s,f(IV)\rangle} \wedge x_{\langle s,e\rangle} \Box \, [be' \, (P) \, (x) \leftrightarrow P \, \{x\}]$

As a result of these postulates and of the usual postulates for first-order extensional reducibility of verbs like s̰t̰ḛa̰l̰, (10) and (11) will have translations equivalent to (12) and (13) respectively; (12) is of course equivalent to the translation of J̰o̰h̰n̰ s̰t̰ḛa̰l̰s̰ ã f̰ḭs̰h̰.

(12) $\vee u_{\langle e\rangle} [\underset{\sim}{fish'}_*(u) \wedge \underset{\sim}{steal'}_*(j,u)]$

(13) $\vee u_{\langle e\rangle} \vee v_{\langle e\rangle} [\underset{\sim}{fish'}_*(u) \wedge \underset{\sim}{steal'}_*(v,u)]$

2. *Rules for Dative Sentences*

Thomason's fragment includes the category TTV (defined as TV/T) containing expressions that combine with a term phrase to produce a 'phrasal' transitive verb, and verbs like *give* are entered as basic expressions in this category. However, I will introduce a second category of three place verbs as well, and I place basic verbs like *give* in this new category instead of the category TTV:

New Categories for Dative Sentences: *Basic expressions:*

TTV   (defined as TV/T, the category   none (for the moment)
          of *double object* verbs)

DTV   (defined as TV//T, the category   (*give, donate,* etc.)
          of *dative transitive verbs*)

The category DTV will be used to produce verb phrases like
give a book to John, whereas TTV will be used to produce verb
phrases like *give John a book.* In lieu of a transformation
which transforms whole sentences like (8) into (9), I will
propose a rule (S20) which simply shifts verbs from the
category DTV into the category TTV, *before* they combine with
either of their objects. Thus we will have analysis trees
like (14) and (15):

(14)

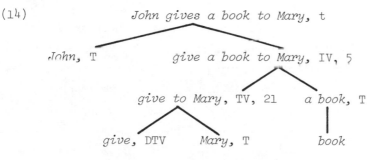

(15)

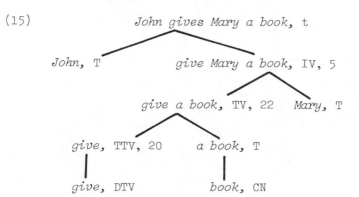

It will be noted that in these trees the rule for combining transitive verb (phrases) with their objects (S5 in PTQ) must combine the TV-phrase *give to Mary* with *a book* to produce *give a book to Mary*, and it must also combine the TV-phrase *give a book* with *Mary* to produce *give Mary a book*. Thus the rule S5 can no longer use simple concatenation as its syntactic operation but must be modified as follows:

S5. If $\alpha \in P_{TV}$, $\beta \in P_T$, then $F_5 (\alpha, \beta) \in P_{IV}$, where (i) if

β is not a variable, then $F_5 (\alpha, \beta) = \alpha'$, and α' is the

result of inserting β after the first basic verb in α,

and (ii) if $\beta = he_n$, then $F_5 (\alpha, \beta) = \alpha''$, and α'' is the

result of inserting him_n after the first basic verb in α.

It might be supposed that this is an unwelcome complication, but in fact just this modification has been proposed on various independent grounds. Thomason (1974) shows that there are syntactic reasons for deriving the IV-phrase *persuade John to leave* by combining the TV-phrase *persuade to leave* with the term phrase *John*. Furthermore, semantic reasons are cited in Dowty 1976 for deriving the IV-phrase *hammer the metal flat* by combining the TV-phrase *hammer flat* with the term phrase *the metal*. The modified S5 generates all these examples correctly.

Transitive verb phrases such as *give to Mary* and *give a book* are, in fact, the key to producing both kinds of passive sentences with Thomason's passive rule alone; since either of these phrases may serve as inputs to his rule (see (16) and (17) on the following page). The new syntactic rules involved in (14) - (17) are as follows:

(16)   *A book is given to Mary by John,* t

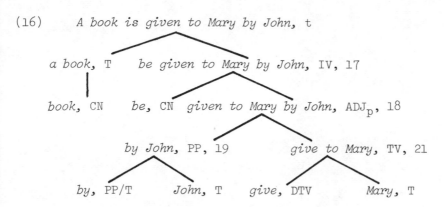

(17)   *Mary is given a book by John,* t

S20. (Dative Shift) If $\alpha \in P_{DTV}$, then $F_{20}(\alpha) \in P_{TTV}$,

where $F_{20}(\alpha) = \alpha$.

Translation: $\lambda \mathscr{P}_{\langle s, f(T)\rangle} \; \lambda \mathscr{Q}_{\langle s, f(T)\rangle} \; \lambda x_{\langle s, e\rangle}$

$[\alpha' \, (\mathscr{Q}) \, (\mathscr{P}) \, (x)]$

Examples: $F_{20}(give) = give$; $F_{20}(sell) = sell$

S21. If $\alpha \in P_{DTV}$, $\beta \in P_T$, then $F_{21}(\alpha, \beta) \in P_{TV}$, where

$F_{21}(\alpha, \beta) = \alpha$ *to* β if β is not a subscripted pronoun,

and $F_{21}(\alpha, he_n) = \alpha$ *to* him_n.

Translation: $\alpha'(^\wedge\beta')$

Examples: $F_{21}(give, Mary) = give\ to\ Mary$; $F_{21}(give, he_2)$

    $= give\ to\ him_2$

S22. If $\alpha \in P_{TTV}$, $\beta \in P_T$, then $F_{22}(\alpha, \beta) \in P_T$, where $F_{22}(\alpha, \beta)$

= $\alpha\ \beta$ if β is not a subscripted pronoun, and $F_{22}(\alpha, he_n)$

= $\alpha\ him_n$.

Translation: $\alpha'(^\wedge\beta')$

Examples: $F_{22}(give, a\ book) = give\ a\ book$; $F_{22}(give, he_2)$

    $= give\ him_2$

To understand the translation of S20, consider first that
Thomason's passive rule is interpreted, in effect, as a semantic operation which reverses the 'grammatical relations'
inherent in the meaning of a transitive verb by purely semantic means; it causes the subject which will later attach to
a passive verb to be interpreted like the direct object of
the original active verb, and causes the object of *by* to be
interpreted like the subject of the active verb.

The translation rule for S20 performs a perfectly analogous
semantic operation on the translation of a verb in the category DTV: its result is that the direct object of the 'shifted'
verb $give \in P_{TTV}$ is interpreted like the indirect object of
the original $give \in P_{DTV}$, and the oblique (i.e., rightmost)
object of $give \in P_{TTV}$ is interpreted as the direct object of
$give \in P_{DTV}$. Once a verb in TTV has combined with a term
phrase to form a transitive verb, it can have its grammatical
relations altered once again by the passive rule.

If we now add the meaning postulate MP10 for extensional, first-order reducibility of verbs like *give*,

MP10. $\forall \mathscr{R}_{\langle s,\langle e,\langle e,\langle e,t\rangle\rangle\rangle\rangle}$ $\wedge \mathscr{P}_{\langle s,f(T)\rangle}$ $\wedge \mathscr{Q}_{\langle s,f(T)\rangle}$

$\wedge x_{\langle s,e\rangle}$ $\Box$ $[\delta\ (\mathscr{P})\ (\mathscr{Q})\ (x) \leftrightarrow \mathscr{P}\{\hat{y}_{\langle s,e\rangle}\ \mathscr{Q}\{\hat{z}_{\langle s,e\rangle}$

$[{}^{\vee}R\ ({}^{\vee}y)\ ({}^{\vee}z)\ ({}^{\vee}x)]\}\}]$

and if we adopt the definitions in (16) (parallel to those in PTQ for 2-place verbs),

(16) *Definition:* $\delta_* = \lambda u_e\ \lambda v_e\ \lambda w_e\ [\delta\ (\hat{P}P\{u\})\ (\hat{P}P\{v\})\ (w)]$

where δ translates *give,* etc.

Definition: $\gamma\ (\alpha,\ \beta,\ \delta) = \gamma\ (\delta)\ (\beta)\ (\alpha)$

then all three of the analysis trees (14) - (16) will have translations logically equivalent to (17):

(17) $\vee u_e\ [book'_*\ (u)\ \wedge\ give'_*\ (j,\ u,\ m)]$

Not all three-place verbs of English are fully first-order reducible, of course. It is well known that the direct-object positions of verbs like *promise* and *owe* are 'intensional contexts', just as the direct object position of the verb *seek* is. Consider *John promised a new coat to Mary,* or *John owes a favor to Mary*. However, these verbs do have the semantic property which we may call (following Montague's terminology) *subject-and-indirect-object-but-not-direct-object-reducibility*.[5] If δ translates *promise* or *owe,* then MP11 must hold for it:

MP11. $\vee S_{\langle s,\langle e\langle\langle s,f(T)\rangle\rangle,\langle e,t\rangle\rangle\rangle\rangle}$ $\wedge \mathscr{P}_{\langle s,f(T)\rangle}$ $\wedge \mathscr{Q}_{\langle s,f(T)\rangle}$

$\wedge x_{\langle s,e\rangle}$ $\Box$ $[\delta\ (\mathscr{P})\ (\mathscr{Q})\ (x) \leftrightarrow \mathscr{P}\{\hat{y}_{\langle s,e\rangle}\ [{}^{\vee}S\ ({}^{\vee}y)\ (\mathscr{Q})$

$({}^{\vee}x)]\}]$

The so-called 'truncated passives' (18) and (19) will receive translations equivalent to (20):

(18) *A book was given to Mary.*

(19) *Mary was given a book.*

(20) $\vee u_e \vee v_e \, [book'_* \, (u) \wedge give'_* \, (v, \, u, \, m)]$

3. *Exceptional Syntactic Behavior of Dative Sentences*

The best-known class of exceptional verbs consists of those which do not undergo Dative Shift and do not have a dative passive form, as in the following example:

(21) a. *John donated the money to the foundation.*

b. **John donated the foundation the money.*

c. *The money was donated to the foundation (by John).*

d. **The foundation was donated the money (by John).*

Such verbs (in fact, the class includes the majority of English three-place verbs) are typically polysyllabic and are of Romance rather than Anglo-Saxon origin. (We will return to the significance of this fact later.) These verbs are 'simple exceptions' to the rule S20. Note that our analysis predicts that if a verb lacks the dative shifted sentence, e.g., (21b), it will lack the dative passive sentence, e.g., (21d), as well, since the dative passive sentence involves a prior application of dative shift. This prediction seems to be correct.

The standard transformational analysis of Dative Movement of course makes the same prediction for parallel reasons.

Some verbs lack an 'unshifted' dative object and the regular passive, but have the dative passive:

(22) a. **The judge spared the ordeal to the defendant.*

     b. *The judge spared the defendant the ordeal.*

     c. **The ordeal was spared to the defendant (by the judge).*

     d. *The defendant was spared the ordeal (by the judge).*

The class of verbs having this pattern is very small: in my
speech it includes, besides *spare* (in the sense exemplified
by *spare me the ordeal,* not as in *spare me a dime*), *refuse,*
deny, envy, and maybe *permit* and *allow,* but surely not many
more. I expect that there will be variation from speaker to
speaker here, so that to some readers the (a) and (c) sentences are acceptable for one or more of these verbs.

In the usual transformational analysis of such sentences
the full power of Lakoff's theory of syntactic exceptions
must be brought in at this point, since these verbs must be
obligatory exceptions to an optional minor rule; that is,
the grammar must require that sentences containing these
verbs obligatorily undergo a transformation which is optional
for many verbs and prohibited for most.

In my proposal, the existence of the two separate syntactic
categories of three-place verbs, DTV and TTV, might have
seemed an unwelcome complication until this point, but now
it is clear what the advantage of having two such categories
is: we can deal with such verbs as *allow, refuse, spare,* etc.,
by entering them as basic expressions of the category TTV,
but not in the category DTV. This step predicts that such
verbs lack the (c) sentence as well as the (a) sentence,
since the (c) sentence is derived ultimately from a basic
verb in DTV.

Of course, the advocate of a dative transformation might
reply by proposing that sentence (22b) is its own deep
structure, so that no application of the Dative Movement

transformation is involved with these verbs, hence no obligatory exception. This approach would require that these verbs
be subcategorized for two noun phrase objects in deep structure, while other verbs (*give*, etc.) are subcategorized for
one object followed by a *to*-phrase. Thus here also, two
distinct subcategories of three-place verbs are postulated,
and this approach is no simpler.[6]

4. *Dative Movement and* Unspecified Object Deletion

Traditional transformational grammar regards (24) as derived
from (23) by the transformation of *Unspecified Object
Deletion:*

(23) *John ate something.*

(24) *John ate.*

In a Montague grammar, it would be possible instead to relate
(23) to (24) by a rule converting transitive verbs directly
to intransitives (or, as traditional grammarians would say,
converting transitive verbs to *transitive absolute* verbs):

S23. If $\alpha \in P_{TV}$, then $F_{23}(\alpha) \in P_{IV}$, where $F_{23}(\alpha) = \alpha$.

   Translation: $\lambda x_{\langle s,e \rangle} \ {}^{\vee}y_{\langle s,e \rangle} \ [\alpha' \ (\hat{P} \ [P \ \{y\}]) \ (x)]$

   Example: $F_{23}(eat) = eat$

By this rule, *John eats* would be derived as in (25) and would
have the translation (26):

(25)

$$
\begin{array}{c}
\textit{John eats, } t \\
\diagup \ \diagdown \\
\textit{John, } T \qquad \textit{eat, IV, 23} \\
| \\
\textit{eat, TV}
\end{array}
$$

(26) ${}^{\vee}u_e \ [eat'_* \ (j, \ u)]$

Of course, not all transitive verbs appear without an object (e.g., *John devoured something* but not **John devoured*), so this rule, like S22, must be subject to a number of exceptions.

When we turn to three-place verbs, the possible 'deletions' multiply:

(27) a. *John served the cake to Mary.*

   b. *John served Mary the cake.*

   c. *John served Mary.*

   d. *John served the cake.*

   e. *John served.*

A transformationalist might propose that (27c - e) should all be derived by an appropriately generalized Unspecified Object Deletion transformation which could delete the first, second, or both noun phrases following a verb. However, this avenue is not open to me; converting a three-place verb to a transitive verb cannot be accomplished by the same rule that converts a transitive verb to an intransitive verb in a Montague grammar, because the categories involved are different in the two cases. Moreover, we must have *two* rules, not just one, converting three-place to transitive verbs, if we are to capture correctly the difference in the normal interpretations of (27c) and (27d): in (27c), the noun phrase remaining denotes the recipient of the serving, in (27d) it denotes the thing served. (Of course, both these sentences could have the unusual interpretations as well — (27c) could have the other interpretation if it were understood that John was preparing a banquet for cannibals, and (27d) could have the abnormal interpretation in a science fiction movie called *The Cake That Ate at 1,000 Gourmet Restaurants.* But the point

is that we must account for *two* interpretations of a sentence
with *serve* followed by a single noun phrase, and these two
interpretations must be provided by different syntactic/seman-
tic rules in Montague grammar, given the constraint that each
syntactic rule has a unique translation rule.)

To make matters more confusing, each of these interpretations could be derived in two different ways, according to
whether the verb which acts as input is from the category DTV
or from the category TTV. That is, to derive the transitive
verb *serve* as it appears in *John served Mary* from the three-
place verb *serve* in DTV we would need a category-shifting rule
with a translation that puts an existentially quantified
variable in place of the *second* argument of the original verb
(i.e., a translation $\lambda \mathscr{P}$ λx $\lor y$ $[\alpha'(\mathscr{P})(\hat{P} P \{y\})(x)]$),
but to derive this same transitive verb *serve* from the verb
serve in TTV would require a different translation, one
placing the quantified variable in place of the first argument
of the input, i.e., $\lambda \mathscr{P}$ λx $\lor y$ $[\alpha'(\hat{P} P \{y\})(\mathscr{P})(x)]$. On
the other hand, to derive the transitive verb *serve* as it
appears in *John served the cake* requires one of the two rules
but with the complementary translation. For reasons that will
become clear later, I adopt the following two rules:

S24. If $\alpha \in P_{DTV}$, then $F_{24}(\alpha) \in P_{TV}$, where $F_{24}(\alpha) = \alpha.$[7]

> *Translation:* $\lambda \mathscr{P}_{\langle s, f(T) \rangle}$ $\lambda x_{\langle s,e \rangle}$ $\lor y_{\langle s,e \rangle}$ $[\alpha'$
> $(\hat{P} P \{y\})(\mathscr{P})(x)]$
>
> *Example:* $F_{24}(serve) = serve$; using this output,
>
> > $F_6(serve, the\ soup) = serve\ the\ soup$ (with 'expected'
> >
> > interpretation).

S25. If $\alpha \in P_{TTV}$, then $F_{25}(\alpha) \in P_{TV}$, where $F_{25}(\alpha) = \alpha$.

   Translation: $\lambda \mathscr{P}_{\langle s,f(T)\rangle}\ \lambda x_{\langle s,e\rangle}\ {}^{\vee}y_{\langle s,e\rangle}\ [\alpha'$
   $(\hat{P}P\ \{y\})\ (\mathscr{P})\ (x)]$

   Example: $F_{24}(serve) = serve$; using this output,

   $F_6(serve, Mary) = serve\ Mary$ (with 'expected'

   interpretation).

With these rules, examples like (27c - e) can be derived as
follows:

(28)

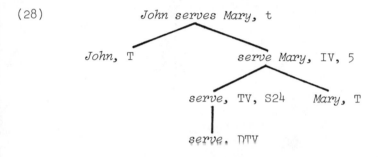

(29)

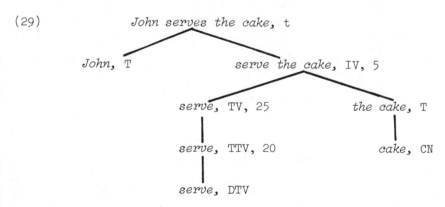

(30)

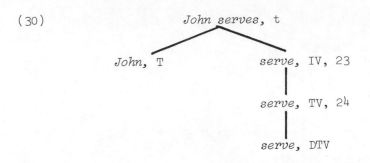

(31)

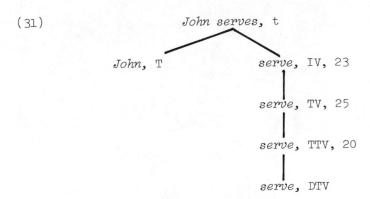

The translations of (28) and (29) will be (32) and (33) respectively, and both (30) and (31) will have translations equivalent to (34).

(32) $\lor u_e [serve'_* (j, u, m)]$

(33) $\lor u_e [\land v_e [cake'_* (v) \leftrightarrow u = v] \land \lor w_e [serve'_*$

$(j, u, w)]]$

(34) $\lor u_e \lor v_e [serve'_* (j, u, v)]$

Of course, the sentences *John serves Mary* and *John serves the cake* will have other analysis trees besides these, analysis trees giving the 'unusual' interpretations of these two sentences discussed earlier.

My reason for adopting S24 in the form given is that it is needed independently to reduce to transitive verbs those three-place verbs that do not undergo dative shift (e.g., *announce*) and thus cannot undergo a rule applying to members of TTV:

(35) a. *John announced the winner to the audience.*

　　b. **John announced the audience the winner.*

　　c. *John announced the winner.*

One final class of 'object deletion' sentences that remains to be accounted for consists of sentences where the *to*-phrase is present but the direct object is absent. This class includes verbs that undergo dative shift (e.g., *rent*) and verbs that do not (e.g., *surrender*):

(36) a. *The general surrendered the fort to the Indians.*

　　b. **The general surrendered the Indians the fort.*

　　c. *The general surrendered to the Indians.*

(37) a. *That landlord doesn't rent apartments to students.*

　　b. *That landlord doesn't rent students apartments.*

　　c. *That landlord doesn't rent to students.*

Such sentences could either be produced by rules already postulated (i.e., by combining the verb *surrender* in DTV with *the Indians* by S21 to give *surrender to the Indians* and then applying S23 to this phrase to give the IV-phrase *surrender to the Indians*), or else they could be produced by new rules taking members of DTV into a new category DIV (= IV///T):

S26. If $\alpha \in P_{DTV}$, then $F_{26}(\alpha) \in P_{DIV}$, where $F_{26}(\alpha) = \alpha$.

　　Translation: $\lambda \mathcal{P}_{\langle s, f(T) \rangle} \; \lambda x_{\langle s, e \rangle} \; {}^{\vee}y_{\langle s, e \rangle}$

　　　　$[\alpha' \; (\hat{P} \; P \; \{x\}) \; (\mathcal{P}) \; (y)]$

　　Example: $F_{26}(surrender) = surrender$

S27. If $\alpha \in P_{DIV}$, $\beta \in P_T$, then $F_{27}(\alpha, \beta) \in P_{IV}$,

where $F_{27}(\alpha, \beta) = \alpha$ *to* β if β is not a variable,
α *to him$_n$* otherwise.

Translation: α' $(^\wedge\beta')$

Example: F_{27} (*surrender, the Indians*) = *surrender to
the Indians*

Postulating these new rules and the new category DIV is of
course a less economical solution than producing (36c) and
(37c) by previously discussed rules, but this latter method
may be preferable for reasons to be discussed below.

5. *Exceptions to the Various Object 'Deletion' Rules*

I have now been forced to propose three or perhaps even four
distinct rules to replace the transformation of Unspecified
Object Deletion, whereas the familiar transformational approach might seem to get by with a single transformation.
However, when we look at the various kinds of exceptions to
object 'deletion' rules, the situation begins to look just as
complex for the transformational approach.

Some verbs, such as *sell*, undergo S21 (from DTV to TV)
but not S22 (from TTV to TV) or S23 (from TV to IV) or S26
(from DTV to DIV):

(38) a.   *John sold the house to Mary.*

   b.   *John sold Mary the house.*

   c.   *John sold the house.*

   d.   **John sold Mary.*

   e.   **John sold to Mary.*

   f.   **John sold.*

On the other hand, the verb *feed* undergoes S22 but not S21
(nor does it undergo S26 or S23):

(39) a. *John fed the cake to Mary.*

    b. *John fed Mary the cake.*

    c. **John fed the cake.*

    d. *John fed Mary.*

    e. **John fed to Mary.*

    f. **John fed.*

Consider how the data in (38) and (39) would have to be
treated in a transformational analysis. If one attempted to
write a single Unspecified Object Deletion Transformation to
perform all these deletions, it would look something like (40):

(40) *Unspecified Object Deletion*

SD: X - $[_{VP}$ V - (NP) - NP - Y $]_{VP}$ - Z

       1   2   3   4   5   6

SC: 1   2   3 $\emptyset$ 5   6

Condition: 4 exhaustively dominates *something* or *someone.*

Though this transformation would be satisfactory for verbs
like *serve* (assuming it could apply to its own output), we
would have to somehow require that the term 3, indicated as
optional in the transformation, must obligatorily be PRESENT
if the verb is *sell*, but must obligatorily be ABSENT if the
verb is *feed*. Thus we cannot simply make certain verbs exceptions to transformations, we must make certain verbs EXCEP-
TIONS TO PARTS OF STRUCTURAL DESCRIPTIONS of transformations.
I leave it to the reader to confirm that tactics such as
ordering the rule extrinsically with respect to Dative Shift
or tinkering with the structural description cannot improve

the situation significantly. Alternatively, we might do away
with the deletion transformation and assume that NP nodes are
allowed to sometimes remain unfilled in deep structure,
appealing to semantic interpretation rules to interpolate
someone or *something* in the appropriate places and to rule out
the starred sentences above as uninterpretable. But as long
as these rules are the general interpretation rules applying
to sentences, rather than the interpretation rules associated
with specific lexical items, there is no reason to believe
that the lexical exceptions to interpretation rules would be
less problematic than the syntactic exceptions under the
deletion hypothesis.

Thus just as was the case with the interaction of Dative
Shift and Passive, we here again see that the added complication of having distinct categories of three-place verbs and
separate syntactic rules for reducing these to transitive and
finally to intransitive verbs is, in a sense, an advantage
when the various classes of exceptions are considered.

Once again, the transformationalist might reply by proposing
that there is not one Unspecified Object Deletion transformation after all, but rather several similar deletion rules.
If so, it would still be necessary to appeal to either
extrinsic rule ordering or else global rules, since the
correct structural descriptions for such transformations
would differ according to whether the optional Dative Movement
Transformation had applied in the case of verbs like *sell* or
feed. Even without a detailed discussion of these possibilities, I think the reader will agree with me that any transformational analysis of these matters will surely turn out
to be almost as complex, if not exactly as complex, as the
Montague grammar analysis I have presented here.

Unfortunately, there are still other exceptional three-place verbs that behave neither exactly like *serve* nor like *sell* nor like *feed*. Of the many possible combinations of simple exceptions to the five rules S20, S23, S24, S25, and S26 that a given verb might have,[8] I believe I have found verbs in at least ten distinct classes (including a class of verbs which undergo all of these rules). These classes are summarized in Table 1. Sentences illustrating the behavior of verbs in each of these classes follow:

I. Verbs undergoing all five rules. For my speech, verbs such as *radio, cable,* and possibly *telephone* and *telegraph* belong to this class.

(41) a. *John radioed the message to Mary.*

b. *John radioed Mary the message.*

c. *John radioed the message.*

d. *John radioed Mary.*

e. *John radioed to Mary.*

f. *John radioed.*

II. Verbs undergoing only S20, S23, S24, and S25: *serve* (cf. 27a‑e; also, **John served to Mary* is not acceptable). Other verbs in this class are *pay, teach*.

III. Verbs undergoing S20, and S24 only: *sell, bring, convey, advance, submit,* and others. (Cf. (38a‑f above.)

IV. Verbs undergoing only S20 and S25; the verb *feed*. (Cf. 39a‑f) above.)

V. Verbs undergoing S20, S23, S24 and S26. Verbs such as *read, shout, whisper, sing, preach,* etc. belong to this class.

Table 1

Rules	I	II	III	IV	V	VI	VII	VIII	IX	X
					Classes					
S20 Dative Shift, i.e., DTV → TTV	✓	✓	✓	✓	✓	✓	✓	×	×	×
S23 Object Deletion for TV, i.e., TV → IV	✓	✓	×	×	✓	×	×	✓	×	×
S24 'Indirect Object Deletion' for DTV, i.e., DTV → TV	✓	✓	✓	×	✓	✓	×	✓	✓	×
S25 'Shifted Indirect Object Deletion' for TTV, i.e., TTV → TV	✓	✓	×	✓	×	×	×	×[†]	×[†]	×[†]
S26 'Direct Object Deletion' for DTV, i.e., DTV → DIV	✓	×[9]	×	×	✓	✓	✓	✓	×	×
Example Verbs:	radio telephone cable	serve pay teach	sell bring convey advance submit	feed	give (give money to a charitable institution) read shout whisper	rent	loan lend allot	surrender confess report propose	transport convey return restore	entrust

† cannot apply

(42) a. *John sang a song to Mary.*

b. *John sang Mary a song.*

c. *John sang a song.*

d. **John sang Mary.*

e. *John sang to Mary.*

f. *John sang.*

VI. Verbs undergoing S20, S24 and S26. The verb *rent* apparently belongs to this class. (Cf. (37a - c) above and *John rents houses* (the reading in which John rents houses FROM rather than TO someone is irrelevant here), **John rents).*

VII. Verbs undergoing S20 (Dative Shift) but none of the 'deletion' rules: *bequeath, leave, will* (as near-synonyms of *bequeath), loan, lend,* and perhaps *allot*:

(43) a. *John loaned five dollars to Mary.*

b. *John loaned Mary five dollars.*

c. **John loaned five dollars.*

d. **John loaned Mary.*

e. **John loaned.*

Note that if a verb does not undergo S20, it cannot (in my analysis) undergo S25, since it can never become a member of the category TTV to which S25 applies.

VIII. Verbs not undergoing S20 but undergoing S23, S24, and S26. This class was illustrated by *surrender* above (cf. (36a - c) and also *The general surrendered the fort, The general surrendered*) and includes also *confess, report,* and perhaps *propose* (in the sense 'propose marriage').

IX. Verbs undergoing only S24. This would appear to be the largest class of three-place verbs of all. It includes *transport, return, restore, explain, deliver, delegate, administer,* etc.

(44) a. *John transported the goods to Mary.*

    b. **John transported Mary the goods.*

    c. *John transported the goods.*

    d. **John transported Mary.*
        (ungrammatical if Mary is recipient)

    e. **John transported to Mary.*

    f. **John transported.*

  X. Verbs not undergoing any of the rules: *entrust.*

(45) a. *John entrusted the package to Mary.*

    b. **John entrusted Mary the package.*
        (but cf. *John entrusted Mary with the package.*)

    c. **John entrusted the package.*

    d. **John entrusted Mary.*

    e. **John entrusted to Mary.*

    f. **John entrusted.*

Two important qualifications must be made about these lists. First, the allowable 'deletions' seem to vary greatly from one speaker to the next, so the reader is unlikely to agree with my judgments for every verb. This is not crucial, nor does it even matter whether as many as ten classes can be distinguished by every speaker; I merely wish to establish that there are more than a few distinct classes of verbs in this respect.

Second, many verbs allow the 'deletions' quite freely in particular discourse contexts *in which the thing or range of things denoted by the 'deleted' term phrase can be implicitly understood by the participants in the discourse in that situation.* For example, I have marked the intransitive use of *sell* as ungrammatical (as in *John sold*) but, for example, it is clear that in a discussion of trading at the stock market it is perfectly natural to say *People are selling like mad today.* All of the judgments in the lists above are intended to apply to the 'out of the blue' context — that is, to a context in which the nature of the thing denoted by the 'deleted' term phrase would *not* be clear to the hearer purely from the context of the discourse.

6. *Dative Shift and Object 'Deletion' Rules as Lexical or Word-Formation Rules*

It is now time to confess that, despite the advantages this formulation of Dative Shift and other rules may have over the usual transformational formulations in the treatment of exceptions, I do not find it completely plausible to suppose that rules with even this idiosyncratic behavior really ought to be considered syntactic rules in English on a par with, say, the subject-predicate rule or the rule for forming relative clauses. From the point of view of language acquisition, it seems questionable that such highly irregular 'rules' reflect, however abstractly, principles a child actually adopts in producing novel English utterances. As C. L. Baker has pointed out to me, it is one thing to suppose children learn exceptions to rules by 'positive information' about their exceptional behavior, but quite another thing to suppose they infer exceptions from the absence of information. That is, it is easy to understand how a child acquiring English past tenses could learn that the past tense of *go* is not **goed* but *went* because sentences produced

by the child's parents systematically have *went* where the
past tense of *go* should occur. However, it is hard to imagine
why a child should infer from merely the absence of sentences
like **Explain me the answer* or **We donated them some money* in
the parents' speech that these particular verbs prohibit a
syntactic rule from applying. After all, it is precisely to
explain how children continually produce novel utterances not
heard in the speech of their parents that we have to postulate
syntactic rules at all to explain language acquisition.

Thus I wish to suggest that S20, S23, S24, S25, and S26
should probably not be considered syntactic rules of a
Montague grammar of English. Rather, there should be five
different basic expressions[10] *serve* occurring in B_{DTV}, B_{TTV},
B_{TV} (two of them in this category), and B_{IV}, respectively.
Other 'verbs' will be represented by basic expressions in
one or more of these various categories, the choice of categories for each 'verb' depending on which of the ten exception
classes it belongs to. There would be no exceptions to these
syntactic rules simply because there would be no such rules.

But this view, on the other hand, seems too extreme as
well. To suggest that there happen to be numerous sets of
completely unrelated basic verbs in different categories that
happen to have the same phonological form and systematically
related interpretations is to ignore important syntactic
patterns of the language. Fortunately, I think there may be
a satisfactory intermediate position on the status of these
rules. What I wish to propose is that the five rules under
discussion might be regarded as rules of *word-formation*, or
lexical rules.

Word-formation is well established in traditional grammar
as the study of how new words of a language are produced from
old either by adding *derivational affixes* to words (e.g.,

verbs *blacken, dampen, flatten* from adjectives *black, damp, flat*; nouns *destruction, decision, rejection* from verbs *destroy, decide, reject*; adjectives *washable, breakable, readable* from verbs *wash, break, read,* etc.) or by *compounding* two words to form a third (e.g., nouns *blackbird, steamboat, pickpocket* from combinations of noun, verb, or adjective with other nouns).

The suggestion that Dative Shift and Object 'deletion' rules are rules of word-formation will initially strike most readers as peculiar, but I will try to show (1) that there can be no good reason from the point of view of Montague for discounting this suggestion if 'word-formation rules' are accepted as a type of rule at all, and (2) that the five rules under discussion have several properties elsewhere associated with word-formation rules rather than syntactic rules.

In early transformational grammar, so-called word-formation rules were assumed to be included among syntactic transformations; cf. the study of English compounding by Lees (1960) and the study of English derivational morphology by Chapin (1967). However, such rules seemed to defy precise systematization, and eventually Chomsky (1970) proposed that rules for forming complex words should be excluded from the syntactic component; rather, complex words were all to be considered independent 'lexical entries', the relationship among morphologically related words being described by a new kind of rule, the 'lexical redundancy rule'. Chomsky's motivations for this new position were (presumably) two-fold. First, word-formation seemed much less systematic than syntax in three ways, in the question of just which derived words in each pattern word-formation are accepted words in the language, in the morphological details of some derived word of a given pattern, and in the syntactic properties of the derived words. Second, the meaning of a derived word is not always completely predictable from the meaning of its parts. For example, *decision* means 'act of deciding' but *delegation* means not just 'act of delegating' but also 'people to whom something is delegated', and *transmission* means not only 'act of transmitting' but also 'thing (namely, part of an automobile) that transmits something'. *Washable* is 'capable of being washed', *breakable* is 'capable of being broken', and this semantic pattern holds for most words in *-able*. Yet *changeable* more often means 'capable of changing' than 'capable of being changed', and various derived words have subtleties of meaning that go beyond these gross paraphrases. As Chomsky notes, *readable* in its usual usage does not simply mean 'capable of being read' but something more like 'capable of being read without undue effort'.

Though articles by proponents of the Extended Standard Theory have recently appeared in which this view is further developed in various ways (cf. Halle 1973; Jackendoff 1975; Aronoff 1976), no significant work on the semantics of word-formation has been offered by these linguists. However, I have elsewhere proposed a semantic theory of word-formation for Montague grammar (Dowty 1975; 1976) which I believe is roughly compatible with the concerns of Chomsky and like-minded linguists.

In my view (and perhaps in the view of Jackendoff and Aronoff as well) a revealing fact about derived words is that a speaker can distinguish between *actual* derived words of his language and *possible* derived words that are not 'real' words, though they may conform to the same patterns as actual words. Thus native speakers of English readily agree that *beautify* is a word of English whereas *uglify* is not, though it conforms to the same pattern of word formation and would

clearly mean 'make more ugly', just as *beautify* means 'make
more beautiful'. This capability suggests that speakers
somehow remember particular derived words that they have
heard other speakers use but are in general cautious about
using a derived word they have not heard in common usage
before, even if it conforms to a familiar pattern. Likewise,
the fact that speakers know idiosyncratic details of the
meanings of various derived words which are not predictable
by rules from the meanings of their constituents suggests
individual learning. This situation is to be contrasted to
that of syntactically complex expressions, since (with the
exception of a few deliberately memorized sentences, poems,
etc.) speakers generally take no notice of whether each
sentence or phrase they use has occurred before, but
presumably rely on general syntactic rules and compositional
semantic rules in some way or other whenever they utter or
understand such phrases.

   If this view is correct, then a primary purpose which
principles of word-formation serve for the speakers of a
language is as an aid in the acquisition of new vocabulary,
i.e., new basic expressions. Knowledge of word-formation
rules and of semantic rules for these makes it possible to
know at least the *approximate* meaning of a new complex word
upon first hearing it (or to make up a new word which one's
audience will understand approximately), but the rules do
not prevent one from deciding that the word has a more
specialized meaning than that specified by a general rule;
these details of its meaning can be inferred by induction
on the contexts in which it is used, by hearing a definition,
etc. As Jackendoff (1975) writes, 'it makes sense to say
that two lexical items are related if knowing one of them
makes it easier to learn the other.'

These observations suggest that we formalize word-formation rules not as part of the grammar of a language proper, but as a means for changing the grammar of a language from time to time by enlarging its stock of basic expressions. Aronoff (1976) apparently has something like this in mind when he refers to word-formation rules as 'once-only' rules, in contrast to syntactic and phonological rules. This approach allows us to adopt Montague's theory to formalize such rules and assign precise semantic interpretations (by way of translation) to them, yet will allow us to avoid the consequence of having to claim that the 'actual' meaning of a derived word is exactly that predicted by the word-formation rule.

In laying out the formal basis for this approach I will first define a *word-formation component* W for a given interpreted language L, then define, relative to L and W, various kinds of *lexical extensions of* L (i.e., languages like L except that additional basic expressions are added). Though I here give the definitions somewhat informally, they can easily be made precise in the general theory of Montague 1970.[11]

Montague's definition of a language L and its interpretation has the following parts:

(L1) A set of names of syntactic categories (*category indices*).

(L2) For each category, the set of *basic expressions* (if any) in that category.

(L3) A set of syntactic rules for L.

Together, (L1 - 3) determine recursively:

(L4) The set of expressions (i.e., basic and derived) in each category.

The interpretation of *L* (i.e., that induced by translation into intensional logic) consists of:

(L5) An interpretation for each basic expression of *L*.

(L6) An interpretation rule (i.e., translation rule) corresponding to each syntactic rule.

Together (L5) and (L6) determine:

(L7) An interpretation for each expression in each category of *L*.

A *word-formation component W* for *L* is a kind of 'pseudo-language' defined independently of *L* but having certain parts identical to those of *L*. *W* consists of:

(W1) The names of syntactic categories of *W* (same as L1).

(W2) Basic expressions in each category (same as L2).

(W3) A set of *word-formation rules*. These are to be defined formally just as Montague defined syntactic rules, i.e., consisting of input categories, output category, and structural operation. (W3) is disjoint from (L3).

Together, (W1 - 3) recursively determine:

(W4) The set of *possible derived words for L* for each category of *W*.

The interpretation for *W* consists of:

(W5) An interpretation for each basic expression (same as L5).

(W6) An interpretation rule (translation rule) corresponding to each word-formation rule.

Together, (W5) and (W6) recursively determine:

(W7) The *derivationally predictable interpretations* for
all possible derived words in all syntactic categories.

A *lexical extension* of an interpreted language *L* is an
interpreted language *L'* exactly like *L* except that *L'* contains
one additional basic expression not found in *L*. Relative to
some *W* for *L*, there are three kinds of lexical extensions:

I. A *semantically transparent lexical extension of L*
   is a *lexical extension L'* of *L* in which (a) the new
   basic expression added is one of the possible derived
   words of *L* according to W, and (b) the interpretation
   assigned to this new expression in *L'* is the interpretation given it by W.

II. A *semantically nontransparent lexical extension of L*
   is a lexical extension of *L* meeting condition (a) but
   not condition (b). (That is, the new basic expression
   has the form of a derived word but not the predicted
   meaning.)

III. A *nonderivational lexical extension of L* is a lexical
   extension of L meeting neither condition (a) nor
   condition (b).

Finally,

A *lexical semantic shift in an interpreted language
L* is an interpreted language *L'* exactly like *L*
except that the interpretation of some basic expression in *L'* is different from the interpretation of
that expression in *L*.

Thus the situation hypothesized above in which a speaker
first guesses the approximate meaning of a new derived word
through knowledge of word-formation rules and then later
refines his understanding of its precise meaning by some other

means can be formally reconstructed as a semantically transparent lexical extension of the speaker's language followed by a semantic shift in the resulting language (i.e., with respect to the new expression just added). The net result of this process would of course be the same as that of a semantically nontransparent lexical extension alone, but the two-stage process reflects the semantic role played by word-formation rules in a way that the one-step process does not.

We can regard an 'adult' grammar with its many derived words as having evolved by a long hypothetical series of lexical extensions in this theory. Alternatively, we may just as well interpret the theory as supplying analyses of many of the basic expressions of a single stage of this 'adult' language: a basic expression α of a language L is given the *analysis* $\mathscr{T}$ by a lexical component W for L (where we may equate 'analysis' with a Montague-type analysis tree, from which the input expressions, their categories, and the rules used are inferable) if and only if $\mathscr{T}$ is an analysis tree in W of which α is the top node. Analyses of this sort may be further classified as semantically transparent or nontransparent, as the interpretation actually given to α in L turns out to match that provided for $\mathscr{T}$ by W.

As an example of a word-formation rule of English, the rule S30 below is offered as a rough formulation of the '-*able*' rule mentioned earlier. (In the translation rule, '$\diamond$' is the possibility operator, which is definable in the intensional logic of PTQ: $\diamond\phi = \neg \Box \neg \phi$.)

S30. If $\alpha \in P_{TV}$, then $F_{30}(\alpha) \in ADJ_p$, where $F_{30}(\alpha) = \alpha + able$.

   Translation: $\lambda x \quad \diamond \vee y [\alpha'(y, \hat{P}[P\{x\}])]$

For example, if *breakable* is added by a semantically transparent lexical extension via this rule, then (46) will have a translation equivalent to (47):

(46) *Every egg is breakable.*

(47) $\wedge u \ [egg'_* \ (u) \ \rightarrow \quad \diamond \vee v \ [break'_* \ (v, \ u)]]$

See Dowty 1975 for examples of other word-formation rules of English formalized in this way, and Aronoff 1976 for more detailed syntactic and morphological descriptions of the English *-able* rule(s).

Traditional grammar recognizes, in addition to derivation and compounding, a third kind of word-formation called *conversion* or *zero-derivation* (cf. Marchand 1969). Such word-formation processes neither combine words nor add affixes but simply change the grammatical category of a word (and its meaning), leaving its form unaffected. Zero-derivation is common in English and languages of similar typology, though it is not characteristic of highly agglutinative languages. Well-known zero-derivation processes of English include: (i) the formation of nouns from verbs, the resulting noun naming the event, process, or state which the verb predicates; the nouns *answer, attack, call, bark, dip, smell, defeat, delight, hope,* etc. are derived from the respective homo-phonous verbs; (ii) the formation of transitive verbs from nouns, the resulting verb often meaning 'put in an α,' where α is the original noun; the verbs *bag, bottle, crate, can, class, corner, file,* etc. derive from nouns in this way.

Most traditional studies of word-formation recognize zero-derivation processes in which a shift of major grammatical category occurs — i.e., a change from one of the categories *verb, adjective, noun, adverb* to another — but not processes which would shift a word from one syntactic 'subcategory' to

another. Thus in Marchand's otherwise exhaustive description
of English word-formation (Marchand 1969) one finds no mention
of a zero-derivation process forming causative transitive
verbs from intransitives, a process which would give transitive *boil* from intransitive *boil* (cf. *The water boils* vs. the
causative *John boils the water*) or transitive *walk* from *walk*
(cf. *The dog walks* vs. the causative *John walks the dog*) or
analogous contrasts with verbs such as *move, cook, burn, run,
grow, break,* etc. Nevertheless, this apparent 'process' has
all the earmarks of a word-formation rule: not every intransitive verb has a causative use (e.g., parallel to *The rabbit
disappeared*, we do not have **The magician disappeared the
rabbit*), and the meaning of the derived verb is not always
exactly predictable on the basis of the basic verb: though
most transitive verbs of this pattern are paraphrasable as
'cause to α' where α is the intransitive verb, and *smoke* as in
The cigarette smokes vs. *John smokes the cigarette* is clearly
an instance of this pattern, the latter use of *smoke* is not
merely 'cause to smoke'; if one throws a cigarette on an open
fire one may have caused it to smoke but one has not smoked
it. Also, this process of causativization is paralleled in
its syntactic properties by causative word-formation processes
in agglutinative languages where a non-null causative suffix
forms transitive from intransitive verbs (Comrie 1976). In
fact, this modern English zero-alternation between transi-
tives and intransitives is simply the final result of the
phonological loss of the old Germanic causative derivational
suffix *-jan*. It is because this suffix originally triggered
changes in the vowel of the root that there are still a few
surviving 'irregular' causative/noncausative pairs in modern
English with different vowels, e.g., *set/sit, lay/lie,
raise/rise,* and *fell* ('to fell a tree')/*fall*.

Thus I see no good reason why the possibility of zero-
derivation rules shifting words from one 'subcategory' to
another should be discounted, particularly in a theory such
as Montague's in which 'subcategories' of verbs must be
recognized for semantic reasons. The rules S23, S24, and S25
that 'reduce' verb categories may be such rules. Like word-
formation rules, these rules are less than fully applicable,
and moreover, they sometimes have semantically unpredictable
results. Consider the intransitive use of *drink*. *John drinks*
is normally used to mean not just that 'John drinks something
or other', but more specifically, that he drinks alcohol,
but this fact is not predictable by any rule.

We noted also that these rules apparently are used more
freely than usual in discourse contexts in which their interpretations would be aided by the context. This too parallels
the situation with word-formation rules. Speakers may judge
certain examples of derived words as unacceptable when
presented with them in isolation, but nevertheless use and
respond to the same or similar examples quite naturally in
the right discourse situation. Zimmer (1971) has studied
these discourse conditions extensively for noun-noun compounds;
among his examples is the compound *pumpkin bus*, which is
unlikely to be judged as an acceptable compound in isolation
by most people (on a par with *school bus* or *steamboat*), but
was nevertheless spontaneously used and understood without
comment in Zimmer's presence.

Likewise, I see no reason why a rule like Dative Shift
converting verbs from DTV to TTV should not conceivably be
considered a word-formation rule, given of course that we
already accept the distinction between DTV and TTV and that
we accept the notion of word-formation rules at all. Dative

shift turns out to have several properties suspiciously suggestive of word-formation.

First, and most important, we have noted that it has numerous unpredictable 'exceptions'.

Second, it applies primarily to verbs of native (Anglo-Saxon) origin rather than verbs of Romance origin. But in fact it has frequently been observed that word-formation distinguishes between these two parts of the vocabulary (cf. Aronoff 1976). Certain derivational affixes such as *-ity* apply much more productively to roots of Romance origin than roots of native origin. However, I know of no other case where a syntactic rule of English depends even partly on whether words involved are of native or Romance origin. (See also the discussion of the history of Dative Shift below.)

Third, we have noted that there is more variation from speaker to speaker on the acceptability of Dative Shift for individual verbs than is normally found with other syntactic rules. But the acceptability of particular derived words is also known to vary greatly from speaker to speaker.

Fourth, we might naturally ask whether there are cases where Dative Shift, like other word-formation rules, alters the meaning of some verbs in unpredictable ways. (It is, after all, this 'failure of compositionality' above all else which forces us to treat word-formation differently from syntactic rules in a Montague grammar.) Strangely enough, the answer to this question seems to depend on who we ask for judgments. There are cases where some speakers of English report a difference in meaning for 'shifted' dative verbs, though other speakers report none at all. Green (1974) reports that though examples like (48) (with 'shifted' *give*) are perfectly acceptable, the examples of (49) are anomalous for her:

(48)   *Mary gave John*
$\left\{\begin{array}{l} a\ bath. \\ a\ kiss. \\ a\ punch\ in\ the\ nose. \\ the\ measles. \\ a\ broken\ arm. \\ an\ inferiority\ complex. \end{array}\right.$

(49)   *Mary gave
$\left\{\begin{array}{l} a\ bath \\ a\ kiss \\ a\ punch\ in\ the\ nose \\ the\ measles \\ a\ broken\ arm \\ an\ inferiority\ complex \end{array}\right\}$ *to John.*

Likewise, the sentences in (51b) are strange in a way that those in (50) and (51a) are not:

(50) a.   *Mary gave John*
$\left\{\begin{array}{l} an\ idea. \\ a\ devastating\ counterexample. \\ a\ clue\ to\ the\ Sphinx's\ riddle. \end{array}\right.$

b.   *Mary gave*
$\left\{\begin{array}{l} an\ idea \\ a\ devastating\ counterexample \\ a\ clue\ to\ the\ Sphinx\ riddle \end{array}\right\}$ *to John.*

(51) a.   *Mary's behavior gave John*
$\left\{\begin{array}{l} an\ idea. \\ a\ devastating\ counter\text{-}example. \\ a\ clue\ to\ the\ Sphinx's\ riddle. \end{array}\right\}$

$$
\text{b. } *Mary\text{'s behavior gave } \left\{ \begin{array}{l} an\ idea \\ a\ devastating\ counterexample \\ a\ clue\ to\ the\ Sphinx\text{'s riddle} \end{array} \right\}
$$

to John.

Green observes that the sentences in (48) differ from all the examples with *give* considered earlier in that the object 'given' (*a bath, a punch in the nose*) is not really transferred from the possession of the subject to the possession of the indirect object, but rather this object denotes an event (*a bath*) which the subject brings about, or an affliction (*an inferiority complex*) that the indirect object comes to have as a result of some action of the subject. Likewise in (51), no change of possession in the literal sense takes place, since the subject of the sentence is abstract (*Mary's behavior*) and never really possesses the objects 'given'. From this Green concludes that (in her speech at least) the 'unshifted' verb *give* (∈ DTV in our treatment) means 'transfer the possession of (an object) from oneself to another'; whereas the 'shifted' verb *give* means something more like 'cause to have'. Green finds similar but not quite parallel subtle distinctions in meaning between the shifted and unshifted verbs *teach, tell, bring,* and others. While it is puzzling that not all speakers detect these differences, it is thus possible for shifted and unshifted verbs to diverge in their meaning for at least some speakers.

    Finally, it is interesting to note that there are at least two languages, unrelated to English and to each other, which have related pairs of sentences syntactically very much like the 'Dative Shift' pairs in English *but in which Dative Shift is accompanied by the addition of a suffix to the verb.* Hawkinson and Hyman (1974) report that in Shona, a Bantu

language spoken in Zimbabwe, indirect objects can be represented as objects of a preposition kù as in (52), or can be
placed directly following the verb if the dative/benefactive
suffix -ér is added to the verb:

(52) Mùrúmê á- kà- nyórá tŝambà kú mwàná.

    man   he-PAST-write letter to child

    'The man wrote a letter to the child.'

(53) Mùrúmê á- kà- nyór -ér-á   mwàná tŝàmbà.

    Man   he-PAST-write-TO/FOR child letter

    'The man wrote a letter to/for the child.'

Chung (1976) reports a parallel case in Bahasa Indonesia, a
Western Austronesian language; indirect objects either follow
the preposition kepada (and come after the direct object), or
else appear immediately after the verb, the verb in this case
having the suffix kan:

(54) Saja mem- bawa surat itu kepada Ali.

    I   TRANS-bring letter the to   Ali

    'I brought the letter to Ali.'

(55) Saja mem- bawa- ken Ali surat ita.

    I   TRANS-bring-BEN Ali letter the

    'I brought Ali the letter.'

Both Hawkinson/Hyman and Chung present various kinds of
evidence showing that, in the respective languages under
discussion, the noun phrase immediately following the suffixed
verb behaves syntactically as a direct object. That is, in
each of the two languages there are several syntactic
processes (including passive) that apply only to the direct

objects of the unsuffixed verbs, and these processes apply
in exactly the same way to the noun phrase immediately
following a suffixed verb. (By drawing attention to this
parallel between English and these other two languages, I do
not wish to suggest that Dative Shift is a word-formation rule
in Shona or in Bahasa Indonesia; this question can only be
decided on the basis of the syntactic and semantic regularity
of the processes in these languages. Rather, I merely wish to
point out that the absence of any morphological evidence in
English that Dative Shift is a rule operating on verbs is
not really evidence against the way I have formulated the
rule, nor is it evidence that it is not a word-formation
rule. Rather, the lack of an affix on dative-shifted verbs
in English may be merely symptomatic of the greater preference
of English for zero-conversion in general, vis-à-vis more
agglutinative languages like Shona and Bahasa Indonesia.

7 For Datives and Their Passives

Though my understanding of *for*-Datives (as in *John baked a
cake for Mary/John baked Mary a cake*) and *to*-Datives that
don't have Dative passives (*Mary tossed John the ball/*John
was tossed the ball by Mary*) is considerably less clear than
my understanding of the examples discussed so far, any
analysis of Dative Shift in English would be incomplete
without mention of these cases as well. Accordingly, I will
sketch what seem to me to be promising approaches to these
two cases, though I cannot at this point give a completely
unproblematic treatment of either.

The most important thing to note about *for*-Datives that
distinguishes them from the *to*-Datives discussed so far is
that *for*-phrases seem to constitute adverbial modifiers,
rather than the third argument place of a three-place verb.

Though a true three-place verb such as *award* (or similarly *feed, lend, send, give,* etc.) may sometimes occur without its direct object, presumably as a result of having a two-place counterpart derived by one of the Object Deletion rules, the truth of such sentences as (56) nevertheless entails the truth of (57) — the meanings of the verb *award* and other such verbs necessarily involves a recipient:

(56) *John awarded the prize.*

(57) *John awarded the prize to someone* (or *to something*).

It is for this reason that I have treated such verbs as fundamentally three-place predicates. However, this is not true of (58) and (59), nor of any other such pairs with *for*-datives; one can bake something whether one has a beneficiary in mind or not.

(58) *John baked a cake.*

(59) *John baked a cake for someone.*

An indication that these *for*-phrases are, furthermore, modifiers of the category IV/IV[12] (rather than, say, TV/TV) is that they seem to occur with verbs of potentially any category with consistent meaning:

(60) a. *John smiled for Mary.*

    b. *John baked a cake for Mary.*

    c. *John tried to walk for Mary.*

    d. *John forced Bill to leave for Mary.*

    e. *John sent a message to Bill for Mary.*

    f. *John claimed that Bill was guilty for Mary.*

(Though (c - f) may also have readings in which the *for*-phrase modifies the complement verb phrase, it is the possibility of taking it to modify the larger IV-phrase that is relevant here.) Of these syntactic possibilities, only the case in which there is a basic transitive verb has an acceptable paraphrase in which the beneficiary noun phrase appears after the verb instead of after *for*:

(61) a. *John smiled Mary.

   b. John baked Mary a cake.

   c. *John tried Mary to walk.

   d. *John sent Mary a message to Bill.

       (Ignore reading in which *a message to Bill* is a term phrase.)

       *John sent a message Mary to Bill.

   e. *John forced Mary Bill to leave.

       *John forced Bill Mary to leave.

   f *John claimed Mary that Bill was guilty.

The complicating factor concerning *for*-datives is the matter of dative passives: are examples like (62) grammatical for all verbs?

(62) *Mary was baked a cake by John.*

Speakers of English differ greatly on this point. For some, such passives of *for*-datives are never acceptable, no matter what the verb. Charles Fillmore is apparently such a speaker, since his treatment of Dative Movement (Fillmore 1965) is deliberately designed to give 'dative passives' for all *to*-datives (e.g., *John was given a book by Mary*) but never for *for*-datives (e.g., (62)). A few other speakers will, to the best of my knowledge, accept such *for*-dative passives for any

verb whatsoever. But the largest class of speakers accept
for-dative passives for some verbs but not for others.

If all speakers shared Fillmore's judgments, the best way
of accounting for examples like (61b) would be a rule like
S27:

(S27) If $\delta \in P_{IV}$, $\beta \in P_T$, and $\delta = \alpha\ \gamma$, where α is a basic

transitive verb, and γ is non-null, then $F_{27}(\delta, \beta) \in P_{IV}$,

where $F_{27}(\delta, \beta) = \alpha\ \beta\ \gamma$ if β is not he_n, $\alpha\ him_n\ \gamma$

otherwise.

Translation: $for'\ (^\wedge\beta')\ (^\wedge\delta')$

Example: $F_{27}(bake\ a\ cake,\ Mary) = bake\ Mary\ a\ cake$;

$F_{27}(smile,\ Mary)$ is undefined.

Note that the form of α is restricted, so F_{27} is only a
partial function; this restriction would appear to be necessary to avoid producing (61a) and (61c - f) while allowing
(61b). If it turns out to be more desirable on general grounds
to allow syntactic rules to give multiple outputs than to
allow them to be partial functions, we would dispense with
S27 and add instead a new condition on the operation combining IV/IV with IV to the effect that when the IV α has
the form specified above and when the IV/IV is *for* β, then
the rule gives both $\alpha\ \gamma$ *for* β and $\alpha\ \beta\ \gamma$ as outputs. This
achieves exactly the same effect as the restricted S27. With
either of these two solutions, no dative passives of *for*-
datives, such as (62), would be produced, since no additional
new TV-expression would be formed. That is, the only passives
possible for sentences with *for*-datives would be the regular
passive *A cake was baked for Mary by John.*

If on the other hand all speakers found *for*-dative passives
acceptable for all verbs, then the obvious solution would be
to add the rule S28, which creates a TTV that will lead to a
new phrasal transitive verb, hence an opportunity for the
additional passive form:

S28. If $\delta \in P_{TV}$, then $F_{28}(\delta) \in P_{TTV}$, where $F_{28}(\delta) = \delta$.

   Translation: $\lambda \mathscr{P} \quad \lambda \mathscr{Q} \quad \lambda x \ [for' \ (\mathscr{Q}) \ [(^\wedge \alpha') \ (\mathscr{P})] \ (x)]$

For example, the TTV *bake* derived by this rule would combine
with *a cake* to give *bake a cake* in the category TV. This in
turn would combine with *Mary* to give *bake Mary a cake* via the
regular verb-object rule. But since *bake a cake* is a TV, it
can alternatively be passivized to produce *be baked a cake*,
which in turn leads to *Mary was baked a cake*. These examples
will receive the expected interpretations.

   Though these two rules S27 and S28 would serve to describe,
respectively, the two extreme idiolects which permit none or
all of the dative passives of *for*-datives, what of the majority
of us who accept shifted *for*-datives with all verbs but accept
for-dative passives with only certain verbs? The only possibility I can see is that such speakers have only the syntactic
rule S27; yet a few verbs that commonly take shifted *for*-
datives have been reanalyzed as belonging to the basic category TTV as well. Something like this has in fact been
suggested by Marchand (1951): 'We see, the currency of a
phrase is not a stable thing, usage is subject to change. In
World War II it was so often repeated how necessary it was
to "find the returning soldiers a job" that it required the
character of a phrase. This paves the way for "*the men would
be found a job*" (*Spectator*, May 18, 1945, 441)." If such
reanalyses are numerous enough to be described by a lexical
rule, then the rule S28 — now as a lexical rule, not a

syntactic rule — would give just the right result. This
approach to the 'mixed' idiolects forces us to posit a
slightly awkward redundancy for certain sentences: if *bake*
is such a reanalyzed (and thus passivizing) verb in some
idiolect, then *John baked Mary a cake* will be produced in two
ways — from the basic TV *bake* via S27, and also from the
basic *bake* in TTV via different rules. But I see no particular
problem with this redundancy nor any alternative to it.

An analogous problem arises with certain *to*-datives that
do allow dative shift but do not allow dative passive (at
least for some speakers): these are verbs that describe the
propelling of an object through space in a particular way,
such as *pitch, toss, throw, roll, slide, hurl, sail,* etc.
Thus everyone accepts *Mary tossed John the apple,* but few
accept (*)*John was tossed the apple* (*by Mary*). Under the
rules given so far, the grammaticality of the first sentence
ought to imply the grammaticality of the second.

I think that a clue to the correct analysis of this class
(whatever that analysis may be) is that the *to*-phrases with
these verbs (like *for*-phrases) are adverbial modifiers and
do not represent the third argument of a three-place predicate.
Whereas any true three-place verb entails the existence of a
recipient even when that recipient is not mentioned (cf.
John awarded the prize above), I believe it can be true that
John tossed (pitched, rolled, etc.) the ball without it being
true that there was someone to whom John tossed (etc.) the
ball. (Note that it is the entailment of an intended *recipient*
(typically animate) of the direct object, that is relevant
here, not just the entailment of an intended *goal*; dative-
shifted verbs are inevitably interpreted as having an intended
recipient, as witnessed by the anomaly of **John tossed the
fence the ball* vis-à-vis *John tossed the ball to the fence,*

or the familiar fact that *John took his pet alligator to the
zoo* is ambiguous, but *John took the zoo his pet alligator* is
not.) Of the *to*-dative listed in the appendices in Green
1974, those that turn out to be two-place rather than three-
place verbs by the entailment test are almost exactly the
ones for which Green marks the dative passive as unacceptable
in her judgment, and I doubt that this correlation can be
accidental. Thus *John tossed Mary the ball* should definitely
not have an analysis parallel to *John gave Mary the book*
(lest the undesirable passive be produced), but one in which
Mary is an adverbial modifier rather than the direct object.
Yet for semantic reasons *Mary* must then probably modify the
TV *toss*, not the whole IV phrase *toss the ball* — else we
could not account for the entailment that Mary was the
intended recipient of the ball rather than merely the
recipient of something or other. If so, I do not yet see
any very natural way of producing a TV phrase *toss Mary* so
that it will combine with a ball to give *toss Mary a ball*
instead of **toss a ball Mary*, since this ungrammatical phrase
is what the verb-object rule should give in such a case.

8. *Intrinsic Ordering Resulting from the Distinction between Syntactic and Word-Formation Rules*

As I have defined word-formation rules, they will apply
only to the *basic* expressions of their input-categories,
never to any syntactically complex expressions in these
categories. This follows from the fact that the word-formation component is a separate 'language' whose syntactic rules
are disjoint from those of the 'real' language. In effect,
all word-formation rules are intrinsically ordered before
all syntactic rules. It is for this reason that I had to
postulate the rule S27 to derive the IV-phrase *surrender to*

the Indians. This last phrase cannot be produced by applying
S23 (the rule that reduces TV-phrases to IV-phrases) to the
TV-phrase *surrender to the Indians* because S23 is a word-formation rule, and therefore syntactically derived TV-phrases
like *surrender to the Indians* are not in its domain. It was
instead necessary to postulate the rule S27 to shift the basic
verb *surrender* into the new category DIV.

Though this additional category and the additional rule may
seem to be an undesirable complication resulting from my separation of the two types of rules, it is in fact an advantage
with respect to certain exceptions. We noted that the phrasal
transitive verb *serve to Mary* cannot be converted to an IV-
phrase by S23 (else the ungrammatical **John served to Mary*
would result), yet the simple transitive verb *serve* does apparently undergo this rule (since *John served* is acceptable).
If the components are separated, then S23 cannot possibly apply
to the syntactically derived phrase *serve to Mary,* though it
can apply to the basic transitive verb *serve*. (Presumably, the
'possible' verb *serve* in DIV is not an actual verb.) If, on the
other hand, we do not separate the components but rather treat
the exceptions by having 'lexically governed' rules à la Lakoff,
then the basic verb *serve* in DTV (from which all 'other' *serve*-
verbs are syntactically derived) must be an exception to S23 in
some derivations but can undergo it in others. A 'global rule'
or some other way of distinguishing the two cases would thus be
necessary.

There are other consequences of the separation of components.
For example, it is not possible to take Passive to be a word-
formation rule under this analysis, since a variety of syntactically derived TV-phrases must serve as its input; to treat
Passive as a word-formation rule would require drastically
complicating the rules S17 - 19 and inventing new rules, so
that the analysis would lose much of its plausibility.

Fortunately, Passive is relatively an exceptionless rule in comparison with Dative Shift and Object Deletion rules, and is semantically completely regular as far as I know. (I doubt that verbs like *weigh* and *cost* should be counted as exceptions to Passive, since the noun phrases that follow them are probably not direct objects but obligatory adverbials of extent like the optional adverbial of extent in *John ran a mile*. Cf. Thomason (ms.) for a treatment of this. Perhaps the only real exceptions are verbs like *have* and *resemble*.) In a related paper (Dowty 1978) I argue that there may in fact be two Passive rules, one a syntactic rule applying to all phrases of the category TV, the other a lexical rule applying only to basic transitive verbs.

Placing Dative Shift and Object Deletion within the lexical component further predicts that their outputs are at least potentially available as inputs to any other lexical rule. It is not clear whether this prediction can be substantiated or not, as quite a number of possible interactions will have to be investigated. It has been observed (Fraser 1970) that so-called 'action nominals' cannot be formed from shifted dative verbs, though they can be formed from unshifted verbs (cf. *His teaching of mathematics to John* vs. **His teaching of John (of) mathematics*) and the same is true of the less productive derived nominal forms (cf. *John's gift of a book to Mary* vs. **John's gift of Mary (of) a book*). Though this might seem at first to be evidence against the classification of dative as a lexical rule, it may simply be an indication that constraints on English derived nominals, whatever the nature of these constraints, simply do not allow derived nominals to have two objects. Note that *John asked Bill a question* is not derived by dative shift, and we still do not have **John's asking of Bill (of) a question*. Similarly, *John envied Bill his new car* would not

be derived by dative shift (unless we want to countenance
positive absolute exceptions, as mentioned earlier), yet
we do not have *John's envy of Bill (of) his new car, though
we do have, significantly, both John's envy of Bill and John's
envy of Bill's new car. An apparent case arguing against
Object Deletion as a lexical rule would be Chomsky's observation (Chomsky 1957) that pre-nominal participles (as in
the sleeping man) can only be formed from basic intransitive
verbs, not from transitive verbs or from verbs that have
lost their objects through Object Deletion (cf. *The eating
man, though we have both the man ate and the man ate lunch).
Treating intransitives and transitive absolutes as equally
basic (as the account I have proposed does) fails to offer
a way to predict this generalization. However, there are
exceptions: McCawley has noticed that visiting (as in the
famous phrase visiting relatives) derives from a transitive
(or transitive absolute) and performing (as in performing
seal) is another such case. Nevertheless, there may well turn
out to be a significant partial generalization in this and
other cases, to the effect that some of what I here class as
'basic' expressions are really 'more basic' than others.
If so, it may be that the only reason for this situation is
that words derived by a sequence of two lexical rules are
somewhat less likely than those derived by one such rule
(given that lexical rules are partially productive and their
outputs individually learned) or that pragmatic factors
of the sort discussed by Green (1974) akew the distribution
for some reason. If on the other hand it turns out that some
of what I call lexical rules are 'more lexical' than others
in an essential way, it might be desirable to postulate a
second 'lexical component' that feeds into the main lexical
component (perhaps relabeled as the 'minor rule component')

in the same way that this component feeds the syntactic
rules; this predicts a potential three-way hierarchy of
ordering among kinds of rules. Perhaps a 'squish' from
quasi-lexical to quasi-syntactic rules would ultimately
describe natural languages most accurately, but I do not see
any way to construct an explicit formal theory of such a
squishy grammar, or any pressing need to do so.

9. *A Note on the History of Dative Shift*
and Dative Passive Sentences in English

In Old English the distinction between direct and indirect
objects was of course made by dative and accusative case
endings on term phrases, rather than by a preposition or a
rigid word order pattern for these term phrases, though
dative objects were more likely to precede accusative objects.
Only accusative objects (direct objects) could normally be
passivized, as is usually the case with languages that
distinguish datives from accusatives (e.g., modern German).
It is known that 'dative passives' begin to appear in significant numbers in English only after the distinction between
dative and accusative cases begin to be neutralized in Middle
English (cf. Visser 1963: 2143 - 2145). If Thomason's
account of passive as crucially involving phrases of the
category TV is correct, then it had presumably become
possible at this point to construe a sequence Verb — Term
Phrase — Term Phrase as 'Verb — Direct Object — Oblique
Object' where the same sequence had originally been analyzed
as 'Verb — Dative Object — Accusative Object.' (Cf. Visser
1963: 662; also Visser suggests (p. 281) that verbs which
originally took only a dative object came to be understood
as having a 'direct object' as a result of this neutraliza-
tion of case endings.) Visser hypothesizes that the adoption

of 'dative passives' was also aided by a passive sentence
pattern, surviving from the freer word order stages, in which
the dative object appears *before* the verb:

> In (1) ['Him was given a book'] the passive sentence opens
> with the indirect object, clearly recognizable as such
> because of its form (a dative). In (1a) ['The king was
> given a book'] it is the zero case; yet was, in the
> beginning apprehended as the direct object. Later,
> however, owing to its occupying the place at the head of
> the sentence (the normal place of the subject in all other
> (non-interrogative) utterances) it tended to be looked on
> as the subject, which became apparent in the use of the
> pronominal forms *I, he, she, we* in this position ['He was
> given a book'] (Visser 1963: 2142).

A fact which cannot be explained very neatly in the
account of the passives of three-place verbs developed here
is that the original, 'direct-object' passives continued to
exist after dative passives became common. And in fact such
sentences (*The book was given John*) exist today, though they
are more characteristic of British than American English and
are not accepted at all by some American speakers. Such
sentences would have to be produced in my approach either
by adding a second Passive rule or by allowing *give Mary a
book* to have two analyses, one with each term phrase as
'direct object'. The survival of this form of passive sentence has no doubt been aided by the influence of prescriptive
grammarians who have repeatedly condemned the dative passive
as ungrammatical. The reason for their prejudice is almost
certainly the fact that dative passives are not possible in
the highly esteemed classical languages, which distinguish
dative from accusative objects by case endings. One can
speculate, therefore, that at the source of the situation
in modern English are two originally distinct dialects, the
'vernacular' one in which *John* is the direct object in *give
John a book,* and the 'literary' one in which *a book* is the

direct object of this phrase. Those of us, perhaps now the
majority of English speakers, who can accommodate both *John
was given a book* and *A book was given John*, have thus been
forced to acquire two Passive rules. Perhaps without the
continuing influence of this 'prestige dialect' through the
written tradition, the second passive would be disappearing
from the language. For me the second passive form connotes
a more formal style than the other forms. However, I have no
further evidence for this 'two-dialect' theory. Relational
grammar, by the way, is presented with the same dilemma by
this second passive form; cf. Johnson 1976 (Appendix I).

   This *Second Passive* rule (giving *be given John*) should
apply to verbs of the category TTV, not DTV; as Green noted,
only verbs which undergo dative shift ever have this second
passive (cf. **Money was donated the hospital*), and this
generalization would not be captured if we derived *be given
John* from *be given to John* by a rule of *to*-deletion (nor if
we derived this passive from DTV). The rule should probably
be a lexical rather than a syntactic rule, since by my
judgments at least, some verbs sound more acceptable than
others with this passive: it is acceptable with verbs such
as *give, send, award, promise, grant, issue,* and others, but
not with *mail, sell, tell, teach, ship,* and others. (This
lexical government could be used as a counterargument to
someone who suggested that the failure of the kind of analysis in this paper to derive both these kinds of passive from
the same rule was evidence in favor of the NP-movement
analysis of passive, for if both passives were to be derived
by the same movement transformation we would again be faced
with a situation in which verbs are lexical exceptions to
some applications of a rule but not to others — e.g., *John
was told the answer* but not **The answer was told John*).

A lexical Second Passive rule (for truncated passives) would convert a verb δ in TTV to the new category ADJ/T, changing the verb to its past participle form, and would yield the translation $\lambda \mathscr{P}$ λx $Vy\ [\delta'\ (\mathscr{P})\ (\hat{P}P\ \{x\})\ (y)]$.

The addition of Dative Shift to the language would have come much later than the reanalysis which created dative passives:

> Here ['He shewed to þe kyng his sweven'] the indirect object is preceded by the preposition *to*. Constructions of this type began to appear — by the side of those without preposition — at the beginning of the Middle English period. Before 1300 the number of examples is very restricted, especially in the poetry ... In the course of the 14th and 15th centuries the number increases with striking rapidity, partly also on account of numerous French verbs which were construed with *à* before a noun complement. (Visser 1963: 624)

Thus I would hypothesize that the category DTV would only have become well-established in the English language in the fourteenth and fifteenth centuries and at first would have contained only verbs of Romance origin. Then Dative Shift would have been added, or more precisely, the *inverse* of the rule S20 I have given here, i.e., a rule shifting members of TTV into DTV. This rule would then allow native three-place verbs to be construed with *to* as well. (The rule S20, like the Dative Movement transformation, can of course be formulated with equal ease in either 'direction' and with just as great a variety of 'exceptions' in each direction; I adopted the S20 version only because it follows the more common transformational version.)

10. *Implications of this Study*

In this paper I have attempted not only to provide a treatment of 'dative movement' sentences compatible with Thomason's

treatment of passive sentences, but also to show that this
treatment of Dative Shift as a category-changing rule has
advantages over the NP-movement analysis in allowing us to
treat the 'exceptions' to this rule and to Object 'Deletion'
in a more satisfactory way.

For those who dislike the proliferation of syntactic
categories in Montague grammar, Robin Cooper (Cooper 1975)
has shown a way of reformulating a Montague grammar that
incorporates Chomsky's notion of a *lexicon* and uses strict
subcategorization features rather than the variety of verbal
categories found in Montague's original system. In such a
system we could have, for example, the various verbs *serve*
represented with the following subcategorization features:

(63) *Montague*
     Grammar   *Subcategorization*
     Category   *Verb*   *Feature*

       DTV   *serve*   [+V, + ____ NP *to* NP]

       TTV   *serve*   [+V, + ____ NP NP]

        TV   *serve*$_1$ [+V, + ____ NP]

        TV   *serve*$_2$ [+V, + ____ NP]

        IV   *serve*   [+V, + ____]

These are all subcategorization features that would be needed
in Chomsky's grammar as well. For those who still are bothered
by the fact that there are 'several' verbs *serve* rather than
just one that can occur in various environments, there would
probably be some notational reformulation under which we
could view the verbs in (63) as comprising a single 'lexical
entry', as long as the translation rules could apply to a
pair consisting of a verb and a subcategorization feature

and could distinguish the two different transitive verbs *serve* (as in *John served Mary* and *John served the soup*).

It might be noted that treatments such as mine and Thomason's comprise a kind of theory of 'grammatical relations' (Subject, Direct Object, Indirect Object) and of rules changing grammatical relations. The theory of so-called relational grammar recently developed by Postal and Perlmutter (Postal and Perlmutter, forthcoming) has called attention to the special status that such notions seem to have in natural languages, and has called attention to apparent inadequacies in the ability of classical transformational grammar to deal with such notions purely in terms of linear ordering of term phrases. It will be noted that the treatment of such notions developed here likewise provides definitions of these relationships independent of the linear ordering of term phrases and of how these relationships are realized in individual languages (i.e., what particular structural operations are used by the rules combining TV with T, TTV with T, etc.). It differs from "relational grammar" in that (1) it uses category-changing rules rather than movement rules, and (2) it is accompanied by (and in fact *motivated* by) an explicit semantic theory, whereas relational grammar is not. The relationships between the two approaches would seem to be a topic deserving further investigation.

Finally, category-changing lexical rules as described in this paper can be used to account for the different homophonous basic expressions Thomason is forced to postulate in his treatment of verb complements and Raising sentences (Thomason 1974). That is, Thomason treats *expect* as a basic expression in three different syntactic categories in order to produce examples like (64):

(64) a. *John expected that Mary would leave.*

   b. *John expected Mary to leave.*

   c. *John expected to leave.*

But we can instead take *expect* in one of these categories as basic and write lexical rules accounting for the change in grammatical category and for the appropriate meaning of the other two verbs in terms of the first. As was the case with the rules discussed in this paper, there are lexical exceptions to the Raising rules, and cases can be found where Raising introduces a subtle unpredictable change in meaning (cf. Postal 1974). Thus the same sort of motivation is present for treating the Raising rules as lexical rules as that observed for Dative and Object Deletion.

   Indeed, it now seems reasonable to me to hypothesize that *all* cases of lexically governed transformations and/or transformations that 'change meaning' can and should be treated as lexical rules along the lines laid out in this paper. The motivation for and implications of this hypothesis are discussed at greater length in Dowty 1978.

Acknowledgments

I would like to thank Barbara Abbott, Stanley Peters, and Richmond Thomason for comments and discussion. Some of the work on this paper was supported by grants from the American Council of Learned Societies and the Institute for Advanced Study.

Notes

   1. A great many of the data in this paper involving three-place verbs of English derive from Green's work, and I am

therefore indebted to her for her thorough study of this problem. However, I do not adopt any of the explanations proposed by Green for the irregular syntactic properties of these verbs. Green's stated thesis is that these syntactic "irregularities" can be predicted on the basis of a proper understanding of the various semantic subcategories to which these verbs belong. However, a look at the summary of her work that Green herself provides in appendices shows immediately that the verbs within each of her semantic classes are still thoroughly heterogeneous in syntactic behavior.

2. The main difference between Thomason's analysis and my simplified version of it is that my version, like PTQ, will give only a *de re* reading to a term phrase in subject position (in nonembedded and nonmodel contexts). This is bad for the nontransformational analysis of passive, since *A unicorn is sought by John* intuitively has a *de dicto* reading. Thomason avoids this consequence by treating the category IV as t/T (rather than as t/e), which means IV-phrases are interpreted as functions applying to the translations of term phrases, rather than vice versa. This method (adopted also in Montague's "Universal Grammar") allows for *de dicto* readings in subject position, though it requires additional meaning postulates for subject position of extensional verbs. To produce the required narrow scope readings for *a unicorn* in example (4), it is also necessary for Thomason to raise the type of infinitives to $\langle\langle s, f(T)\rangle, t\rangle$. In the version I give, the category ADJ_p would also have to be raised to this type to achieve the proper semantic effect. Another difference is that Thomason apparently no longer thinks that all readings of passive sentences can be derived through a category of adjectives (my ADJ_p, his ACN); a second path of derivation

is also to be provided. (Cf. Thomason ms. July 1976, pp.
69 - 72. See also Dowty 1978, where this dual derivation of
passives is adopted.)

3. I simplify the statement of this and all other translation rules in what I hope will be an obvious way: the
notation "α'(^β')" is understood to mean "if α and β (i.e.,
the inputs to the syntactic rule in question) translate
into α' and β' respectively, then the output of the syntactic
rule just described translates into α'(^β')."

4. In Thomason's original, more complex system (cf. n. 2)
these meaning postulates would have roughly the following
form; assume here that IV is defined as t/T, so that IV-
phrases translate into expressions of the type $\langle\langle f(T)\rangle, t\rangle$:

MP8.1'. $\wedge\mathcal{R}_{\langle s,f(TV)\rangle}\ \wedge\mathcal{P}_{\langle s,f(T)\rangle}\ \Box\ [en'\ (\mathcal{R})\ (\mathcal{P})\ \leftrightarrow$

$\qquad \vee y_{\langle s,e\rangle}[\vee\mathcal{R}\ (\mathcal{P})\ (\hat{P}P\ \{y\})]]$

MP8.2'. $\wedge\mathcal{R}_{\langle s,f(TV)\rangle}\ \wedge\mathcal{P}_{\langle s,f(T)\rangle}\ \wedge\mathcal{Q}_{\langle s,f(T)\rangle}$

$\qquad \Box\ [by'\ (\mathcal{P})\ (\mathcal{R})\ (\mathcal{Q})\ \leftrightarrow\ \vee\mathcal{R}\ (\mathcal{Q})\ (\mathcal{P})]$

MP9. $\qquad\wedge X_{\langle s,f(IV)\rangle}\ \wedge\mathcal{P}_{\langle s,f(T)\rangle}\ \Box\ [be'\ (X)\ (\mathcal{P})\ \leftrightarrow\ X\ \{\mathcal{P}\}]$

5. Here again my simplification of Thomason's system is
slightly inadequate because it will not give a *de dicto*
reading for the subjects of these verbs in their passive
forms. But, intuitively, *a new coat* should have a *de dicto*
reading in *A new coat was promised to John by Mary* just as
it does in *Mary promised John a new coat.* As before, raising
the translation type of IV from $\langle\langle s, e\rangle, t\rangle$ to $\langle\langle s, f(T)\rangle, t\rangle$
will allow us to circumvent this difficulty.

6. Alternatively, it might be suggested by the transformationalist that examples like *The guard allowed the prisoner
a cigarette* are not derived from **The guard allowed a
cigarette to the prisoner* by Dative Movement but rather by a

have-Deletion transformation from *The guard allowed the prisoner to have a cigarette.* Whatever the merits of this suggestion, it does not solve the problem of syntactic exceptions but only complicates it. Though *allow* and *permit* might undergo this rule, similar verbs in similar syntactic constructions do not, since we do not get **John persuaded the prisoner a cigarette* from *John persuaded the prisoner to have a cigarette,* nor **The guard wanted the prisoner a cigarette* from *The guard wanted the prisoner to have a cigarette.* This last failure is all the more remarkable since *want* is one of the verbs claimed to undergo *have*-Deletion in different circumstances, i.e., in *John wants a new car* from *John wants to have a new car.* Also, the example *The guard refused the prisoner a cigarette* would have to be derived not by *have*-Deletion but by *give*-Deletion from *The guard refused to give the prisoner a cigarette.* But again, similar cases fail to give rise to this "deletion." Cf. **The guard hesitated the prisoner a cigarette* vs. *The guard hesitated to give the prisoner a cigarette,* or **The guard condescended the prisoner a cigarette* vs. *The guard condescended to give the prisoner a cigarette.* The semantic relationships that hold between these isolated cases of paraphrases with *allow* and *have, refuse* and *give* are probably best captured by semantic means, e.g., by meaning postulates.

7. Rules S24 and S25 as I have stated them literally use the identity function and so cause the same expressions to appear in more than one category. While the general theory in Montague 1970 does not, as I understand it, strictly prohibit this, it does apparently require that the expression would have to have one and the same interpretation in all categories in such cases. Since this obviously cannot be the

case for the outputs of S24 and S25, we must invent some
trivial way of distinguishing these outputs from the inputs
to satisfy this requirement. One could do this in various
ways, such as by taking expressions to be not ordinary English
expressions simpliciter but rather pairs consisting of an
'ordinary' expression and some kind of index. A variant of
this procedure would be to adopt Barbara Partee's proposal
to let the grammar produce labeled bracketed expressions
instead of just strings. Thus each basic expression would
have a bracket labeled with its category, and any syntactic
rule would add a new outer bracket with the category of its
output expression as label. For example, $[serve]_{DTV}$ would
be a basic expression; the result of applying S20 to it
would be $[[serve]_{DTV}]_{TTV}$, and the result of applying S25
to this new expression would be $[[[serve]_{DTV}]_{TTV}]_{TV}$, etc.

8. Not literally all 32 (2^5) combinations of exceptions
would be possible, because if a verb failed to undergo S20,
converting it to TTV, then it could not undergo S25, which
applies to the category TTV, since there would be no way for
it to enter the category except by S25.

9. It might seem that the ungrammatical sentence *John
served to Mary* would be produced even if *serve* does not
undergo S26, since the phrase *serve to Mary* would be produced
in P_{TV}, and *serve* is supposed to allow S25 to apply,
converting TV-phrases to IV-phrases. Though this is indeed
a problem here, it is not a problem in the revised view of
these rules discussed later on, for reasons explained in
section 8.

10. As pointed out in note 7, the "Universal Grammar"
theory does not literally allow the same basic expression in
more than one category, so some distinction must be invented
among these expressions.

11. The formal definitions based on Montague 1970 (henceforth UG) are as follows:

1. Assume L is a *language* (as defined in UG) and $L = \langle\langle A, F_\gamma, X_\delta, S, \delta_o \rangle_{\gamma\in\Gamma, \delta\in\Delta}, R\rangle$.

   Assume $\mathscr{B}$ is a *Fregean interpretation* (as in UG) for L and $\mathscr{B} = \langle B, G_\gamma, f\rangle_{\gamma\in\Gamma}$.

   Then an *Interpreted Word-Formation Component* $\mathscr{W}$ for L is an ordered pair $\langle L', \mathscr{B}'\rangle$ such that (1) L' is a disambiguated language and $L' = \langle A', F'_\gamma, X_\delta, S', \delta_o \rangle_{\gamma\in\Gamma, \delta\in\Delta}$, (2) ' is a Fregean interpretation for L' and $\mathscr{B}' = \langle B', G'_\gamma, f\rangle_{\gamma\in\Gamma}$, and (3) the type assignment from Δ into T is the same for L' as for L. Comment: Note whereas Δ, X_δ for $\delta \in \Delta$ and f are required to be the same in $\mathscr{W}$ as the corresponding elements in L and $\mathscr{B}$, it need not be the case (and in all nontrivial cases will not be the case) that A', F'_γ for $\gamma \in \Gamma'$, S', B', and G'_γ for $\gamma \in \Gamma'$ equal A, F_γ for $\gamma \in \Gamma$, S, B, and G, respectively. The family of syntactic categories C' generated by $\mathscr{W}$ is to be regarded as the set of *possible words of L*.

2. *A lexical extension of an interpreted language L* is a pair $\langle L'', \mathscr{B}''\rangle$ such that (1) $L'' = \langle\langle A'', F''_\gamma, X''_\delta, S'', \delta_o \rangle_{\gamma\in\Gamma'', \delta\in\Delta''}, R''\rangle$, where L'' is exactly like L except that for some $\delta \in \Delta$, X''_δ contains exactly one more member than X_δ. (2) $\mathscr{B}''$ $(= \langle B'', G''_\gamma, f''\rangle_{\gamma\in\Gamma''})$ is exactly like $\mathscr{B}$ except

that f" assigns an interpretation also to the new member of X''_δ.

3. We distinguish three kinds of lexical extensions of a language L relative to its interpretation $\mathcal{B}$ and to an interpreted word-formation component $\mathcal{W}$ for L:

I. A *semantically transparent lexical extension* of L relative to $\mathcal{B}$ and $\mathcal{W}$ is a pair $\langle L'', \mathcal{B}'' \rangle$ such that (1) L" contains the basic expression α not contained in L and for some C'_δ ($\delta \in \Delta$) of the family of syntactic categories C' generated by $\mathcal{W}$, $\alpha \in C_\delta$; and (2) if g is the meaning assignment for L' determined by $\mathcal{B}'$, then $f''(\alpha) = g(\alpha)$.

II. A *semantically nontransparent lexical extension* of L relative to $\mathcal{B}$ and $\mathcal{W}$ is a lexical extension of L meeting condition (1) but not condition (2) in I above.

III. A *nonmorphological lexical extension* of L relative to $\mathcal{B}$ and $\mathcal{W}$ is a lexical extension of L which meets neither condition (1) nor condition (2) in I above.

12. For that matter, *for*-phrases may turn out to be of the category t/t rather than IV/IV.

References

Aronoff, Mark. 1976. *Word Formation in Generative Grammar*. Linguistic Inquiry Monographs I. Cambridge, Mass.: MIT Press.

Chapin, Paul. 1967. *On the Syntax of Word-Derivation in English*. Information System Language Series 16. Bedford,

Mass.: MITRE Corp.

Chomsky, Noam. 1957. *Syntactic Structures*. The Hague: Mouton.

———. 1970. "Remarks on Pronominalization." In R. A. Jacobs and P. S. Rosenbaum, eds., pp. 184 - 221. *Readings in English Transformational Grammar*. Waltham, Mass.: Ginn and Co.

Chung, Sandra. 1976. "An Object-Creating Rule in Bahasa Indonesia." *Linguistic Inquiry* 7 (1): 41 - 89.

Comrie, Bernard. 1976. "The Syntax of Causative Constructions: Cross-Language Similarities and Divergencies." In M. Shibatani, ed. *The Grammar of Causative Constructions*. New York: Academic Press.

Cooper, Robin. 1975. "Montague's Semantic Theory and Transformational Syntax." Ph.D. dissertation, University of Massachusetts, Amherst.

Dowty, David R. 1975. "Toward a Semantic Theory of Word Formation for Montague Grammar." *Texas Linguistic Forum* 2: 69 - 96.

———. 1976. "Montague Grammar and the Lexical Decomposition of Causative Verbs." In B. Partee, ed., *Montague Grammar*, pp. 201 - 246. New York: Academic Press.

———. 1978. "Governed Transformations as Lexical Rules in a Montague Grammar." *Linguistic Inquiry* 9 (3) (Summer): 393 - 426.

Fillmore, Charles. 1965. *Indirect Object Constructions in English and the Ordering of Transformations*. Monographs on Linguistic Analysis 1. The Hague: Mouton.

Fraser, Bruce. 1970. "Some Remarks on the Action Nominalization in English." In R. A. Jacobs and P. S. Rosenbaum, eds., *Readings in English Transformational Grammar*. Waltham, Mass.: Ginn and Co.

Green, Georgia. 1974. *Semantics and Syntactic Regularity*.
    Bloomington: Indiana University Press.

Halle, Morris. 1973. "Prolegomena to a Theory of Word Forma-
    tion." *Linguistic Inquiry* 4: 3-16.

Hawkinson, Annie K., and Larry M. Hyman. 1974. "Hierarchies
    of Natural Topic in Shona." *Studies in African Linguistics*
    5 (2) (July 1974): 147-170.

Jackendoff, Ray. 1975. "Morphological and Semantic Regulari-
    ties in the Lexicon." *Language* 51: 639-671.

Johnson, David Edward. 1976. "Toward a Theory of Relationally-
    Based Grammar." Ph.D. dissertation, University of Illinois.

Lakoff, George. 1967. *Irregularity in Syntax*. Ph.D. disser-
    tation, Indiana University. Published 1970 by Holt,
    Rinehart and Winston.

Lees, Robert B. 1960. *The Grammar of English Nominalizations*.
    The Hague: Mouton.

Marchand, Hans. 1951. "The Syntactical Change from Inflec-
    tional to Word Order System and Some Effects of This Change
    on the Relation 'Verb/Object' in English: A Diachronic-
    Synchronic Interpretation." *Anglia* 70: 70-89.

———. 1969. *The Categories and Types of Present-Day
    English Word Formation*. Munich: Beck.

Montague, Richard. 1970. "Universal Grammar." *Theoria*
    36: 373-398.

———. 1973. "The Proper Treatment of Quantification in
    Ordinary English." In K. J. J. Hintikka, et al., eds.,
    Approaches to Natural Language. Dordrecht: D. Reidel
    Publishing Co.

Postal, Paul M. 1974. *On Raising*. Cambridge, Mass.: MIT Press.

Postal, Paul M., and David Perlmutter. Forthcoming.
    Relational Grammar.

Thomason, Richmond. 1974. "Some Complement Constructions in
    Montague Grammar." In *Proceedings from the 10th Regional
    Meeting of the Chicago Linguistic Society*, pp. 712 - 722.

———. 1976. "Some Extensions of Montague Grammar." In
    Barbara H. Partee, ed., *Montague Grammar*, pp. 77 - 117.
    New York: Academic Press.

———. Ms. May 1976. "Montague Grammar and Some Transforma-
    tions."

———. Ms. July 1976. "On the Interpretation of the
    Thomason 1972 Fragment."

Visser, F. Th. 1963. *An Historical Syntax of the English
    Language*. Leiden: Brill.

Zimmer, Karl E. 1971. "Some General Observations about
    Nominal Compounds." *Stanford Working Papers on Language
    Universals* 5: C1 - C21.

6

Measure Adjectives in Montague Grammar
Muffy E. A. Siegel

1. *Introduction*

Measure adjectives are adjectives that cannot be interpreted
straightforwardly because their extensions depend upon such
things as the determination of a measurement scale, a comparison class, and a norm for the class for the measured
property. For instance, in order to determine the truth value
of the sentence *Gladys is tall*, one would have to identify
height as the relevant dimension, but one would also have to
know what or who Gladys is (a woman? a child? a duck?) and
the normal height for members of her group. Consequently, a
good informal test for identifying an expression containing
a measure adjective is to see whether it can be accurately
paraphrased by an expression of the form 'ADJ for a CN,'
where CN stands for a common noun picking out the comparison
class:

(1) Irene is tall.   (tall for a woman)

(2) The library is tall.   (tall for a building)

(3) Erica is a tall child. (tall for a child)

Other common measure adjectives are *heavy, short, fat,* and
appropriate readings of *clever, strong,* and *intelligent.*

The purpose of this paper is to discuss the incorporation of measure adjectives into a grammar of a fragment of English based on that in Montague (1974b) and the transformational extensions suggested in Partee (1975b; 1976). I argue that measure adjectives constitute a class of the simple predicative adjectives that are usually called absolute adjectives and are not directly related to other relative adjectives, which are best analyzed as being intensional ad-common nouns.

2. *Adjectives in Montague Grammar*

2.0. *Introduction*

In order to develop a treatment of measure adjectives within a Montague framework, it is necessary first to discuss adjectives in general. I have treated the problem of fitting adjectives into a Montague framework at length elsewhere (Siegel 1976a), but I will summarize the results here.

2.1. *The Two-faced Adjective and the Categorial Component*

In traditional grammar, an adjective is a word that modifies a noun of some sort and appears either in the predicate or next to the noun as part of the noun phrase:

(4) The house is *red*.

(5) The *red* house

One of the characteristics of the adjective as a part of speech, then, is that it is a word which can occupy two quite different syntactic positions, although not every adjective can appear in both positions. The categorial component of the Montague syntax will assign adjectives to two different syntactic categories. Predicate adjectives will belong to a one-place predicate category to be called t///e in order to distinguish it syntactically from intransitive verb phrases (t/e) and common noun phrases (t//e). The predicate adjectives will combine with a semantically empty *be* by syntactic rule (6) to form a t/e phrase (that is, an IV phrase) and then with a term phrase to form a sentence. Consequently, they will, in effect, be translated by translation rule (7) (Montague 1974b; rule T4) like any other one-place predicate.

(6) If $\alpha \in P_{t///e}$, then $F_{20}(\alpha) \in P_{IV}$, where $F_{20}(\alpha) = \alpha'$ and

   α' is be α.

(7) If $\delta \in P_{t/IV}$ and $\beta \in P_{IV}$ and δ, β translate into δ',

   β', respectively, then $F_4(\delta, \beta)$ translates into $\delta'(^\wedge\beta')$.

Adjectives in attributive position will belong to the category t//e / t//e, abbreviated CN/CN, since such adjectives combine with common nouns to make more complex common nouns, as in syntactic rule (8) and the corresponding translation rule (9).

(8) If $\alpha \in P_{CN/CN}$ and $\beta \in P_{CN}$, then $F_{21}(\alpha, \beta) \in P_{CN}$,

   where $F_{21}(\alpha, \beta) = \alpha \beta$.

(9) If $\alpha \in P_{CN/CN}$ and $\beta \in P_{CN}$ and α, β translate into α',

   β', respectively, then $F_{21}(\alpha, \beta)$ translates into $\alpha'(^\wedge\beta')$.

   Each of these syntactic categories, t///e and CN/CN, has at some time been employed alone as the adjective category (Dowty 1976; Montague 1974c; Partee 1975a). However, many linguists, including Bolinger (1967), Jackendoff (1972), and Winter (1965), have argued that adjectives must originate in both positions. Moreover, within a Montague framework, if all adjectives were to belong to the same underlying syntactic category, either t///e or CN/CN, we would expect them to behave uniformly semantically as well, in the absence of any interfering meaning postulates. In fact, though, there is

a clear semantic duality among adjectives. The two semantic
roles that adjectives can play are exactly those of the two
semantic types that correspond to the two syntactic categories predicted for adjectives. This semantic duality has
long been noticed.[1] It can be stated this way: The property
that an adjective represents may be bound to the meaning of
a common noun it modifies in some way or it may be free, a
simple predicate. A fairly clear example of this distinction
in English appears in the following sentence:

(10) Marya is a beautiful dancer.

The reading of (10) in which the meaning of *beautiful* is bound
to that of *dancer* means that Marya is beautiful as a dancer.
She dances beautifully, although she may not be beautiful to
look at. The other, free, reading of (10) means that Marya
is beautiful and a dancer. She is a member of the intersec-
tion of the sets of beautiful things and dancers and, consequently, must be beautiful in general. From now on, I will
call readings of adjectives that are bound to the meanings
of their common nouns in this way *relative* and those that
are not so bound and therefore subject to a conjunctive paraphrase, *absolute*. The list in (11) includes examples of
adjectives that are absolute, ones that are relative, and
ones that, according to the present analysis, constitute a
pair of homonyms that are absolute and relative, respectively.

In order to see that the Montague semantics predicts from
the two syntactic adjective roles that adjectives will have
just these two sorts of meanings, consider the semantic types
that will be assigned to the syntactic categories t///e and
CN/CN by Montague's function f (Montague 1974b: 260). t///e's
will, like IV's and CN's, be assigned the type $\langle\langle s, e\rangle, t\rangle$
a characteristic function of a set of individual concepts.

(11) *absolute*   *relative*   *both*

speckled	rightful	beautiful	clever
rancid	former	good	present
carnivorous	veteran	big	intelligent
nearby	actual	navigable	representative
nude	consummate	skillful	public
four-legged	inveterate	local	stupid
aged	blithering	old	handy
rife	mere	responsible	terrible
asleep	veritable	crazy	rabid
touched (mad)	ostensible	true	definite
loath	alleged	final	close
remise	chief	faint	present
naughty		ready	current
drunk			

Through the translation rule (7) and the use of definitions, conventions, and meaning postulates, the translation of a sentence with a predicate adjective, like one with an ordinary intransitive verb, will eventually reduce to a simple extensional predicate applied to an individual.

(12a) beautiful'$_*$(m)

Marya is beautiful. (absolute)

This constitutes part of the translation of the absolute reading of (10), which says simply that Marya, the individual, is beautiful as well as being a dancer:

(12b) beautiful'$_*$(m) ∧ dancer'$_*$(m)

Marya is a beautiful dancer. (absolute)

In parallel fashion, it can be seen that the semantic type corresponding to the CN/CN category for adjectives is appropriate to the relative meaning of adjectives. Function f will assign to CN/CN (as to IV/IV) the semantic type ⟨⟨s, ⟨⟨s, e⟩, t⟩⟩, ⟨⟨s, e⟩, t⟩⟩, a function from properties of individual concepts to characteristic functions of sets of them. This matches perfectly the relative meaning of *beautiful*, in which the adjective combines with the property of being a dancer (the intension of the common noun) to form an expression, *beautiful dancer*, that picks out a new subset of dancers. The translation rule (9) used with the definitions, conventions, and meaning postulates of Montague 1974b will yield the following translation for such a prenominal adjective:

(13) (beautiful' (^dancer'))$_*$(m)

 Marya is a beautiful dancer. (relative)

Here, the adjective does not modify an individual, but applies instead to the intension of the common noun, thus formalizing the observation that in relative readings, the meaning of the adjective is relative to the meaning of the common noun that it applies to.

2.2. *Transformations*

The two semantic roles of adjectives, then, can be seen as a natural consequence of their two syntactic roles. However, it is not the case, at least in English, that all and only predicate adjectives have the absolute reading, while all and only prenominal adjectives have the relative reading.[2] We have already seen that in (10) prenominal *beautiful* is ambiguous. Nevertheless, it is true, as predicted, that those adjectives that can appear only in predicate position have only the absolute reading, while those adjectives that can appear only in prenominal position have only the relative reading. In (14) are some adjectives that can occur only predicatively.

(14)   the baby is asleep   the boat is afloat
    *the asleep baby   *the afloat boat

    my brother is touched   corruption is rife
    *my touched brother   *rife corruption

Unlike *beautiful*, the adjectives in (14) cannot have a reading
where the meaning of the adjective is relative to that of the
common noun:

(15) The dancer is beautiful. (as a dancer, not as a person)

    The baby is asleep.   (*as a baby, not as a female)

    The boat is afloat.   (*as a boat, not as a hotel)

    My brother is touched.   (*as my brother, not as a pilot)

On the other hand, none of the adjectives in (16), adjectives
which can appear only prenominally, has an absolute sense,
one which is not relative to the meaning of the common noun.

(16)   a veteran manager   the rightful king
    *the manager is veteran   *the king is rightful

    the inveterate cheat   the consummate liar
    *the cheat is inveterate *the liar is consummate

It seems correct to suppose, then, that adjectives which
originate in predicate position are all and only ones that
have the absolute reading that the Montague semantics accords
predicate adjectives, while adjectives that originate in
prenominal position are all and only those that exhibit the
relative, intensional reading that the semantics automatically
accords them. The English word *beautiful* would be translated
into two constants of the intensional logic, one a member of
the category t///e, and the other, of CN/CN. We can account
easily enough for the fact that absolute versions of adjectives

can sometimes appear in prenominal position and relative ones
in predicate position with the following syntactic rules,
both of which are semantically empty. The first rule is a
version of the old transformational rule of relative clause
reduction and preposing, which was first proposed as a way
to derive all adjectives from underlying predicates.[3] It
avoids the pitfalls of earlier rules of its type, since it
applies only to t///e adjectives.[4] Since such adjectives are
never relative to a modified common noun, they produce
synonymous expressions in relative clauses or preposed, as
in *food that is rancid* and *rancid food*. Rule (17) will
account for the fact that *dancer such that she is beautiful,
beautiful dancer, beast such that it is carnivorous,* and
carnivorous beast all have readings which should be translated conjunctively.

(17) If $\alpha \in P_{CN}$ and α is of the form β such that he_n be γ

where $\beta \in P_{CN}$ and $\gamma \in P_{t///e}$, then $F_{22}(\alpha) \in P_{CN}$,

where $F_{22}(\alpha) = \alpha'$ and α' is $\gamma \beta$.

The second rule, the one that accounts for the presence
of some relative readings in predicate position, deletes a
dummy common noun. That is, as far as the semantics is
concerned, the relative reading of *The dancer is good* will
be something like 'The dancer is a good Δ' where Δ ranges
over CN's, but is uniquely interpreted for any utterance
in terms of the context. *The dancer is good* is most likely
to be interpreted as 'The dancer is good as a dancer'; that
is, the Δ is most likely to be interpreted as being co-
intensional with the common noun of the subject. However,
The dancer is good could, in the right context, mean 'The
dancer is good as a checker player'. This would be the most
reasonable reading if the sentence were uttered while the

speaker was watching a checker tournament among show people.
Notice that such an interpretation is impossible for a prenominal adjective. One would not say, 'That's a good dancer'
while watching a checker tournament. This fact provides
independent evidence for the existence of a contextually
interpreted dummy CN in the structure of sentences with
relative adjectives in predicate position. Of course, syntactically, the dummy CN must be deleted, by a rule such as
(18).

(18) If $\alpha \in P_{t/e}$ and α is of the form $\underset{\sim\sim}{be}$ a β $\underset{\sim}{\Delta}$ where

   $\beta \in P_{CN/CN}$ and Δ is a variable ranging over P_{CN},

   then $F_{23}(\alpha) \in P_{t/e}$, where $F_{23}(\alpha) = \alpha'$ and α' is $\underset{\sim\sim}{be}$ β.

3. *Measure Adjectives as Members of Category t//e*

3.0. *Introduction*

Let us return now to the measure adjectives. If some adjective readings are absolute and arise from extensional one-
place predicates, while others are relative and arise from
intensional ad-common nouns, where do the measure adjectives
fit in? The measure adjectives have traditionally been called
'relative',[5] for they are interpreted relative to a measurement scale and comparison class. Because of this, sentences
containing them are not accurately translatable conjunctively,
as are sentences containing absolute adjectives like *speckled*.
That is, something that is a speckled hen is speckled and a
hen, while something that is a big hen is not simply big and
a hen, since it might not be big in absolute terms or
compared to a hippopotamus. As noted in section 2, the
expressions which I have called relative adjectives also
resist a conjunctive translation. A veteran manager is not

veteran and a manager, but veteran as a manager. However,
I will argue that expressions with CN/CN adjectives and
expressions with measure adjectives cannot be translated
conjunctively for different reasons. In fact, I will argue
that measure adjectives are not relative in my sense at all.
They are members of the absolute category, t///e. There is
both semantic and syntactic evidence for this conclusion.

3.1. *Extensionality of Measure Adjectives*

Absolute adjectives combine with term phrases and modify
their extensions, individuals. Relative adjectives apply
instead to the intensions of common nouns. It can be seen
informally that measure adjectives are not interpreted
relative to the intension of a common noun in the same way
that CN/CN's are. Compare the following two expressions:

(19) a good car (good as a car)   CN/CN

(20) a fast car (fast for a car)   Measure Adjective

In (19) the reading of *good* is an intensional, CN/CN reading.
To understand the meaning of *good* here, you must know the
meaning of *car*, what, exactly, is expected of a car. On the
other hand, *fast* in (20) is a measure adjective. In order to
understand the meaning of *fast* in (20), one needn't know
much about what a car is. One need only know about how fast
things called cars normally go. Apparently, this particular
piece of information isn't essentially part of the meaning
or intension of *car*. Cars that don't go at all are still
called cars, and so are cars that go nearly seven hundred
miles per hour.

Examples (21) and (22) give another indication that the
relativity of measure adjectives is not relativity to the
meaning of the modified common noun.

(21) bad library   CN/CN

(22) tall library   Measure Adjective

In (21) the most natural reading of *bad* is the intensional one, 'bad as a library', where *bad* applies to the meaning of *library*. The whole expression is most likely to mean that the library's book collection is scant, ill-chosen, or inaccessible, although it might mean in addition that the physical surroundings are such that they make it difficult to do what one normally does in a library. In contrast, the interpretation of *tall* in (22) has nothing to do with the meaning of *library*. The whole expression means something like 'library that is tall for a building'. Its interpretation depends upon the selection of the comparison class 'building' and the placement of the library relative to some norm. The only knowledge about libraries necessary for these decisions is that many libraries happen to constitute entire buildings. Such knowledge is knowledge about things in the extension of *library*, not about its intension.

More direct evidence of the extensionality of measure adjectives is difficult to find. Because of the indeterminacy of measure adjectives, the usual test for extensionality, substitutability in the expression being tested of co-extensional items, will not work quite correctly. For instance, if, for some reason, exactly the same people played trombone as sang bass in the chorus, we could use the co-extensive items *trombone player* and *bass singer* to test for extensionality. In testing the adjectives *dead* and *good*, for instance, we would find that (23) holds, but that (24) does not.

(23) Clay is a dead trombone player if and only if Clay
     is a dead bass singer.

(24) Tim is a good trombone player if and only if Tim is a
     good bass singer.

The two clauses in (23) will always have the same truth values,
even though the referent in their predicates is referred to
by two different common nouns. We can conclude from this that
dead is extensional, an absolute adjective. The two clauses
of (24), on the other hand, will not necessarily have the same
truth value, so the whole of (24) will not necessarily be
true. Even though *trombone player* and *bass singer* are co-
extensional, they are not mutually substitutable after *good*.
This is because *good* has a CN/CN version, so it can be
intensional; that is, its meaning can be relative to that of
the particular common noun employed.

    Unfortunately, being intensional like *good* in (24) is not
the only way that an adjective can fail the substitution test
for extensionality. Measure adjectives fail the test, when
they do so, not because their meanings are interpreted relative to those of the modified common nouns, but for independent
reasons suggested earlier. Consider once more the example
where the same group of people constitute both all the trombone players and all the bass singers. Let us submit a
measure adjective like *tall* to the extensionality test of
substitution of co-extensive expressions. Is it true that Ray
is a tall trombone player if and only if he is a tall bass
singer, under the assumption that all and only trombone
players are bass singers? At first, it might seem as if it
would have to be true. But suppose some stubborn observer[6]
cherished a theory that trombone players ought to be very
tall on the average (perhaps because long arms are useful to
them), that, in the future, perhaps, they will be taller,
at least, than the average bass singer. This observer might
not accept as true the proposition that X is a tall trombone

player (tall for a trombone player) if and only if X is a
tall bass singer (tall for a bass singer).

The measure adjective *tall* has failed the substitution
test, but not because it is interpreted relative to the intension of the common noun it modifies. It has failed the test
because, with measure adjectives, there is some leeway as to
what individuals will be included in the comparison class for
the adjective and what norm will be picked for the dimension
that the adjective represents. Our difficult observer in the
case of the trombone players and the bass singers has happened
to include hypothetical trombone players in the comparison
class, something that is fairly natural to do. The observer
consequently chose a higher norm for tallness in trombone
players than the norm that would have been chosen by someone
who did not share her theory about trombone players. This
norm also turned out to be higher than the norm for bass
singers, so truth value was not preserved when one expression
was substituted for the other, and the bi-conditional did
not hold.

It is important to remember, however, that this failure
to preserve truth value under substitution is not due to
relativity to the intension of the modified common noun. Just
as in the earlier examples (19) - (22) speed was not part of
the intension of *car* and the height of buildings was not part
of the intension of *library*, height is not relevant to the
meaning of *trombone player*. The indeterminacy of measure
adjectives has to do with the selection of a comparison class
that may or may not coincide with the extension of the
modified common noun and of a norm for the class along the
adjective's dimension. These are quite different activities
from relativizing the meaning of *good* in *good trombone player*
to the meaning of *trombone player*. I return in section 3.3

to ways of accounting for the selection of comparison classes, dimensions, and norms.

3.2. *Membership in Category t///e*

If the indeterminacy in the interpretation of measure adjectives is not due to their being intensional, then it is reasonable to believe that measure adjectives are vague in certain defined respects, but extensional. There is nothing to be gained and something to be lost by assigning measure adjectives to the category CN/CN. This is not to say that they could be so assigned. Although the general form of semantic rules predicts that CN/CN's will be intensional, and the other words which we have reason to call CN/CN's are in fact intensional, it would still be possible, in theory, to assign measure adjectives to the category CN/CN, and to have a meaning postulate like (25), which would ensure that they were interpreted extensionally, like t///e's.

(25) $\lor M$ $\land u \,\square\, [(\alpha \, (^\wedge \beta))_* \, u \leftrightarrow {}^\lor M \, (u) \land \beta_* \, (u)]$

where $\alpha \in P_{CN/CN}$

$\beta \in P_{CN}$

M is a variable over properties of individuals (extensional, one-place predicates).

u is a particular individual variable.

However, there are serious problems with such an approach. A meaning postulate like (25) violates the reasonable constraint that meaning postulates must not have the effect of translating an expression of one category as if it were a member of another, existing category. Meaning postulate (25) is designed to make measure adjectives, once they have been classified as CN/CN's, behave semantically like t///e's.

None of Montague's meaning postulates does such a thing, and any constraints actually observed in our already too powerful theories of language should be preserved, if possible.

The desire to constrain the meaning postulates might be reason enough to conclude that it is not a good idea to classify measure adjectives as CN/CN's. They are not like other CN/CN's semantically, since they are extensional. But there is more direct evidence that they must not be classified as CN/CN's. Measure adjectives are not like CN/CN's syntactically, either. In fact, they are just like t///e's. Measure readings emerge only in environments where t///e adjectives are permissible. There are even some constructions where only t///e's are permissible, and measure adjectives occur there, too. Some of these constructions include the *see-catch-find* construction (Dowty 1972; 1975), the *there* construction (brought to my attention by John Goldsmith), and nonrestrictive adjectives.

(26) The warden caught the swimmers nude.

(27) There is a bat asleep in the bathroom.

(28) We all know naughty Nancy.

We must first establish that these concentrations do indeed act as a diagnostic for t//e adjectives, before we can use them to tell us anything about measure adjectives. At first glance, it is reasonable to expect the constructions illustrated in (26) - (28) to accept only adjectives of the category t///e and to reject those of category CN/CN. The adjectives do not seem to be combined with CN's. In fact, in (28), the adjective clearly combines with a term phrase. Furthermore, if we examine the particular non-measure adjectives that can appear in these three constructions, our expectation is borne out. Adjectives that are always absolute, such as those in the examples above, are permissible, but adjectives that are always relative (CN/CN's) are not:

(29) *The warden caught the swimmers veteran.

(30) *There are several crimes actual in the story.

(31) *We all know ostensible Jonathan.

In addition, adjectives that, like *beautiful*, seem to have both absolute and relative versions always have only their absolute readings in the constructions in question, thus supporting the view that these constructions accept only t///e adjectives.

(32) I've seen several of my teachers old.

   (*Old* has to mean 'aged' (old in general) and not
   'former' (old as a teacher) as it might in *old teacher*.)

(33) There is always a hammer handy.

   (*Handy* has to mean 'nearby' (handy in general) and
   not 'useful' (handy as a hammer) as it might in *handy
   hammer*.)

(34) We all love responsible Fred.

   (*Responsible* has to mean 'trustworthy' (responsible in
   general) and not 'concerned' (responsible as something)
   as it might in *responsible party*.)

It seems then, that all these constructions accept only, though not all, t///e adjectives. The assumption that they do makes possible fairly simple accounts of each of them not otherwise possible in the grammar.[7] The fact that measure adjectives routinely appear in all three constructions constitutes evidence that measure readings adhere to t///e versions of adjectives.

(35) I've often seen the grass tall around that house.

(*Tall* means 'tall for grass'.)

(38) There were two pigs clean in the whole pen.

(*Clean* means 'clean for a pig'.)

(37) We're all afraid of big Bertha.

(*Big* means 'big for a woman' or 'big for a steam engine', etc.)

While the fact that the particular measure adjectives appearing in (35) - (37) must be t//e's since they appear in these constructions does not prove that there are no measure adjectives that are CN/CN's, it does show that the relativity of measure adjectives is not relativity to the meaning of a common noun as it is with CN/CN's. In (37), *big* does not even combine with a common noun, but with a full term phrase, *Bertha*. Nevertheless, its meaning is relative to the normal size of individuals of whatever class Bertha belongs to, a class not even hinted at in the syntax of (37).

An examination of the particular adjectives that can have measure readings also supports the idea that such readings arise from a special interpretation of t///e adjective. Only those adjectives that have absolute readings ever have measure readings. Adjectives that are relative in the intensional, CN/CN sense and never absolute do not develop the measure kind of relativity, the one paraphrasable by expressions of the form 'ADJ for a CN'.

(38) Jack is a blithering fool, but he's not a blithering idiot.

(*blithering for a fool, but not blithering for an idiot)

(39) This is the actual design that was used, but it's not the actual building.

(*actual for a design, but not actual for a building)

Similarly, for adjectives which have both a relative and an absolute reading, the measure interpretation is associated with only the absolute reading. Notice, in the sentences below, how thinking of the 'for a' measure paraphrase changes the interpretation of the adjective from the relative interpretations dominant in the (a) sentences to the absolute interpretations that emerge in the t///e diagnostic environments of the (c) sentences.

(40) a. Marilyn is a crazy mother (crazy as a mother), but she's not a crazy artist (crazy as an artist).

   (Marilyn is not necessarily insane in general, just an unconventional parent.)

b. Marilyn is a crazy mother (crazy for a mother), but she's not a crazy artist (crazy for an artist).

   (Marilyn must be at least a little generally insane compared to other mothers, although not compared to other artists.)

c. I've seen those mothers crazy.

   (*Crazy* here must mean insane in general, not just unconventional.)

(41) a. Herb is an old lover (old as a lover; former or veteran lover), but he's not an old teacher (old as a teacher, former or veteran teacher).

b. Herb is an old lover (old for a lover; aged compared to other lovers), but he's not an old teacher (old for a teacher; aged as teachers go).

c. I've seen a lot of my teachers old.

(*Old* here means aged only.)

Finally, measure interpretations share idiosyncratic syntactic restrictions of t///e adjectives. The t///e version of *close*, for instance, is an exception to the relative clause reduction and preposing rule, (17). In (42) below, *close* can have either the absolute meaning of 'nearby' or the relative meaning of 'intimate (as a collaborator)'. In (43), though, *close* can have only the relative meaning; the absolute version cannot get to prenominal position.

(42) The collaborator was close.

(43) the close collaborator

As always, the measure reading appears only where the absolute meaning, the one not relative to the meaning of *collaborator*, can appear. Only in (42) can *close* mean 'close for a collaborator' that is, perhaps five to one hundred miles away. In (43) *close* has the relative reading, 'close as a collaborator', not the measure reading, 'close for a collaborator'. We can compare the situation with *close* with the one we find with *clever*. The t///e version of *clever* does prepose. We get absolute, relative, and measure readings both predicatively and prenominally.

(44) The sociologist is clever.

(45) That's a clever sociologist.

In both (44) and (45) the speaker could be saying that the individual is clever in general and a sociologist (absolute), clever as a sociologist (relative), or clever for a sociologist (measure).

In section 3.1 the semantic evidence that measure adjectives are not intensional made it seem inconvenient to
classify them as CN/CN's. Such a move would have necessitated
a new and undesirable kind of meaning postulate. The syntactic evidence in section 3.2 shows that measure readings are
associated with t///e's and not with CN/CN's syntactically
as well.

It should be added that not all t///e adjectives have
associated with them a measure interpretation. The ones that
do not are the adjectives that cannot be taken as picking
out any kind of a measurement scale. *Present,* for instance,
has an absolute meaning ('present in space'; 'here') as well
as a relative meaning ('present in time'; 'currently in the
position of'). Yet it has no measure interpretation, even
predicatively, where only the absolute version appears:

(46) She is a present employee (*present for an employee).

(47) The employee is present (*present for an employee).

Other adjectives that have absolute meanings but do not pick
out a measurement scale include *rancid, carnivorous. nude,
navigable, rabid, final, artificial, local, ready.* However,
any adjective that has a t///e version and also has the
lexical property of picking out some kind of measurement
scale can yield a measure interpretation in contexts where
the t//e version is syntactically permissible. If measure
adjectives are to be classified as t///e's, both their
extensionality and their syntactic behavior will automatically
be accounted for. What remains is to examine the sense in
which measure adjectives are relative, or, more accurately,
vague, in spite of their t///e status.

3.3. *Analyses of Measure Adjectives*

Several linguists and philosophers have advanced theories of
measure adjectives, often under the title of theories of
relative, or attributive adjectives. Jerrold Katz (1972), for
instance, suggests a theory which is supposed to account for
both measure adjectives and my relative adjectives, all under
the rubric of relative adjectives. I have shown here and
elsewhere (Siegel 1976a; 1976b) that there are important
systematic differences in the syntax and the semantics of
these two groups of adjectives. What I have called relative
adjectives are intensional ad-common nouns; measure adjectives
are extensional predicates and, hence, share more with
absolute adjectives than with relative ones. Katz's theory
treats adjectives as extensional predicates and so, while it
cannot account for relative adjectives in my sense, it does
shed some light on the interpretation of measure adjectives.

(48) Skyscrapers are tall.

(49) Skyscrapers are GREATER in VERTICAL SIZE than
     the average BUILDING.

Example (49), Katz's semantic representation of the sentence
in (48), at least sets out the basic tasks in interpreting a
measure adjective: designating the category of comparison
(BUILDING), choosing the relevant dimension (VERTICAL SIZE),
and giving the subject's relation to the comparison class
along the dimension (GREATER than average). Unfortunately,
Katz's theory does not really tell us satisfactorily where
the kinds of information in (49) come from. Katz's method
of predicting the comparison class is especially troublesome.
Consider sentence (50) and its putative representation, (51).

(50) He's a crazy one.

(51) He is GREATER in CRAZINESS than the average HUMAN.

Prenominal *crazy* does admit of a measure interpretation; a
crazy artist might just be 'crazy for an artist'. Katz's
theory should work on it. The comparison class according to
Katz, is the lowest-order category included as a semantic
marker for the subject. If the subject is *he*, as in (50),
the lowest order category is HUMAN, or possibly, ANIMATE.
Yet (50) might well mean 'he's crazy for a doctor', as in
If he's a doctor, he's a crazy one! It seems that the comparison class actually comes from the situation and the linguistic
context rather than from any semantic markers on the subject.

The situation is similar with prenominal measure adjectives with less empty common nouns. One might think that
Katz's theory would have no trouble giving the comparison
class for such measure adjectives. A tall man is simply
GREATER in VERTICAL SIZE than the average MAN. Actually,
though, comparison classes for prenominal measure adjectives
can be thoroughly idiosyncratic. Double prenominal adjectives
afford a clear demonstration of the difficulty of determining
the comparison class of measure adjectives systematically.

In order to appreciate the vagaries of double measure
adjectives, we must first consider double adjectives in
general. A second regular t///e, like *nude* or *drunk*, for
instance, just adds another property of individuals to a set
of conjoined properties (see (52) and (53) below). This is
as predicted by our syntactic and semantic rules. Examples
(52) and (53) are synonymous; their corresponding translations
are clearly logically equivalent. An extra CN/CN, on the
other hand, modifies the intension of whatever maximal
CN-phrase it combines with (see (54) and (55) below).

(52) drunk nude executive

    Translation: $\hat{x}_1$ [executive' x_1 ∧ nude' x_1 ∧ drunk' x_1]

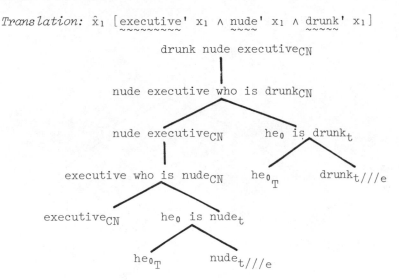

(53) nude drunk executive

    Translation: $\hat{x}_1$ [executive' x_1 ∧ drunk' x_1 ∧ nude' x_1]

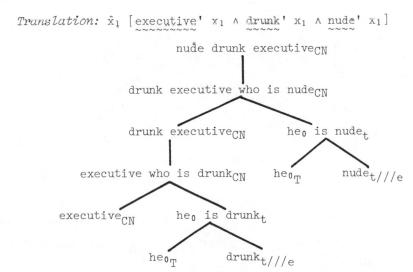

(54) nude chief executive

Translation: $\hat{x}_1$ [chief' (^executive') $x_1 \wedge$ nude' x_1]

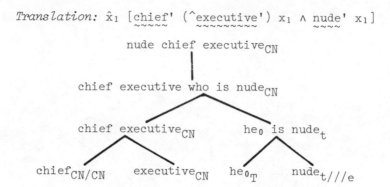

(55) chief nude executive

Translation: (chief') (^ $\hat{x}_1$ [executive' $x_1 \wedge$ nude' x_1])

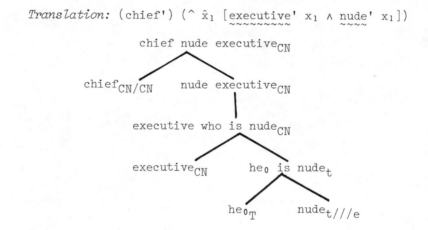

Examples (54) and (55) are not synonymous, and their respective translations reflect this fact.

It is also interesting to note that the interpretation of sequences like *chief nude executive* or *genuine carnivorous cow*, sequences of the form $ADJ_{CN/CN}$ $ADJ_{t///e}$ CN, bears on the question of how relative clauses are to be analyzed.[8] Such double adjective sequences are always interpreted as if the CN/CN applies to the entire reduced and fronted relative clause with its head, as in (55). We get readings corresponding to [chief$_{CN/CN}$ [nude executive]$_{CN}$] or [genuine$_{CN/CN}$ [carnivorous cow]$_{CN}$]. If a CN/CN applies to an expression, that expression must be a phrase of the category CN, so the relative clause with its head must be a common noun phrase. This fact supports an analysis of relative clauses where relative clauses with their heads are common noun phrases, as in Montague grammar. A theory that analyzes relative clauses as having the structure [NP [S]]$_{NP}$ (as in Ross 1967) would be incompatible with the idea that these CN/CN adjectives combine with common nouns.

Let us now consider double measure adjectives.

(56) heavy fast runner

$\hat{x}_1$ [runner' x_1 $\wedge$ fast' x_1 $\wedge$ heavy' x_1]

(57) fast heavy runner

$\hat{x}_1$ [runner' x_1 $\wedge$ heavy' x_1 $\wedge$ fast' x_1]

If the measure adjectives *heavy* and *fast* are actually t///e's, as I've argued that they must be, then (56) and (57) should be translated as above. In fact, (56) does have a reading that roughly corresponds to the given translation: 'runner that is both heavy and fast for a runner'. This is the reading upon which (56) is synonymous with (57), as in the translations above. A theory of measure adjectives would just have to explain where the comparison clause 'for a runner' comes in. This wouldn't be too difficult for Katz's or other theories. However, a complete theory would also have to explain why it is that (56) may also mean 'heavy for a fast runner'. Such a reading is quite different from the translation given above; it is also different from a translation appropriate to a CN/CN, since it is extensional. Presumably, it is the context of utterance that allows us to understand how much is included in the comparison class.

It would appear that with prenominal measure adjectives, the comparison class may be taken as being the set picked out either by the basic common noun modified, or by another, more complex common noun to the right of the measure adjective. The ambiguity must be resolved in context. One might think that a system using Katz's semantic markers could at least systematically predict the available options, from the broadest comparison class, the basic common noun, to the narrowest, the maximal common noun phrase to the right of the measure adjective. In fact, though, there seems to be no way to predict formally the set of possible comparison classes for a prenominal measure adjective. Apparently, whatever picks out the comparison class can actually skip through a complex common noun, omitting adjectives that are irrelevant to the dimension of the measure adjective.

(58) Billy is a tall little red-headed basketball player.

Sentence (58) is meant to be a description of a child who plays basketball. It means that Billy is tall for a little basketball player. The interpretation of *tall* seems to have skipped over *red-headed* in the collection of a comparison class, presumably because hair color isn't relevant to height. CN/CN's enjoy no such selectivity. They are bound by syntactic-semantic rule to modify the entire following common noun phrase:

(59) Billy is a former little red-headed basketball player.

(60) Billy is our top little red-headed basketball player.

Both (59) and (60) are strange things to say unless you want to suggest in (59) that Billy isn't red-headed any more, and,

in (60), that Billy is, in some sense, top in his capacity
as a red-head.

The measure adjectives, then, are alone in depending crucially for the determination of their comparison classes upon
contextual disambiguation and lexical peculiarities. If it
is to be a theory of measure adjectives, Katz's system with
its semantic markers fails to provide the necessary mechanisms
to determine comparison class. Another problem with Katz's
system is that the relevant dimension is supposed to be part
of the meaning of the adjective. In fact, it will usually
turn out to be all of the meaning of the adjective, and so,
not be very illuminating. For *clever*, the dimension will be
CLEVERNESS, for *beautiful*, BEAUTY, and, in (50), the dimension for *crazy* is CRAZINESS. Once again, the semantic markers
as such haven't helped much. CRAZINESS remains an untrans-
lated, unquantifiable quality. Finally, the relation between
the subject and its comparison class is elusive. Calling
someone or something crazy I think requires that the person
or thing be somewhat more than crazier than average. Someone
who is only a tiny bit crazier than average would be merely
odd.

The Bartsch and Vennemann (1972) theory is somewhat similar
to the Katz theory in that the relative adjectives are meant
to include words like *good, heavy, big, beautiful,* and *intelligent,* but they are all treated strictly as measure adjectives. No 'ADJ as a CN' readings or other intensional
readings are considered. Therefore, the theory is best
considered as a theory of measure interpretations. A representation of a sentence like (61), for instance, would be
(62).

(61) John is tall.

(62) f_T^M (John) > N

f^M is a measure function that assigns numbers to sets.
Specifically, in (61), f^M is assigning a degree of tallness
(the dimension is indicated by the subscript T) to John. The
formula in (62) says that John's degree of tallness is greater
than the context-specific or socially determined norm of a
contextually determined comparison class. N, representing
this norm, is really a function of all the sets relevant to
the discourse: people in general, John's relatives, John's
contemporaries, or whatever.

As a theory of measure adjectives, this one has some
advantages over Katz's. It is less linguistically determined.
Both the dimension of comparison and the norm or average are
to be contextually, not lexically, given. Consequently, in
this theory, there would be no special problems with (50),
either in defining the comparison class for the nonlexical
subject or in allowing for broader standards of craziness
than just greater or less than average. Unlike Katz, Bartsch
and Vennemann unabashedly choose tallness as the relevant
dimension for *tall*. There is no attempt to analyze the adjective further. In fact, both because of the reliance on
contextual input and the absence of abstract semantic markers,
the Bartsch-Vennemann theory seems more like a theory of
strategies of interpretation of sentences in context than a
theory of underlying structure. It seems to take the structure and the lexicon of the language for granted. If the
scope of this theory is limited, as it must be, to measure
adjectives, its approach is consistent with my findings that
measure adjectives are special cases of absolute adjectives,
picked out from their category-mates by the idiosyncratic
property of being able to designate measurement scales.

Another theory of measure adjectives that allows for contextual disambiguation is presented in Wheeler (1972). This theory is meant to account for all attributive adjectives, but an attributive is first defined as 'an adjective or adverb which, when paired with a substantive or stuff-predicate or verb, yields sentences which cannot correctly be given a conjunctive account' (Wheeler 1972: 311). This definition includes both my relative adjectives and my measure adjectives. However, later, the definition is narrowed to include extensional modifiers only. This immediately excludes adjectives with 'as a' readings like *good* and other CN/CN adjectives (*former, alleged, blithering, mere*) from the class of attributive adjectives. It narrows the class, in fact, to what I have called measure adjectives, the only ones to be extensional but not subject to a conjunctive translation.

According to Wheeler, the kind of adjective that he is dealing with is a 'two-termed relation between an individual and a class of individuals, plus a membership sentence saying that the individual belongs to the class to which it is related' (1972: 315). Thus, the logical form of (63) is (64).

(63) John is a tall man.

(64) Tall (John, x̂ (x is a man)) & John ∈ x̂ (x is a man))

Since Wheeler is concentrating on attributive, as opposed to predicative, adjectives, there is rarely any problem with determining the comparison class. As in (63), the comparison class is given by the modified noun. However, Wheeler does want to account for the relativity of (65), as in (66).

(65) That lobster is red.

(66) Red (that lobster, $\hat{x}$ (x is a lobster)) & (that

   lobster $\in \hat{x}$ (x is a lobster))

Probably, he would also represent (67) as in (66), if it were said while pointing at a lobster.

(67) It's red.

So it seems that the comparison class is meant to be contextually determined, as in the Bartsch-Vennemann theory. The dimension of comparison, however, is given here in even more surfacy terms than in the Bartsch-Vennemann theory. We get not 'tallness', but *tall*. It is not really a dimension, but a relation between the individual and the comparison class. The nature of this relation is not given at all, but left to be contextually determined. Wheeler avoids saying anything about John being taller than any average or norm in (64). He observes, rightly, I think, that such a norm may be nowhere to be found, yet we can still use measure adjectives: 'The population of acrobats consists of 101 individuals, 51 of which are exactly seven feet tall. It seems to me that the 51 are tall acrobats, but they are not any taller than most acrobats' (Wheeler 1972: 319).

   The last theory of measure adjectives to be considered is that in Kamp (1975). Kamp's theory of measure adjectives is at once the most explicit and the least linguistically determined. It is also the only one of these theories meant by its author more or less as a theory of measure adjectives. Kamp first considers the prenominal adjective theories of Montague (1974c) and Parsons (1971), in which all adjectives are treated as CN/CN's. He then offers his own theory of adjectives that can act like vague one-place predicates, although he is not sure how far the domain of such a theory extends. As examples of adjectives that would definitely not

be in its domain, he mentions *alleged, fake, skillful, good,*
and *four-legged.* This list includes paradigm examples of
relative adjectives (CN/CN's: *alleged, fake, skillful, good*),
as well as nonmeasuring absolute adjectives (*four-legged*).
In my terms, this leaves as the domain for Kamp's theory only
measure adjectives, those t///e's with a 'for a' interpretation.

Kamp gives no translations of English into a logic. Rather,
he gives model-theoretic truth definitions to account for the
use of sentences with measure adjectives, which he takes to
be, basically, simple one-place predicates. Kamp, then, is
trying more to develop a theory of use of a type of predicate
than a grammar of adjectives. This fits in nicely with the
notion of measure adjectives as a peculiar subset of the
t///e's. Also, a theory of use seems to be the proper realm
in which to treat the problems of measure adjectives. Damerau
(1975) comes close to this conclusion in a critique of various
formal syntactic-semantic proposals for dealing with measure
adjectives. He criticizes a proposal set out in Lakoff (1972)
and Zadeh (1974) to use fuzzy sets. The proposal relies too
heavily on linguistic variables like *height* and also lacks
the notion of a comparison class. Similarly, Damerau regards
the choice of comparison class, norm or average, and dimension in Katz's system as too linguistically determined to
represent the facts accurately. He concludes that all aspects
of the interpretation except, perhaps, the polarity of the
adjective, must be open to contextual influence, but he
mourns the fact that such an approach won't make for very
convenient syntactic deep structures: 'The difficulty, of
course, is formulating a grammar capable of deriving correct
surface structures from such a deep structure ... In the
absence of such a grammar, any evaluation of the validity of

possible semantic deep structures ... is really empty of
content' (Damerau 1975: 5). In contrast, Kamp embraces the
conclusion that measure adjective interpretation is not only
a matter of syntax: 'The idea of a predicate being true of
an entity to a certain degree ... is closely related to such
general features of natural language as vagueness and contextual disambiguation' (Kamp 1975: 128 - 129).

Kamp's truth definitions for sentences with measure adjectives are given in terms of graded context-dependent models.
Given a model (an incomplete one) of the actual world, the
context of use determines a slightly less vague ground model,
as well as a set of possible further sharpenings or modifications of the model. In some cases, the context-determined
ground model will be explicit enough about the standard of
comparison, the dimension of comparison, and the subject's
place on the dimension to provide a truth value for a sentence
like (68).

(68) Harry is heavy.

Harry will be in either the positive or the negative extension of the predicate *heavy* in the ground model, and the
sentence will be true or false, accordingly.

If, however, the standard of comparison and, consequently,
the subject's relation to it aren't fully determined in the
ground model by the context, an intermediate truth value can
be determined by examining the truth of the sentence in the
possible models less vague than the ground model, that is,
in the possible sharpenings and modifications of the ground
model that the context has determined. In this way it is
possible to calculate the degree of truth for the sentence
(a number between 0 and 1) based on the frequency with which
possible standards of comparison would make the sentence true.

If, on the other hand, the relevant dimension isn't picked out in the ground model, the truth of the sentence may actually be undecidable. Kamp agrees with the others that there is little trouble identifying the relevant dimensions with a one-dimensional adjective like *heavy* or *tall*. However, unlike the others, Kamp isn't satisfied with saying that cleverness, which is multidimensional, is the relevant dimension in (69).

(69) Harry is clever.

The truth of (69) would be undecidable in Kamp's theory unless some single-scaled attribute like problem-solving ability or quick-wittedness is contextually selected for primary attention. I am not at all sure that problem-solving ability or quick-wittedness is particularly more single-scaled than cleverness, but I think that this treatment of dimension in Kamp's theory does capture the fact that we can't use a measure adjective as such unless we have some idea of a scale in mind.

Kamp's theory is built on vagueness and operates by contextual disambiguation. It shares none of the problems of the others, and succeeds in building in a scalability requirement for dimensions of comparison. One might suggest that Kamp's theory runs into fewer problems because it attempts less, that is, it does not constitute a grammar of adjectives, or even a logical structure for them, beyond that of a simple predicate. In fact, though, the goals of this theory are simply different. Kamp considers the measure-adjective problem to be related, not so much to the syntactic and logical role of the adjective, but to vagueness and contextual disambiguation. His theory does provide a framework for the treatment of these latter phenomena.

3.4. *Measure Adjectives and Comparison*

The theories of measure adjectives, then, seem to get more
correct as they get more vague. That is, the more they allow
the comparison class, the dimension, and the position along
the dimension to be contextually determined, the better they
account for the facts. The various logical forms given for
measure adjectives are not representations to be built into
a grammar. Rather, they are models of what we mean when we
use measure adjectives, no matter what their underlying grammatical structure might be.

I have tried to show that adjectives with a measure interpretation are a subset of the t///e adjectives. As far as the
workings of the grammar go, the distinction between t///e's
and CN/CN's is the fundamental one. Aside from their t///e
characteristics, measure adjectives show no uniform syntactic
behavior. Much of the supposed importance of measure adjectives as a class comes from the role they are supposed to
play in comparatives. In a discussion of why nouns don't
often have comparative forms, Kamp hypothesizes that a word's
ability to produce reasonable comparatives depends upon its
having a sizable extension gap (it must not be too clear what
is and what is not in its extension) and on its determining
a dimension or a few dimensions of measurement. Among adjectives, these two features would be determined by facts about
the world and the lexical properties of the words. Yet, many
writers, including Sapir (1944), as well as Katz, Bartsch and
Vennemann, and Wheeler, have maintained that adjectives that
can participate in comparative constructions are exactly the
category of measure adjectives which characteristically allow
a 'for a' interpretation in the positive. Even Kamp explains
comparatives as part of the same phenomenon as the measure

readings, although he claims no grammatical significance for
the category so determined.

However, many adjectives that cannot have a measure interpretation can appear in comparatives:

(70) a. Bowser is a speckled poodle, but he's not a speckled
dalmation.

(*Bowser is speckled for a poodle, but he's not
speckled for a dalmation.)

b. Spot is more speckled than Bowser.

(71) a. This is a public restroom but it's not a public
auditorium.

(*This is public for a restroom, but it's not public
for an auditorium.)

b. Let's go someplace more public.

There are many other adjectives, absolute, relative, and
homonym pairs, that can be used in comparatives but not as
measure adjectives:

(72)

speckled	temporary	navigable	handy
angry	forcible	representative	rabid
remiss	rightful	customary	sorry
loath		public	close
		local	ready

This list of non-measure adjectives that permit comparatives
even includes some exclusively relative adjectives, words of
a category, CN/CN, incapable of yielding a 'for a' measure
interpretation:

(73) I will follow Peter, because he is the more rightful king.

Further evidence that comparatives are not, like measure
interpretations, limited to t///e adjectives can be found in
the comparatives of doublets. We saw in (40) and (41) that

the measure interpretation of a doublet automatically selects
the t///e version of the doublet. Comparative constructions
show no such behavior. The sentences below are ambiguous. The
adjectives can have their CN/CN interpretations or the t///e
interpretations of the (b) sentences.

(74) a. I've never seen a sorrier artist.

(*Sorry* can mean either 'bad specimen of' or
'regretful'.)

b. I've never seen that artist sorry ('regretful' only).

(75) a. Kim is looking for a handier tool.

(*Handy* can mean either 'useful' or 'conveniently
nearby'.)

b. There's always a hammer handy in this house
('conveniently nearby' only).

Comparison, then, is not part of the same phenomenon as
measure interpretation. It is much more widespread, occurring
in more than one grammatical category, including non-adjective
categories. Measure interpretation, now on its own, looks
even more like a special way of interpreting t///e's. Wheeler
observes that some adjectives, like *red*, which can have a
measure interpretation more often have an absolute interpretation. He proposes to account for this by saying that, for
the absolute reading, the comparison class is everything.
One could extend this hypothesis to account for t///e's and
t///e versions of doublets that never allow a measure interpretation by saying that such adjectives help determine a
context in which the comparison class is always everything.
This way, we can think of whatever theory best explains the
interpretation of measure adjectives as part of a general
strategy for using t///e's.

Acknowledgments

This paper is an expanded and slightly revised version of
Chapter IV of my doctoral dissertation (Siegel 1976a). I
would like to thank the members of my dissertation committee,
Emmon Bach, Terence Parsons, and, especially, Barbara Partee
for their help and encouragement in this project.

Notes

1. Some who have treated the semantic duality among
adjectives in various languages include Babby (1971; 1973);
Bartsch and Vennemann (1972); Berman (1974); Bolinger (1967);
Fornaciari (1884); Kamp (1975); Katz (1972); and Parsons
(1970).
   2. See Siegel (1976a; 1976b) for an account of other
languages in which this prediction is more nearly borne out.
   3. Proposed in Chomsky (1957) and Smith (1961).
   4. The problems involved in deriving all adjectives this
way have been discussed by Bolinger (1967), Jackendoff (1972),
and Winter (1965), among others.
   5. See Russell (1945); Wheeler (1972); and Bartsch and
Vennemann (1972).
   6. Terry Parsons brought this possibility to my attention.
   7. See Siegel (1976a), section III.31.
   8. Thanks to Emmon Bach, who pointed this out to me.

References

Babby, Leonard. 1971. "A Transformational Analysis of Russian
    Adjectives." Ph.D. dissertation, Harvard University.
————. 1973. "The Deep Structure of Adjectives and Participles
    in Russian." *Language* 49: 349 - 360.

Bartsch, Renate, and Theo Vennemann. 1972. *Semantic Structures*. Frankfurt: Athenaum Verlag.

Berman, Arlene. 1974. "Adjectives and Adjective Complement Constructions in English." Report No. NSF-29. Department of Linguistics, Harvard University.

Bolinger, Dwight. 1967. "Adjectives in English: Attribution and Predication." *Lingua* 18 (1): 1 - 34.

Chomsky, Noam. 1957. *Syntactic Structures*. The Hague: Mouton.

Damerau, Fred J. 1975. "On 'Fuzzy' Adjectives." IBM Research Report RC 5340. Thomas J. Watson Research Center, Yorktown Heights, New York.

Dowty, David. 1972. "Temporally Restrictive Adjectives." In John Kimball, ed., *Syntax and Semantics I*. New York: Seminar Press.

————. 1975. "The Stative in the Progressive and Other Essence/Accident Contrasts." *Linguistic Inquiry* 6 (4).

————. 1976. "Montague Grammar and the Lexical Decomposition of Causative Verbs." In Barbara H. Partee, ed., *Montague Grammar*. New York: Academic Press.

Fornaciari, R. 1884. *Sintassi italiana dell'uso moderno*. Florence, Italy.

Jackendoff, Ray S. 1972. *Semantic Interpretation in Generative Grammar*. Cambridge, Mass.: MIT Press.

Kamp, J. A. W. 1975. "Two Theories about Adjectives." In Edward B. Keenan, ed., *Formal Semantics of Natural Language*. Cambridge: Cambridge University Press.

Katz, Jerrold. 1972. *Semantic Theory*. New York: Harper & Row.

Lakoff, George. 1972. "Hedges: A Study in Meaning Criteria and the Logic of Fuzzy Concepts." In *Papers from the Eighth Regional Meeting of the Chicago Linguistics Society*.

Montague, Richard. 1974a. "English as a Formal Language." In *Formal Philosophy*, ed. Richmond Thomason. New Haven:

Yale University Press.

————. 1974b. "The Proper Treatment of Quantification in
Ordinary English." In *Formal Philosophy,* ed. Richmond
Thomason. New Haven: Yale University Press.

————. 1975c. "Universal Grammar." In *Formal Philosophy,*
ed. Richmond Thomason. New Haven: Yale University Press.

Parsons, Terence. 1970. "Some Problems Concerning the Logic
of Grammatical Modifiers." *Synthèse* 21 (3-4): 320-334.

————. 1971. "Meanings of Adjectives in Attributive Position."
Preliminary notes, University of Massachusetts, Amherst,
mimeo.

Partee, Barbara. 1975a. "John Is Easy to Please." Ms.,
University of Massachusetts, Amherst.

————. 1975b. "Montague Grammar and Transformational Grammar."
Linguistic Inquiry 6: 203-300.

————, ed. 1976. *Montague Grammar.* New York: Academic Press.

Ross, John Robert. 1967. "Constraints on Variables in Syntax."
Ph.D. dissertation, MIT; available from the Indiana
University Linguistics Club.

Russell, Bertrand. 1945. *A History of Western Philosophy.*
New York: Simon and Schuster.

Sapir, Edward. 1944. "Grading: A Study in Semantics."
Philosophy of Science 11: 93-116.

Siegel, Muffy E. A. 1976a. "Capturing the Adjective." Ph.D.
dissertation, University of Massachusetts, Amherst.

————. 1976b. "Capturing the Russian Adjective." In
Partee 1976.

Smith, Carlota S. 1961. "A Class of Complex Modifiers in
English." *Language* 37 (5).

Wheeler, Samuel. 1972. "Attributives and Their Modifiers."
Nous 6 (4).

Winter, Werner. 1965. "Transforms without Kernels." *Language*
    41 (31): 484 – 489.
Zadeh, L. 1974. "The Concept of a Linguistic Variable and
    Its Application to Approximate Reasoning." IBM Research
    Report RJ 1355, San Jose, California.

7

Mass Nouns and Mass Terms in Montague Grammar

Michael Bennett

For a long time I have wanted to get clearer about the
relationships among mass nouns and their quantifiers, mass
terms, measure phrases, the Partee puzzle about temperature,
and related topics. (Incidentally, I am using 'measure phrase'
loosely to refer to expressions like weigh ten grams and
temperature in degrees Fahrenheit.) A useful way to get
straight about such matters is to construct a fragment.
I have such a fragment and occasionally I will refer to it
(Bennett 1977b).

I feel quite uncertain about the results. We are all aware
of the enormous literature on these topics in both linguistics
and philosophy. The subject is notorious for its metaphysical
difficulties. I know of no other topic in syntax and semantics that ushers one so quickly into the metaphysical sub-
structure of English. I am not a clever ontologist and I
easily get lost in these catacombs. Let me apologize in
advance if I have made any obvious blunders.

Difficulties are compounded by the fact that many of the
mass noun quantifiers are vague. Let me say right off that I
do not have a theory of vagueness, and the framework I am
working with is incomplete in this respect. Hans Kamp has
argued that a theory of vagueness underlies any adequate
account of adjectives (Kamp 1975). If this is correct, again

my framework has serious shortcomings; for I am employing the
old Montague-Kamp-Parsons theory of adverbial and adjectival
modification.

Montague himself took a shot at mass nouns and mass terms
(Montague 1973b), when he commented on Moravcsik's paper at
the conference where he presented 'Proper Treatment' (Montague
1973a). However his discussion is very tentative and incomplete. A classic paper on the subject is Terence Parsons'
"An Analysis of Mass Terms and Amount Terms" (1970). I now
find myself in agreement with most of that paper; in fact,
Parsons' views have pervaded my thinking on the subject. But
Parsons says very little about how to treat the quantifiers
for mass nouns. We are told that the mass noun quantifiers
all and some get the same treatment as the corresponding
count noun quantifiers, but that the mass noun quantifier most
differs from its count noun counterpart. It was Parsons'
discussion of most which led me to see the important role
that mereology plays in our subject.

I was drawn to the present topic because I had previously
worked on some of the exotic plural quantifiers such as
few, a few, several, and many. I was struck by the remarkable
parallel between the plural quantifiers and the quantifiers
for mass nouns. In fact, every plural quantifier has a mass
noun counterpart except several. I became convinced, and I
still am, that the key to understanding mass noun quantification lies in an understanding of the plural quantifiers.
Indeed, it seems to me that one should first study the plural
in English, and then turn to mass nouns. I find the first
topic much easier than the second, and the second, in a sense,
a generalization of the first.

Because of the limitations on space, I have decided not
to say very much about the quantifiers for mass nouns.

Actually, my ideas about how they should be treated are
sketched in my dissertation (Bennett 1974, section 4.7).
Basically I still believe what I said there about *quantifi-*
cation. But at that time I accepted Montague's proposal that
mass terms denote properties of individuals. That is, he
proposed that substances be analyzed by such functions. I
now have doubts that this is correct, and this will be my
main topic in this paper.

There are several terms in use such as 'noun', 'term',
'nominal', etc. I had better explain how I want to use these
words or there might be confusion.

$\langle e, t \rangle$

T (terms)	CN (count nouns and count noun phrases)
John	man
a man	tall man
every man	man who is a spy
MT (mass terms)	MN (mass nouns and mass noun phrases)
water	water
little water	blue water
all water	water that is pure

Count nouns and mass nouns correspond to the semantic type
$\langle e, t \rangle$. They denote sets of individuals. Intuitively the
proper name John denotes an individual. But, as we know,
Montague gave proper names a more complicated denotation
so that proper names and quantifier phrases like every man
could be regarded as being of the same syntactic category.

I am not going to say anything about quantifier phrases here, so when I use the word 'term', think of proper names like *John* and mass terms like *water*. A clear example of a use of a mass term is:

> *gold is one of the elements*

Forgetting Montague's complications, basically a proper name denotes an individual, an entity of type *e* in the ontology for intensional logic. But what should a mass term like water denote? In his little paper on this logic, Montague proposes that it denotes a property of individuals, a function from points of reference to sets that consist of the quantities of water at the point of reference in question. Quantities or bits of water are taken to be individuals of type *e*. The corresponding mass noun water denotes at a point of reference the set of quantities of water at that point of reference. This is in contrast to Parsons' proposal that mass terms denote individuals, *the substances*, and that there exists a relation-in-intension, *being a quantity of*, that 'provides' the quantities of a substance at each point of reference.[1] Montague took the virtue of his proposal to be that he had given an analysis of substances in terms of their possible quantities and, as a consequence, had analyzed the relation *being a quantity of*. I doubt that Montague's analysis is correct, but before I give my reasons, I want to consider another question.

Does every expression that functions as a mass noun, or mass noun phrase, also function as a mass term? We must remember that mass nouns can be modified by adjectives and relative clauses. We can have the following terms:

> most (blue water)
>
> the (water in the glass)

> some (water that is impure)

But do the mass noun phrases involved correspond to mass terms? Do the following sentences make sense?

> blue water is a liquid
>
> water in the glass is a liquid
>
> water that is impure is a liquid

It is very possible that such sentences can be derived from sentences involving quantified mass noun phrases. For example, it might be possible to derive the first sentence from

> all blue water is a liquid

by some kind of a deletion rule. But I am not questioning this possibility. The clearest way I can put the question is as follows: do these sentences have readings where the subject term is regarded as denoting a substance? Do these sentences have readings that are roughly of the same logical form as the following?

> gold is one of the elements

Rather surprisingly, I think, Montague argues in a footnote that they do not:

> It should also be pointed out that blue water is a liquid turns out meaningless, but I think that on reflection this will be found compatible with intuition. ('How many liquids are there and how many metals?' 'Umpteen and phumpteen.' 'Did you count water?' 'Yes.' 'How about blue water?' 'Oh, I forgot.' 'And red water, and green water, and ...') Of course, heavy water is different; heavy is here syncategorematic and heavy water an unanalyzed mass noun [*sic*]. (Montague 1977b, p. 294, n. 1)

I happen to believe that Montague's conclusion is right — blue water is not a mass term and blue water is a liquid is

ungrammatical on the intended reading. But I am not confident
that my reasons for accepting this are the same as Montague's.
I said that I was surprised that Montague gave this argument.
This is because there is no technical obstacle for Montague
to allow all mass noun phrases to have mass term counterparts.
A natural way of doing this is to have in the lexicon basic
mass nouns, just as we have basic count nouns.

$$B_{MN} = \{water, gold, \dots \}$$

These can be modified by adjectives and relative clauses to
form complex mass noun phrases.

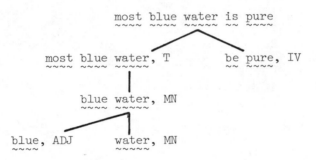

All mass terms can be derived from mass noun phrases by
promotion.

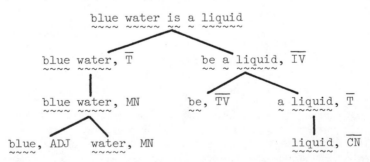

The mass noun phrase blue water has the translation blue'
([^water']). The corresponding mass term is given the translation

$$\lambda PP \{[\hat{}blue' ([\hat{}water'])]\}$$

where P is a variable of type $\langle s, \langle\langle s, \langle e, t\rangle\rangle, t\rangle\rangle$ which
ranges over properties of properties of individuals. The
analysis tree corresponds to a translation that is logically
equivalent to the following:

$$liquid' ([\hat{}blue' ([\hat{}water'])])$$

I do not have a knock-down argument against this view that
every mass noun phrase corresponds to a mass term. But I do
have a half-baked argument. The objection is really Montague's
argument in a slightly different form. Remember that Montague
is proposing to analyze substances as properties of individuals. We might say that in the semantics, substances are being
represented by properties of individuals. The objection is
this: if we regard all mass terms as denoting substances,
then the grammar is generating mass terms that denote
properties of individuals that intuitively do not represent
any substance. For example, gold that weighs (exactly) one
gram will denote a certain property of individuals, a different one than that denoted by gold.[2] But what substance does
the property of being a quantity of gold that weighs one
gram represent? I don't think it represents any substance.
Notice that on this theory, in a rich enough model, we are
going to have an infinite number of substances: gold that
weighs two grams, gold that weighs three grams, etc. It's
not clear to me that a semantics should decide such a matter.

A natural reply to this argument grants that the property
of individuals denoted by the mass term gold that weighs one
gram does not represent a substance in the ordinary sense.
But the property of individuals in question is a perfectly
good one and we ought to have ways to talk about it. Using

the mass term gold that weighs one gram is just one way of
doing that.

   It is difficult to answer this reply; many issues are
involved. Certainly I agree that we can talk about this
property of individuals. But I don't think that we do it with
a mass term. Talk about properties usually takes place in a
metalanguage when we are explaining our semantics. For example,
we might say in the metalanguage that verb phrases express
properties of individuals. We might even use a sentence like

>   the property of being sold that weighs one
>   gram is exemplified

But I am inclined to think of such a sentence as being extra-
ordinary; it is one that a philosopher would use in the metalanguage. Even so, the occurrence of gold that weighs one
gram here is most naturally analyzed as a mass noun phrase,
not a mass term. There might be ordinary sentences that
contain terms that denote properties of individuals. The
sentence

>   to walk is easy

might be analyzed as containing a term to walk that, from
the point of view of the semantics, denotes a property of
individuals. But this doesn't necessarily support the claim
that there are mass terms like gold that weighs one gram
that function semantically in the same way.

   I believe that Montague is right to delimit the mass
terms to just the basic ones — to count water as a mass term
and to rule out blue water. But I have doubts about his
proposal to analyze substances as properties of individuals.
Again I do not have any knock-down arguments, but I want to
express my misgivings. My doubts stem from beliefs about
how mass terms are introduced into the language. My picture

of how this works is the view developed by Saul Kripke (see
Kripke 1972a and 1972b). Probably no introduction of a mass
term really happens just like this, but a paradigm gives the
flavor. We identify some sample of stuff. We believe that the
sample, or almost all of it, has certain properties that set
it off from all previously identified substances. So we
baptize the new substance as follows: 'Gold is the substance
instantiated by the stuff over there, or at any rate, by
almost all of it.' Kripke's view allows for a term to be
introduced that fails to refer to anything. Someone can introduce an empty term into the language by making up a story and
pretending to refer to something, or perhaps the speaker is
trying to deceive and the empty name is slipped in among
a web of lies. Then there is the fellow who thinks he is
naming some new substance, but he is hallucinating his
sample; the description which he is employing to fix a
referent is improper. What I fear is that in these cases,
Montague's theory gives us a referent — namely, the function
from points of reference to sets of individuals, the individuals with all the right properties at the point of
reference.

Kripke considers the example of the mythical species
unicorn. Suppose that all we are told in the story about
unicorns is that they are a definite species, they resemble
horses except that they have a long horn on their head, and
something about maidens which I can't go into here. Kripke
argues that it is incorrect to think that unicorn is a count
noun that fails to have anything in its extension in the
actual world, but might have something in its extension in
some possible world. It is very tempting to think that
something might be a unicorn in another world; just imagine
a world where there are things having all the characteristics

in the story. Kripke's argument is that the story has not
told us enough about the species unicorn; the account is too
indefinite. For example, it has been left undetermined what
the internal characteristics of unicorns are like. Are they
mammalian, reptilian, or what? The story does not describe a
particular species. As Kripke puts it, 'we cannot say with
propriety that there are any definite circumstances under
which unicorns would have existed.' We can imagine situations
where there are several different species that have the
characteristics of unicorns given in the story. But we can't
say which are the unicorns. We cannot say that all of them
are unicorns because this would violate the characteristic
supplied by the story that the unicorn is a definite species.

We are in a similar situation with respect to fictional
substances. Let's consider the fictional substance kryptonite,
famous from the Superman comic books. Presumably the writers
of the Superman comics were pretending to refer to a substance
when they wrote the stories.[3] I have forgotten most of the
details, but the stories probably gave some characteristics
of kryptonite like the following: it's a metal that resembles
silver, it is scarce on the planet Earth, it is radioactive,
and it glows in the dark. The argument made about unicorns
should be made here. It is incorrect to say that the mass
noun kryptonite has an empty extension in the actual world
but could have something in its extension in some possible
world. The stories don't tell us enough about its chemical
structure. The stories just give us some surface characteristics which might be true of any number of substances. It
won't do to say that all of them are kryptonite because this
would violate the characteristic that kryptonite is a particular substance. It is true that the characteristics mentioned in the comics fix a definite property of individuals;

just take their conjunction.[4] But this property of individuals doesn't represent in any natural way a definite substance. Here I am appealing to our intuitive notion of a substance. A substance is something such that all of its quantities have a certain definite internal structure in common.[5]

There is a certain use of the mass term kryptonite where it does refer. This is when one uses the term *outside* the stories to refer to the fictional substance that was introduced by the Superman comics. Earlier I used the term this way myself. I was referring to an existing entity, the fictional substance kryptonite. Kripke has talked a little bit about this special use (1972b). But it is not to be confused with the use of the mass term *within* the stories. There the term fails to denote and the writers are only pretending to refer to a substance. But I suspect that Montague would say that even in the context of the stories, kryptonite is a denoting term.

My suspicions are to some degree confirmed by Montague's argument against the view that mass terms denote the set of quantities of the substance in question,

> For consider the example brought up in the September workshop session of two never-to-be-realized (but describable and realizable) substances called Kaplanite and Suppesite. The two sets in question would then be identical, but Kaplanite is a liquid might be true and Suppesite is a liquid false. (Montague 1973b, p. 290)

I accept this argument under certain conditions. It depends on what Montague means by 'describable and realizable'. Suppose that it could be theoretically proved that if certain steps were taken, then quantities of a hitherto-unrealized substance would be created. By using descriptions which involve the subjunctive, possibly we could fix a referent for a baptism. This kind of case is similar to the

one Kripke considers when Leverrier dubs the planet Neptune
even though he has never seen the planet through his telescope.
The referent is fixed by a description that describes a planet
that causes such and such discrepancies in the orbits of
certain other planets (Kripke 1972a, p. 347, n. 33). I am not
confident that Montague has in mind such a restricted interpretation of 'describable and realizable'. I believe that his
proposal that mass terms denote properties of individuals
lends itself to treating Kaplanite and Suppesite on a par
with kryptonite. His theory suggests that for a mass term to
have a denotation, it is sufficient to tell a story, as in
the Superman comic books.

Of course this is not a conclusive argument against the
proposal. One can imagine maintaining Kripke's views about
reference as well as Montague's proposal about what mass
terms denote. The Kripkian part of the theory would then
check the excesses of the Montague part, and kryptonite
would fail to refer. I now want to give a second half-baked
argument against analyzing substances as properties of
individuals.

There is a family of arguments against various proposals
about what mass terms denote. They all take the form that the
proposal will identify substances x and y when intuitively
x has a property which y does not have, i.e., when x and y
are intuitively distinct. Parsons persuasively argued that
mass terms cannot denote the mereological sum of their
quantities. Remember the wood-furniture example (Parsons
1970, pp. 376 - 377). We just considered Montague's argument
that mass terms cannot denote the set of their quantities.
Certainly this proposal will not work if there are such
things as extinct substances and we take the denotations of
the corresponding mass terms to be the set of quantities of

the substance *at* the point of reference. Characteristically, Montague proposed that we turn to an intensional entity, the function from points of reference to sets of quantities. I believe that an argument in the same style as those just mentioned can be made against Montague's own proposal.

Kaplan made such an argument against the treatment of groups in my dissertation (Bennett 1974). There I proposed that groups be represented by sets of individuals. When he pointed out that two committees could have exactly the same members, I replied that we could represent a group by a property of individuals, a function from points of reference to sets where the set consists of the membership of the group at the point of reference. Sound familiar? But Kaplan persevered. He argued that you might have two committees that are instituted in such a way that their memberships must always coincide, no matter what happens. Whoever serves on the first committee must serve on the second and vice versa. Here, the memberships of the two committees necessarily coincide. Kaplan's view was that groups are just individuals that persist through worlds and times changing their memberships. I didn't take Kaplan's advice when I wrote my dissertation, but I am prepared to take it now.[6]

My hunch is that a similar argument can, and should, be made against Montague's proposed analysis for mass terms. But I can never convince myself that *two* material substances could necessarily have the same quantities. Surely if they were two, they would differ in their quantities at some world-time.

It occurred to me that we might find a counterexample by shifting from material substances to 'immaterial' or 'abstract' substances. Recall Plato's concern with the virtues in the

Protagoras, 349b - c. Socrates is addressing the Sophist Protagoras.

> The question, if I am not mistaken, was this. Wisdom, temperance, courage, justice, and holiness are five terms. Do they stand for a single reality, or has each term a particular entity underlying it, a reality with its own separate function, each different from the other? [Hmmm, a function from what to what? — M.B.] Your answer was that they are not names for the same thing, but that each of these terms applies to its own separate reality, and that all these things are parts of virtue, not like the parts of a lump of gold all homogeneous with each other and with the whole of which they are parts, but like the parts of a face, resembling neither the whole nor each other and each having a separate function.

Socrates challenges this picture by forcefully arguing that if we consider *instances* of the virtues, persons and their deeds, it is difficult to find an instance where one virtue is exemplified and not another. Rather than compare two individual virtues, let's compare justice and virtue. There is some plausibility to saying that necessarily John is just if and only if he is virtuous. Yet intuitively there are differences between justice and virtue. Protagoras would put it as follows: justice is a part of virtue but virtue is not a part of justice. I would like to put the difference as follows: justice is one of the virtues but virtue is not one of the virtues. The point is that justice seems to have a property that virtue does not.

What does this have to do with Montague's analysis of mass terms? Justice and virtue appear to function like mass nouns and mass terms. We can say things like

> justice is a virtue
>
> there is little virtue in Las Vegas

Montague is not opposed to applying his analysis to certain
abstract mass terms (Montague 1973b, p. 293), and I see no
reason why he wouldn't apply it in these cases. Justice
would denote the property of being an instance of justice,
and likewise for virtue. The difficulty is that justice and
virtue might denote the same property. But justice is one of
the virtues might be true and virtue is one of the virtues
false.[7]

I have criticized two theses: first, that every mass noun
phrase has a mass term counterpart; second, Montague's proposal that mass terms be regarded as denoting properties of
individuals. I did not give knock-down arguments against
these theses, but I believe that my arguments can be refined
and made more forceful.

A different kind of criticism of Montague's analysis of
mass terms is that difficulties arise because of the type-
theoretic framework. The count noun liquid is supposed to
be a higher-order noun that has properties of individuals in
its extension. Is liquid to have the same semantic type as
an ordinary count noun like table or a different type? There
are ways of making the two have the same type. One is
Thomason's proposal to expand the entities of type e to
include properties of individuals (Thomason 1976, p. 83).
Another is Montague's method of representing basic individuals
as entities of a more complicated type, as he did in Montague
1973a when he represented individuals as individual concepts.
I don't want to claim that these approaches are wrong, but I
do find them to be unnatural. There is the possibility of
maintaining a split-level syntax in which liquid and table
have distinct semantic types. But this approach differs from
problems of duplication. Both kinds of count nouns can take
the same adjectives, for example rare. The split-level

approach forces the duplication of an adjective like rare
when there is no natural way to link the two words semantically (cf. Bennett 1974, section 4.2).

A way of avoiding the various difficulties that we have
considered concerning reference and levels is to treat mass
terms as denoting individuals — that is, to regard substances
as being of type *e*. This is Parson's line in his paper, and
I think it is right. We must then follow Parsons and introduce a relation-in-intension, *being a quantity of*, that tells
us the quantities of any substance at the point of reference.
Of course I disagree with Parsons about how many mass terms
there are. Parsons allows that every mass noun phrase can
generate a mass term by way of his substance abstraction
operator (Parsons 1970, section V).[8] Since I am not generating
complex mass terms, I am not employing such an operator.
Parsons might ask how I am going to explain examples like:

>   ice is frozen water
>
>   zinc is leaded tin that has been annealed
>
>   muddy water is widespread

In all these cases I believe that there are implicit quantifiers and that we are dealing with mass nouns or mass noun
phrases. The first example might be elliptic for:

>   all ice is frozen water

and the third example is elliptic for the following (cf.
Bennett 1974, section 4.7):[9]

>   the muddy water is widespread

There are some mass terms that appear to be syntactically
complex: heavy water, dry ice, and liquid oxygen. But I
would take Montague's line on these. They are unanalyzed mass

terms that appear in the lexicon as basic expressions. For example, dry ice is a basic expression of category MT, and it is not to be derived from the adjective dry and the mass noun ice. Richmond Thomason tells me that quantities of dry ice are not even ice; but all dry ice is ice would be true if dry ice were treated as nonbasic.

Let's consider some of the details of the fragment that I have constructed. Simple mass terms like water and gold are basic expressions in the lexicon.

$$B_{MT} = \{water, gold, oxygen, dry ice, hydrogen$$
$$dioxide, ...\}$$

There are no basic mass nouns in the lexicon. Mass nouns are created by a syntactic rule that transforms a basic mass term into a 'basic' mass noun.

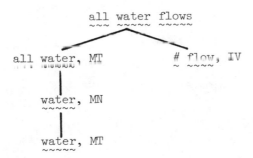

all water flows

all water, MT   # flow, IV

water, MN

water, MT

The mass term water has the translation $\lambda P P(w)$ where P is a variable of type $\langle e, t \rangle$ and w is an individual constant. The corresponding mass noun has the translation:

quantity of' $([\hat{P}P(w)])$

Here quantity of is a basic expression of category CN/T. The analysis tree corresponds to a translation that is logically equivalent to the following:

$$\wedge x [quantity of' ([\hat{P}P(w)])(x) \rightarrow \# flow'(x)]$$

This is one way of implementing Parsons' ideas into the Montague framework.

Let me conclude with a few speculations. For a long time I was unclear about the relationship between the Kripke picture of reference and Montague grammar. I was troubled about how one might formally represent Kripke's remarks about the mythical species unicorn and his tentative idea that a sentence like

there are some unicorns

might not express a proposition at all. For if it did, then we are able to say with propriety that there are definite circumstances under which unicorns would have existed. I think we now have one way of representing this. Suppose we have a way of treating empty terms so that when a sentence contains such a term, then it doesn't express a proposition. Thus

kryptonite is a substance

for example, might not express a proposition. But because of the dependency of mass nouns on mass terms,

John has a little kryptonite

will also fail to express a proposition. There might be a similar dependency between species names and certain count nouns. The meaning of the count noun tiger might depend on the meaning of the species name tiger in the following way: the count noun means *member of the species tiger*.[10] We now see how

there are some unicorns

can fail to express a proposition. I think this picture comes close to what Kripke and Kaplan have in mind (cf. Kripke 1972a and Kaplan 1973, p. 518, n. 31).[11] Kaplan makes

a remark that suggests that this picture should be extended
to 'almost all single words other than particles'. We should
think about this.

Acknowledgments

Except for a few notes, this is a talk that was delivered at
the conference on Montague Grammar, Philosophy, and Linguistics
at the State University of New York at Albany in April 1977.
I am very grateful to Richmond Thomason for some helpful
comments. At the conference I learned that Alice ter Meulen
has been working in the same area (ter Meulen 1976).

Notes

1. Some caution must be taken in interpreting Parsons in
this way, for he says in Parsons 1975 that his view in
Parsons 1970 is compatible with Montague's.

2. I am indebted to Jacques Desrosiers for this example
and for putting me on the road to the objection that follows.

3. This example of a fictional substance is somewhat
marred by the fact that there is a substance called krypton.
Possibly the writers of the Superman comics were referring
to this actual substance. But if I recall correctly, Krypton
was the planet on which Superman was born, and the substance
that took away his powers was called 'kryptonite'. It is
difficult for me to check on these matters.

4. Actually there might be some difficulties here. Some
of the properties of kryptonite might be explained in terms
of other fictional entities: the planet Krypton, Gotham
City, and Superman. We could either take only those properties that are not explained in these terms or we could
consider a different case to make our point. We can imagine

different stories that are very much like the Superman stories except that they involve actual entities like Mars, New York City, and Saul Kripke.

5. I am not intending to restrict the notion of substance to 'natural kinds', whatever these are. I am willing to count mud and garbage as substances. But quantities of garbage can be quite diversified in their internal structure. I definitely want to count garbage as both a mass term and a mass noun. This leaves me unclear about how the notion of substance is to be extended to include garbage.

6. This view about groups will be incorporated into Bennett 1977a. A common noun phrase like group of men will have individuals, entities of type e, in its extension. However, plural definite descriptions and lists, like the trees in the park and Tom, Dick, and Harry, will denote classes, as in Bennett 1974. Gerald Massey (1976) has proposed that these latter expressions should denote individuals which are the mereological sums of the corresponding classes. But this approach cannot account for the fact that (1) implies (2).

(1) Tom is not Dick

(2) Tom and Dick are two in number

7. I am nagged by the question as to how the Kripke theory of reference explains how terms like justice and virtue get their separate denotations.

8. Parsons yielded to the temptation to promote every mass noun phrase into a mass term. We should not be surprised if others succumb to a similar temptation: promoting every plural count noun phrase into a species term. Indeed, Carlson (1977), to some extent, has already committed this sin.

The parallels between mass constructions and the plural are many. We advocate introducing a primitive relation-in-

intension, *being a quantity of*, that tells us the quantities
of any substance at any point of reference; similarly, we
advocate introducing a primitive relation-in-intension, *being
a member of*, that tells us the membership of any species or
group at any point of reference. Of course species, groups,
and substances are all regarded as individuals of type *e* (cf.
n. 6).

9. I am unclear whether the sentence

water is widespread

on its true reading is derived from

the water is widespread

or as follows (or both):

water is widespread

water, MT   be widespread, IV

etc.

The second alternative is not so absurd if we understand the
verb phrase in this context as expressing the property: is
a substance such that the sum of its quantities is widespread.

10. Some count nouns might get introduced into the
language on their own hook — bachelor, for example, by way
of a definition.

11. Actually Kaplan's picture is that penguin in Peter is
a penguin is itself a rigid designator that refers to the
species.

References

Bennett, Michael. 1974. "Some Extensions of a Montague
    Fragment of English." Ph.D. dissertation, UCLA; available
    from the Indiana University Linguistics Club.
————. 1977a. "The Plural in Montague Grammar." In prepara-
    tion.
————. 1977b. "Mass Nouns and Their Quantifiers in Montague
    Grammar." In preparation.
Carlson, G. 1977. "Reference to Kinds in English." Ph.D.
    dissertation, University of Massachusetts, Amherst.
Kamp, Hanso. 1975. "Two Theories about Adjectives." In Edward
    B. Keenan, ed., *Formal Semantics of Natural Language*, pp.
    123 - 155. Cambridge: Cambridge University Press.
Kaplan, D. 1973. "Bob and Carol and Ted and Alice." In
    K. J. J. Hintikka et al., eds., *Approaches to Natural
    Language,* pp. 490 - 518. Dordrecht: D. Reidel Publishing Co.
Kripke, Saul. 1972a. "Naming and Necessity." In D. Davidson
    and G. Harman, eds., *Semantics of Natural Language,* pp.
    253 - 255. Dordrecht: D. Reidel Publishing Co.
————. 1972b. "Existence: Vacuous Names and Mythical Kinds."
    Talk delivered at the Oberlin Philosophy Colloquium,
    April 1972.
Massey, Gerald. 1976. "Tom, Dick, and Harry, and All the
    King's Men." *American Philosophical Quarterly* 13: 89 - 107.
Montague, Richard. 1973a. "The Proper Treatment of Quantifi-
    cation in Ordinary English." In K. J. J. Hintikka et
    al., eds., *Approaches to Natural Language*, pp. 221 - 242.
    Dordrecht: D. Reidel Publishing Co.
————. 1973b. "Comments on Moravcsik's Paper." In K. J. J.
    Hintikka et al., eds., *Approaches to Natural Language,*
    pp. 289 - 294. Dordrecht: D. Reidel Publishing Co.

Parsons, Terence. 1970. "An Analysis of Mass Terms and Amount
Terms." *Foundations of Language* 6: 362 - 388.
————. 1975. "Afterthoughts on Mass Terms." *Synthèse* 31:
517 - 521.
ter Meulen, Alice. 1976. "Mass Nouns in English: A Proposal
for the Analysis in Montague Grammar." Doctoraalscriptie,
Universiteit van Amsterdam.
Thomason, Richmond. 1976. "Some Extensions of Montague Grammar."
In Barbara H. Partee, ed., *Montague Grammar*, pp. 77 - 117.
New York: Academic Press.

8

Infinitives and Context in Montague Grammar

Jeroen Groenendijk and Martin Stokhof

0. *Introduction*

In this paper we will discuss the main aspects of a proposal
for the analysis of infinitives in the framework of Montague
grammar. To give a brief characterization: in this proposal
infinitives are translated directly into expressions which
denote propositions and which contain in subject position a
new type of expression of intensional logic. The denotation
of this new type of expression depends on the context in
which the infinitive occurs. A context will be defined as an
ordered sequence of entities. Roughly stated, expressions
will be evaluated with respect to a context which is built
up systematically by preceding expressions. This kind of
notion of context differs from several others, such as context as the physical properties of the speech situation, or
as the knowledge which the speaker and the hearer have in
common. The present notion of context is meant to be additional to these and other notions, and may, in the end, be
incorporated in an overall notion of context.

In this paper we will be concerned mainly with the role
this notion of context plays in the analysis of infinitives.
Other problems for which it might be useful are mentioned in
section 3.

The main idea behind our proposal is to analyze infinitives
in such a way that it is expressed *directly* that infinitives
denote propositions. This association of infinitives with
propositions is generally accepted. But the two analyses in
the framework of Montague grammar that have been proposed,
those of Barbara Partee (1976) and of Richmond Thomason (1976a;
1976b), do not account for this. In Partee's analysis no
relation between infinitives and propositions is established
at all. And in Thomason's proposal the relation is made only
indirectly. In his syntax Thomason treats infinitives as
derived indirectly from a sentential basis: sentences containing syntactic variables are transformed into what he calls
abstracts, and a certain subclass of these abstracts is the
infinitives. However, this syntactic analysis implies that in
the semantics infinitives turn out to be expressions which
denote properties and not, as one would wish, expressions
denoting propositions. In order to achieve that in the end
infinitives *are* related to propositions, Thomason has supplied
his analysis with a set of meaning postulates which associate
certain relations between individuals and a property, with
relations between individuals and a proposition. We have no
objection of principle against such an approach, but, still,
we would like to develop an alternative. There are three
reasons for this. First, we consider the very indirect relation between infinitives and propositions to be unintuitive.
Second, we would like to avoid the syntactic complications of
Thomason's proposal which do not seem to have a syntactic
motivation. Third, we would like to avoid using the meaning
postulates Thomason needs in order to account for the relation between infinitives and propositions, because they are
of a rather unusual kind.

1. *Syntax*

Our proposal is to generate infinitives directly in the syntax
by means of simple concatenation of a basic expression *to* and
an IV-phrase of arbitrary complexity. Categories are assigned
in such a way that the result of this concatenation is translated into an expression of intensional logic which denotes
the characteristic set of properties of the proposition expressed by the infinitive. The main task of the analysis is
to give an adequate account of the nature of the propositions
expressed by infinitives.

The well-known fact that which proposition is expressed
by an infinitive depends on the sentence in which it occurs
is illustrated by the following two sentences:

(1) John promises Mary to go.

(2) John permits Mary to go.

In (1) the infinitive *to go* expresses the proposition that
John goes; in (2) it expresses the proposition that Mary goes.
So, the semantic content of an infinitive taken in isolation
will have to be variable in some sense of the word.

Our analysis postulates the existence of a third kind of
expression in the language of intensional logic: besides
constants and variables we introduce so-called *context expressions*.[1] Context expressions are expressions the denotation of
which depends in a systematic way on the context. Restricting
ourselves to infinitives, the context relevant for the interpretation of context expressions which occur in the translation of infinitives is determined by the expressions occurring
in the matrix sentence. The context will consist of the denotation of these expressions. So, what has to be defined is
the contribution of expressions to a context. Given such a

definition, we then have to define what the denotation of a context expression given a certain context is.

The syntactic part of our proposal is rather straight-forward. Expressions behaving syntactically more or less like terms, and being semantically interpretable as expressions denoting propositions, have been introduced by Enrique Delacruz in his paper on factives (1976). In this paper he introduced the category of *proposition level terms*. We follow his suggestion to assign infinitives to a similar category. Whereas *that*-phrases are assigned to the category $\overline{T}$, infinitives are assigned to the category $\overline{\overline{T}}$. Their categorial definitions are as follows: $\overline{T} = t/\overline{IV}$ and $\overline{\overline{T}} = t//\overline{IV}$, where the category $\overline{IV}$, the category of proposition level intransitive verbs, as Delacruz calls them, is defined as $t//t$. Consequently, the expression *to* is to be an expression which takes intransitive verb phrases into expressions of category $\overline{\overline{T}}$, i.e., it is to be assigned to the category $\overline{\overline{T}}/IV$. It should be noted that this categorization is chosen mainly for reasons of convenience. We could have analyzed infinitives differently, as ordinary terms, using Thomason's method of leveling in the semantics (1976b). Our semantic analysis is neutral with respect to this choice.

Let us now consider the question how to generate sentences containing infinitives. In this paper we will concentrate on the two simple examples (1) and (2), given above. Although they are simple, these two sentences suffice to illustrate the problems we want to discuss at this moment. In order to be able to generate sentences such as (1) and (2) we have to decide upon the categorization of verbs such as *promise* and *permit*. Consider the following alternatives:

(A) *promise* $\in B_{(IV/\overline{\overline{T}})/T}$; *permit* $\in B_{(IV/T)/\overline{\overline{T}}}$

(B) *promise, permit* $\in B_{(IV/T)/\overline{\overline{T}}}$

The usual strategy is to create a categorial difference
between such verbs as *promise* and *permit* as in (A). Usually
this is motivated by pointing out that these two verbs behave
differently with respect to reflexivization, as the following
examples illustrate:

(3) John promises Mary to shave $\left\{ \begin{array}{l} \text{*him} \\ \text{himself} \\ \text{her} \\ \text{*herself} \end{array} \right\}$.

(4) John permits Mary to shave $\left\{ \begin{array}{l} \text{him} \\ \text{*himself} \\ \text{*her} \\ \text{herself} \end{array} \right\}$.

The asterisk indicates the impossibility of interpreting the
pronoun as being coreferential with *John* or *Mary*. In our
opinion, the strength of this argument for (A) should not be
overestimated. It could well be argued for that reflexive
pronouns should be introduced not as derivatives from syntactic variables (as is done both in Michael Bennett's (1976)
and in Richmond Thomason's (1976a) analyses), but as basic
expressions, syntactically functioning as place reducers on
verbs. In that case, the unacceptability of a sentence like:

(5) Mary washes himself.

would not be explained as an instance of syntactic un-well-
formedness, but as an instance of semantic, sortal incorrectness. Given our analysis of infinitives, a similar explanation
could be given for the unacceptabilities in (3) and (4).

Given the possibility of a satisfactory analysis of
reflexives along these lines, and given the fact that there
seem to be no convincing arguments in favor of (A), we prefer
to base our analysis on (B), according to which there is no
categorial difference between such verbs as *promise* and *permit*.
The syntax of infinitives and sentences containing them has
no further problems to offer. An analysis tree for both (1)
and (2) is:

(6)

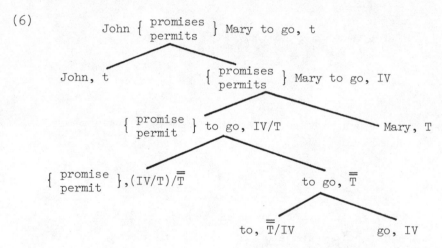

2. *Semantics*

Let us now turn to the semantics of infinitives. To the
language of intensional logic, we add for type e, a set CE_e
of context expressions. We let the expression v_c be an element
of that set. Further, we introduce the following particular
variables:

(7) $P = v_{0,\langle s,\langle\langle s,e\rangle,t\rangle\rangle}$

$P = v_{0,\langle s,\langle\langle s,t\rangle,t\rangle\rangle}$

$P = v_{0,\langle s,\langle\langle s,\langle\langle s,e\rangle,t\rangle\rangle,t\rangle\rangle}$

$Q = v_{0,\langle s,\langle\langle s,\langle\langle s,t\rangle,t\rangle\rangle,t\rangle\rangle}$

Further, we add the following translation rules:

(8)   *to* ⤳ $\hat{P}$ [$\hat{Q}$ [Q {^(P {^v_c})}]]

   that ⤳ $\hat{P}$ [$\hat{Q}$ [Q {p}]]

The resulting translation of an infinitive such as *to walk*
is as follows:

(9) $\hat{P}$ [$\hat{Q}$ [Q {(P {^v_c})}]] (^walk')

By means of the usual rules for lambda conversion and the
usual meaning postulates this can be reduced to:

(10) $\hat{Q}$ [Q {^walk$'_*$ (v_c)}]

In other words, the translation of the infinitive *to walk*
results in an expression which denotes the characteristic set
of properties of the proposition that v_c, some contextually
specified individual, walks. If one compares this with the
translation of the *that*-phrase: *that John walks,*

(11) *that John walks* ⤳ $\hat{P}$ [$\hat{Q}$ [Q {p}]] (^walk$'_{\parallel}$ (j))

which reduces to:

(12) $\hat{Q}$ [Q {^walk$'_*$ (j)}]

one sees that already at this stage the similarity between
infinitives and *that*-phrases is made clear: they denote the
same kind of set-theoretical object.[2]

   Let us now consider the translation of a complete sentence.
Having categorized *promise* and *permit* in the same way, as given
under (B) above, the sentences (1) and (2) translate into the
formulas (13) and (14) respectively:

(13) promise' (^$\hat{Q}$ [Q {^go' {^v_c}}]) (^$\hat{P}$ [P {^m}]) (^j)

(14) permit' (^$\hat{Q}$ [Q {^go' {^v_c}}]) (^$\hat{P}$ [P {^m}]) (^j)

This is of course not yet the result we want. What we want is
promise and *permit* as relations between two individuals and
a proposition. We need the following meaning postulate to
obtain these corresponding extensional relations:

(15) $\lor$M $\land$x $\land P$ $\land Q$ $\Box$ [γ (Q) (P) (x) $\leftrightarrow$ Q {$\hat{p}$ P {$\hat{y}$ M {$^\lor$x,

$$^\lor\text{y, p}\}\}\}]$$

> where γ translates *promise* or *permit* and M is a variable
> of type $\langle$ s, $\langle\langle$ s, t$\rangle$, $\langle$ e, $\langle$ e, t$\rangle\rangle\rangle\rangle$.

Combining this meaning postulate with the substar notation
convention results in the following logically true formula:

(16) $\Box$[λ(Q) (P) (x) $\leftrightarrow$ Q {$\hat{p}$ P {$\hat{y}$ γ_* ($^\lor$x, $^\lor$y, p)}}}]

> where γ translates *promise* or *permit*.

With the help of (15) and (16), (13) and (14) can be reduced
to (17) and (18) respectively:

(17) ((promise$_*^!$ ($^\wedge$go$_*^!$ (v_c))) (m)) (j)

(18) ((permit$_*^!$ ($^\wedge$go$_*^!$ (v_c))) (m)) (j)

For example, (17) expresses that the promise relation holds
between the individual John, the individual Mary, and the
proposition that some contextually specified individual goes.
This is of course not yet exactly what we want to end up with,
because the corresponding sentence (1) expresses that the
promise relation holds between John, Mary, and the proposition
that John goes. If this result is to be obtained, we have
to make sure that in (17) John is the contextually specified
individual to which the context expression v_c refers. In
(18), however, Mary must be the contextually specified individual to which the context expression v_c refers, if this
formula is to express what the corresponding sentence (2)

expresses. Only if we succeed in obtaining these interpretations for arbitrary models, we will have captured the full
meaning of the sentences (1) and (2).

Let us therefore now turn to the model theory. What we need
to obtain these interpretations is the following. First, we
need a definition of what a context is. Second, we need to
know what kinds of expressions contribute to the context, and
what their contribution consists of. This information will be
given in the form of a definition of *context change*. And,
finally, we need a definition of the denotation of context
expressions. To this purpose we introduce the notion of a
context assignment function. It should be noted that context
expressions are 'context dependent' in two senses. Not only
are their denotations to be taken from contextually introduced
individuals, but also which such individual has to be taken
depends on the context. In the case of infinitives it depends
on the meaning of the main verb of the matrix sentence.

So what has at least to be accounted for is the contribution to the context of expressions denoting individuals and
of expressions such as promise' and permit'. Expressions
denoting individuals will contribute their denotation to the
context. It is their denotations that are needed in the
interpretation of context expressions. The predicate constants
translating verbs such as *promise* and *permit* will contribute
the relations in intension which they express. For it is
their meaning which plays a role in the interpretation of
context expressions.

The notion of a context based on a model is defined by the
following two definitions. In what follows τ stands for the
type $\langle s, \langle\langle s, t\rangle, \langle e, \langle e, t\rangle\rangle\rangle\rangle$.

Definition 1: Let 𝔄 be a model; then the *set of i-place*

contexts based on $\mathfrak{A}$, $C^{(i),\mathfrak{A}}$, is the set $(D_e \cup D_\tau)^i$, in which D_e and D_τ are domains based on $\mathfrak{A}$.

Definition 2: Let $\mathfrak{A}$ be a model; then the *set of all contexts based on* $\mathfrak{A}$, $C^{\mathfrak{A}}$, is the set $\underset{i \geq 0}{U} C^{(i)}$.

So a context is an ordered sequence consisting of individuals (elements of D_e) and relations in intension between two individuals and a proposition (elements of D_τ). At this moment, these are the only things we need, but the definition of context can easily be generalized to contain entities of domains corresponding to other types as well. The role of the individuals in the context will be clear: they constitute the possible denotations of subsequently occurring context expressions. The role of the relations in intension is to specify under the scope of which predicate, if any, certain individuals are introduced, and under the scope of which predicate a suitable denotation for a context expression is to be found. This last aspect will enable us to account for the different so-called control properties of verbs such as *promise* and *permit*.

Having defined what a context is, let us now consider how it is built up. The definition of this process takes the form of a recursive definition of the context change brought about by an expression in a given context, relative to a certain set of parameters. In what follows, σ stands for the type $\langle\langle s, f(\overline{\overline{T}})\rangle, f(IV/T)\rangle$.

Definition 3: The *context change* of an expression α in a context c, relative to a model $\mathfrak{A}$, an index k, an assignment function g, and a context assignment function f, $K^{\mathfrak{A},k,g,f}$, is that function from $(ME_a \times C) \rightarrow C$ such that:

(i) If $\alpha \in CON_e$, then $K^{\mathfrak{A},k,g,f}(\alpha, c) = c^* \langle F(\alpha)(k) \rangle$.

(ii) If $\alpha \in VAR_e$, then $K^{\mathfrak{A},k,g,f}(\alpha, c) = c^* \langle g(\alpha) \rangle$.

(iii) If $\alpha \in CE_e$, then $K^{\mathfrak{A},k,g,f}(\alpha, c) = c^* \langle f(\alpha, c) \rangle$.

(iv) (a) If $\alpha \in CON_\tau$, then $K^{\mathfrak{A},k,g,f}(\alpha, c) = c^* \langle F(\alpha) \rangle$.

  (b) If $\alpha \in CON_\tau$, then $K^{\mathfrak{A},k,g,F}(\alpha, c) = c^* \langle F(\alpha_*) \rangle$.

(v) If α is a constant, variable, or context expression other than specified under (i)-(iv), then
$K^{\mathfrak{A},k,g,f}(\alpha, c) = c$.

(vi) If $\alpha = \beta(\gamma)$ and α is of the form $(\dots(\delta(\gamma_1))\dots)(\gamma_n)$, $n \geq 1$, then

  (a) If $\delta \in (CON_a \cup VAR_a)$, then $K^{\mathfrak{A},k,g,f}(\alpha, c) =$
  $K^{\mathfrak{A},k,g,f}(\gamma_1, (\dots, K^{\mathfrak{A},k,g,f}(\gamma_{n-1},$
  $K^{\mathfrak{A},k,g,f}(\delta, K^{\mathfrak{A},k,g,f}(\gamma_n, c)))\dots))$.

  (b) If δ is of the form $\lambda \nu \mu$, then $K^{\mathfrak{A},k,g,f}(\alpha, c) =$
  $K^{\mathfrak{A},k,g,f}(\alpha', c)$, where

$$\alpha' = \beta(\gamma)\left[\frac{\delta(\gamma_1)}{\mu[\nu/\gamma_1]}\right].$$

(vii) If $\alpha = \wedge \nu \phi$, $\vee \nu \phi$ or $\neg \phi$, then $K^{\mathfrak{A},k,g,f}(\alpha, c) =$
$K^{\mathfrak{A},k,g,f}(\phi, c)$.

(viii) If $\alpha = \phi \wedge \psi$, $\phi \vee \psi$, then $K^{\mathfrak{A},k,g,f}(\alpha, c) =$
$K^{\mathfrak{A},k,g,f}(\psi, c), K^{\mathfrak{A},k,g,f}(\phi, c)$.

(ix) If $\alpha = {}^{\wedge}\beta$, ${}^{\vee}\beta$, $\lambda\nu\ \beta$, then $K^{\mathfrak{A},k,g,f}(\alpha,\ c) =$

$K^{\mathfrak{A},k,g,f}(\beta,\ c)$.

In this definition * is the concatenation operation on sequences. According to clauses (i)-(iv), the only basic expressions that change the context are, for the moment, constants, variables, and context expressions of type e, and constants of the types τ and σ (e.g., 'promise$_*^!$ and promise'). According to clause (v), all constants and variables of other types give rise to a null change. Clauses (vi)-(ix) define the context change of compound expressions in terms of the context change of their compounds. The most important clause is clause (vi). It defines the context change induced by expressions which have a function argument structure.[3] To see what it says, consider the translation of sentence (1), which has a function argument structure:

(17) $((\text{promise}_*^!\ ({}^{\wedge}\text{go}_*^!\ (v_c)))\ (m))\ (j)$

According to clause (vi), first the individual constant j, then the predicate constant promise$_*^!$, then the constant m, and finally the proposition ${}^{\wedge}\text{go}_*^!\ (v_c)$ contribute to the context. The reason for this is that in the evaluation of formulas such as (17), the infinitive has to be evaluated with respect to a context to which the main predicate and also the subject and indirect object have already contributed. A strategy in which, quite generally, first the argument of a function argument expression contributes, and then the function expression, does not give the right results. In that case the main predicate would contribute after the infinitive had contributed. The inverse strategy of letting quite generally first the function expression contribute, and then the argument, does not work either. In that case the

subject and indirect object would contribute after the
infinitive, giving wrong results as well. What seems to be
needed, and what is expressed in this definition, is that
the order in which the parts of a complex function argument
expression contribute to the context reflects the linear
order of the corresponding expressions in the surface structure of natural language. And if you think of the way in which
a context is built up in psychological terms, as it would be
built up by an actual language user, this seems a quite natural
thing.

Let us now turn to the definition of a context assignment
function. As we have said above, which contextually introduced individual is assigned to a context expression depends
on the meaning of the predicate under the scope of which that
context expression occurs. This is expressed in the definition
below. In order to be able to formulate the appropriate
restrictions on context assignment functions, it is convenient
to have means to refer to the different elements of a certain
context. If $c^{(i)}$ is an i-place context, then $c_k^{(i)}$ is the k-th
element of that context.

Definition 4: Let $\mathfrak{A}$ be a model; then a *context assignment
function* f based on $\mathfrak{A}$ is a function from $(CE_e \times C) \to D_e$
such that if $\alpha \in CE_e$ and $c^{(i)} \in C$, then either

   (i) $\exists k$: $c_k^{(i)} = F \text{ (promise}_*^!) \text{ \& } [\forall \ell: \ell > k \Rightarrow c^{(i)} \notin D_\tau]$

       & $f(\alpha, c^{(i)}) = c_{k-1}$, or

  (ii) $\exists k$: $c_k^{(i)} = F \text{ (permit}_*^!) \text{ \& } [\forall \ell: \ell > k \Rightarrow c^{(i)} \notin D_\tau]$

       $f(\alpha, c^{(i)}) = c_{k+1}$, or

 (iii) $f(\alpha, c^{(i)})$ is undefined.

So a context assignment function will always assign to a
context expression which occurs directly under the scope of
the predicate $promise_*^!$, that element in the context that
immediately precedes the contribution of $promise_*^!$. Definition
4 guarantees that this element of the context will always be
the individual denoted by the subject of $promise_*^!$. If the
context expression occurs directly under the scope of $permit_*^!$,
then it is assigned the element of the context immediately
following the contribution of $permit_*^!$, being the individual
denoted by its indirect object. These clauses suffice for the
limited number of infinitive-taking verbs under consideration
here. The definitions can easily be extended to deal with the
control properties of other such verbs.

Given these definitions of context, context change, and
context assignment function, we can now state the following
general definitions of the denotation of expressions:

Definition 5: Let $\mathfrak{A}$ be a model, k an index, g an ordinary
assignment function, and c a context based on $\mathfrak{A}$, then the
denotation of α with respect to $\mathfrak{A}$, k, g, f, and c,
written as $\alpha^{\mathfrak{A},k,g,f,c}$, is defined as follows:

(i) If $\alpha \in \mathrm{CON}_a$, then $\alpha^{\mathfrak{A},k,g,f,c} = F(\alpha)(k)$.

(ii) If $\alpha \in \mathrm{VAR}_a$, then $\alpha^{\mathfrak{A},k,g,f,c} = g(\alpha)$.

(iii) If $\alpha \in \mathrm{CE}_a$, then $\alpha^{\mathfrak{A},k,g,f,c} = f(\alpha, c)$.

(iv) If $\alpha = \beta(\gamma)$, and α is of the form $(\ldots (\delta(\gamma_1)) \ldots)$
(γ_n), $n \geq 1$, then:

(a) If $\delta \in (\mathrm{CON}_a \cup \mathrm{VAR}_a)$, $a \in$ Type, then
$$\alpha^{\mathfrak{A},k,g,f,c} = ((\ldots (\delta^{\mathfrak{A},k,g,f,c^1}(\gamma_1^{\mathfrak{A},k,g,f,c^n}))$$

$$\ldots)\ (\gamma_{n-1}^{\ \mathfrak{A},k,g,f,c^2}))\ (\gamma_n^{\ \mathfrak{A},k,g,f,c}),$$

where $c^1 = K^{\mathfrak{A},k,g,f}\ (\gamma_n,\ c)$

$c^2 = K^{\mathfrak{A},k,g,f}\ (\delta,\ c\ )$

$c^m = K^{\mathfrak{A},k,g,f}\ (\gamma_{n-(m-2)},c^{m-1}),$

for all m: $2 < m \leq n$.

(b) If δ is of the form $\lambda\nu\ \mu$, then $\alpha^{\mathfrak{A},k,g,f,c} = \alpha'^{\ \mathfrak{A},k,g,f,c}$, where

$$\alpha' = \beta\ (\gamma)\ \left[\frac{\delta\ (\gamma_1)}{\mu\ [\nu\ /\ \gamma_1]}\right]\ .$$

(v) If $\alpha = \phi \wedge \psi$, then $\alpha^{\mathfrak{A},k,g,f,c} = 1$ iff $\phi^{\mathfrak{A},k,g,f,c} = 1$

and $\psi^{\mathfrak{A},k,g,f,c'} = 1$, where $c' = K^{\mathfrak{A},k,g,f}\ (\phi,\ c)$.

(vi) If $\alpha = \vee\nu\ \phi$, then $\alpha^{\mathfrak{A},k,g,f,c} = 1$ iff there exists

an x in D_a (ν being a variable of type a) such that

$\phi^{\mathfrak{A},k,g',f,c} = 1$, where g' is like g except for the

possible difference that g' $(\nu) = x$.

The clauses for the other connectives and identity are
analogous to clause (v), those for lambda expressions, negation, the cap- and cupoperators and the universal quantifier
are analogous to clause (vi).

The complexity of clause (iv) in this definition has
essentially the same source as the complexity of clause (vi)
in Definition 3, the definition of context change. It is
caused by the discrepancy which exists between the linear

order of the various expressions in the surface structure and the function argument structure of the corresponding translation. The linear order of surface structure plays an essential role in the evaluation of corresponding formulas; it determines what the context in each step of the evaluation process is.[4]

Let us consider some examples in order to illustrate the workings of these definitions. The first example considers the evaluation of the formula which translates sentence (1), *John promises Mary to go.*

Example 1:

$$[\![((\text{promise}_*^! (^{\wedge}\text{go}_*^! (v_c))) (m)) (j)]\!]^{\mathfrak{u},k,g,f,c} = 1 \text{ iff}$$

$$(([\![\text{promise}_*^!]\!]^{\mathfrak{u},k,g,f,c^1} ([\![^{\wedge}\text{go}_*^! (v_c)]\!]^{\mathfrak{u},k,g,f,c^3}))$$

$$([\![m]\!]^{\mathfrak{u},k,g,f,c^2})) ([\![j]\!]^{\mathfrak{u},k,g,f,c}) = 1$$

where $c^1 = K^{\mathfrak{u},k,g,f} (j, c) = \langle ..., F (j) (k) \rangle$

$\qquad c^2 = K^{\mathfrak{u},k,g,f} (\text{promise}_*^!, c^1) = \langle ..., F (j) (k),$

$\qquad\qquad F (\text{promise}_*^!) \rangle$

$\qquad c^3 = K^{\mathfrak{u},k,g,f} (m, c^2) = \langle ..., F (j) (k),$

$\qquad\qquad F (\text{promise}_*^!), F (m) (k) \rangle$

Let F (j) (k) be the individual John, and F (m) (k) the individual Mary.

$[\![^{\wedge}\text{go}_*^! (v_c)]\!]^{\mathfrak{u},k,g,f,c^3}$ is that element ρ from 2^I (I is the set of indices such that ρ (i) = 1 iff $[\![\text{go}_*^! (v_c)]\!]^{\mathfrak{u},i,g,f,c^3} = 1$, i.e., iff $[\![\text{go}_*^!]\!]^{\mathfrak{u},i,g,f,c^4} ([\![v_c]\!]^{\mathfrak{u},i,g,f,c^3}) = 1$

where $[\![v_c]\!]^{\mathfrak{u},i,g,f,c^3} = f (v_c, c^3) = F (j) (k),$

which is the individual John.

So, the conditions under which the formula representing the sentence *John promises Mary to go* is true are such that it is true in an arbitrary model, with respect to an index, an assignment function, a context assignment function, and a context if and only if the individual John, the individual Mary, and the proposition that John goes stand in the promise relation.

Let us now consider the evaluation of the translation of sentence (2), *John permits Mary to go*.

Example 2:

$$[\![((permit_*^! \ (^\wedge go_*^! \ (v_c))) \ (m)) \ (j)]\!] \ ^{\mathfrak{A},k,g,f,c}$$

The evaluation of this formula runs completely parallel to that of the previous example, but now $c^3 = \langle \ ..., F \ (j) \ (k),$ F (permit$_*^!$), F (m) (k)$\rangle$ and, therefore, $f \ (v_c, \ c^3) = F \ (m) \ (k)$, being the individual Mary.

So, the sentence *John permits Mary to go* is true if and only if the individual John, the individual Mary, and the proposition that Mary goes stand in the permit relation. So, these two examples show that our analysis treats correctly the differences between the sentences (1) and (2).

It can also be shown that more complex sentences, such as (19) - (21) are treated in the right way:

(19) John promises Mary to promise Bill to go.

(20) A man promises Mary to go.

(21) Every man promises Mary to go.

We will end this section by giving the evaluation of the formula representing sentence (21):

Example 3:

$[\![\; \wedge u \; [man_*^! (u) \to [((promise_*^! (^\wedge go_*^! (v_c))) (m))$

$(u)]]]\!] \; ^{\mathfrak{A},k,g,f,c} = 1$ iff for all $x \in D_e$:

$[\![man_*^! (u) \to ((promise_*^! (^\wedge go_*^! (v_c))) (m)) (u)]\!] \; ^{\mathfrak{A},k,g',f,c} = 1$,

where g' is like g except for the possible difference that

g' (u) = x

$[\![man_*^! (u) \to ((promise_*^! (^\wedge go_*^! (v_c))) (m)) (u)]\!] \; ^{\mathfrak{A},k,g',f,c} = 1$

iff it is not the case that $[\![man_*^! (u)]\!] \; ^{\mathfrak{A},k,g',f,c} = 1$ and

$[\![((promise_*^! (\hat{g}o_*^! (v_c))) (m)) (u)]\!] \; ^{\mathfrak{A},k,g',f,c'} = 0$

where $c' = K \; ^{\mathfrak{A},k,g',f} (man_*^! (u), c) = \langle ..., g' (u) \rangle$

In order to see that the context-expression v_c is interpreted

correctly, consider the case where $[\![man_*^! (u)]\!] \; ^{\mathfrak{A},k,g',f,c} = 1$ and

$[\![((promise_*^! (^\wedge go_*^! (v_c))) (m)) (u)]\!] \; ^{\mathfrak{A},k,g',f,c'} = 1$ iff

$(([\![promise_*^!]\!] \; ^{\mathfrak{A},k,g',f,c'^1} ([\![^\wedge go'(v_c)]\!] ^{...,c'^3}))$

$\quad ([\![m]\!] ^{...,c'^2})) ([\![u]\!] ^{...,c'}) = 1$

where $c'^1 = K \; ^{\mathfrak{A},k,g',f} (u, c') = \langle ..., g' (u), g' (u) \rangle$

$\quad c'^2 = K \; ^{\mathfrak{A},k,g',f} (promise', c'^1) =$

$\quad\quad\quad \langle ..., g' (u), g' (u), F (promise') \rangle$

$\quad c'^3 = K \; ^{\mathfrak{A},k,g',f} (m, c'^2) = \langle ..., g' (u), g' (u),$

$\quad\quad\quad F (promise'), F (m) (k) \rangle$

$[\![^\wedge go_*^! (v_c)]\!] \; ^{\mathfrak{A},k,g',f,c'^3}$ is that element ρ from 2^I such that

$\rho (i) = 1$ iff $[\![go_*^! (v_c)]\!] \; ^{\mathfrak{A},i,g',f,c'^3} = 1$, i.e., iff

$$[\![go^!_*]\!]^{\,\mathfrak{u},i,g',f,c'^4} ([\![v_c]\!]^{\,\mathfrak{u},i,g',f,c'^3}) = 1$$

where $[\![v_c]\!]^{\,\mathfrak{u},i,g',f,c'^3} = f\,(v_c,\,c'^3) = g'\,(u)$

So, the sentence (21) is true if and only if for every individual x which is a man, the individual x, the individual Mary, and the proposition that x goes stand in the promise relation.

3. *Concluding Remarks*

In this section we will make a few remarks about the application of context expressions in other cases than the analysis of infinitives. An important case concerns the interpretation of reduced verbs. One might translate a sentence like *John gives a book,* in which apparently a three-place verb has been reduced to a two-place verb, in such a way that a context expression occurs in the place of the indirect object. This would mean that the syntactic operation of place reduction semantically amounts to the introduction of a context expression. This would explain two things. First, it would explain why *John gives a book* is appropriate only if it is part of a larger stretch of discourse. For only in that case can a suitable denotation for the context expression be found. Second, it would explain the difference in meaning between *John gives a book* and *John gives someone a book.* [5]

Other possible applications of the notions context and context expression concern anaphoric pronominal reference. As we have mentioned above, since we do not make a categorial difference between verbs like *promise* and *permit,* the usual strategy of deriving reflexives from syntactic variables seems no longer available. In the spirit of the present proposal, one could consider reflexive pronouns to be basic expressions, syntactically functioning as place reducers, and being semantically interpreted as a special kind of context expression which takes its denotation from that part of the context which is built up by expressions occurring in the smallest sentence in which the reflexive itself occurs. Assuming the domain of individuals to be divided into male, female, and other individuals, the sentence *Mary washes himself* would lack a truth value, because within the context built up by the expressions occurring in this sentence no male individual has been introduced. The unacceptability of sentences such as *John promises Mary to wash herself* and *John permits Mary to wash himself* would be explained in a similar way.

Yet another kind of context expression may be exemplified by nonreflexive anaphoric pronouns. They would have to be assigned an individual which occurs only in that part of the context which is built up by expressions which are outside the smallest sentence in which the anaphoric pronoun occurs. Interpreting reflexive and nonreflexive pronouns in this way would mean that sentence boundaries must be reflected in the context, but this does not seem to be a substantial problem. This way of handling anaphoric reference, which seems to resemble an interpretative-semantics point of view, may be more appropriate for treating some of the notoriously diffi- cult cases of pronominal reference, such as pronouns of laziness and anaphoric reference in longer discourse.[6] Another advantage might be that the syntax will be more like a surface syntax.

A last remark concerns the context contribution of quantified term-phrases. Consider indefinite term-phrases, which are analyzed by means of the existential quantifier. As far as the interpretation of context expressions occurring in

infinitives is concerned, clause (vii) of Definition 3,
according to which quantifiers as such do not contribute to
the context, gives the right results. However, if we introduce anaphoric context expressions, it will become necessary
to refer to the context contribution of quantified sentences
as such. Their context contribution seems to consist in the
introduction of some individual for which the sentence in the
scope of the existential quantifier holds. This is expressed
in the following definition.

Definition 6: $K^{\mathfrak{A},k,g,f}(\vee\nu\ \phi,\ c) = K^{\mathfrak{A},k,g',f}(\phi,\ c)$,

where g' is like g except for the possible difference that:

either, there is an x in D_a (if ν is a variable of type a)

such that g' $(\nu) = x$ and $\phi^{\mathfrak{A},k,g',f,c} = 1$, or g' $(\nu) = \not\!c$,

where $\not\!c$ is a special null individual.

So, if there is no individual for which the sentence in the
scope of the quantifier is true (i.e., if the quantified
sentence as a whole is false), then a special null individual
is introduced in the context. If the definition of denotation
is changed in such a way that any sentence containing an
expression which refers to this null individual is false, then
the unacceptability of the sentence *Mary didn't kiss a boy
and he had red hair* can be explained by showing that it is a
contradiction.

We hope that these short and rather speculative remarks
provide some support for the claim that the notions of context
and context expression can be adequate instruments for the
analysis of other phenomena than infinitives.

Acknowledgments

The preparation of this paper was supported by the Netherlands
Organization for the Advancement of Pure Research (Z.W.O.).
We would like to thank Renate Bartsch, Theo Janssen, and Ewan
Klein for their comments on an earlier version of this paper.

Notes

1. These context expressions should not be confused with
Roland Hausser's context variables (see Hausser 1978). In some
respects Hausser's approach is akin in spirit to ours, but
there is a fundamental difference: Hausser's context variables
are in a reconstruction process replaced by linguistic entities
from the linguistic context. In our approach, as will become
clear later in this paper, the denotations of context expressions are identified with the denotation of other expressions
in the context. We think that our kind of approach is more
natural and is less likely to break the law of compositionality
of interpretation.

2. This means that verbs which take both a *that*-complement
and an infinitival complement, although for syntactic reasons
assigned to different syntactic categories, on the semantic
level express the same relation.

3. A reason for the rather complicated formulation of this
clause is that if it is formulated this way, the validity
(under the usual conditions) of lambda conversion is guaran-
teed also for expressions containing context-expressions.

4. Another, related reason is the one given in note 3.

5. As a matter of fact, David Dowty (see his article in
the present volume) has proposed a treatment of place reduction of verbs semantically amounting to existential quantification. Such an analysis would make *John gives a book*

and *John gives someone a book* equivalent, which clearly
is not the case.

6. Jim McCawley suggested that another application might
be the analysis of phenomena usually analyzed as cases of
Super Equi-NP Deletion such as *John thinks that it is wise
to promise Bill to go.*

References

Bennett, Michael. 1976. "A Variation and Extension of a
Montague Fragment of English." In Partee, ed., 1976.

Delacruz, Enrique B. 1976. "Factives and Proposition Level
Constructions in Montague Grammar." In Partee, ed., 1976.

Hausser, Roland R. 1978. "How Do Pronouns Denote?" In Frank
Heny and Helmut Schnelle, eds., *Syntax and Semantics,
Vol. 10: Selections from the Third Groningen Round Table.*
New York: Academic Press.

Partee, Barbara H. 1976. "Some Transformational Extensions
of Montague Grammar." In Partee, ed., 1976.

————, ed. 1976. *Montague Grammar.* New York: Academic Press.

Thomason, Richmond H. 1976a. "Some Extensions of Montague
Grammar." In Partee, ed., 1976.

————. 1976b. "On the Semantic Interpretation of the
Thomason 1972 Fragment." Ms.

A PTQ Semantics for Sortal Incorrectness

James Waldo

In this paper I propose a way of dealing, in a Montague
framework, with sentences which are sortally incorrect. I take
as paradigms of sortally incorrect sentences strings such as

(1) The theory of relativity is shiny.

(2) The taste of lemon is breakable.

On a very rough, intuitive level, one can characterize
sortally incorrect sentences as those which are deviant
because they predicate of an object some property which
cannot be either sensibly affirmed or sensibly denied of
that object because the object is of the wrong sort.

For philosophical foundation this paper relies heavily
on Thomason's work on sortal incorrectness (1972). Specifically, I will assume that Thomason has established the
following:

I. Simple sentences (i.e., those that do not translate into
a formal language as having a truth value determined by
some truth function of components) which are sortally
incorrect have no truth value.

II. A nonsimple sentence whose components are sortally
incorrect may be true, false, or neither true nor false.

III. Since sortal incorrectness is closely tied to the truth
     of a sentence, the proper place to deal with sortal
     incorrectness in a grammar is the semantic component
     of that grammar.

I will also follow Thomason's lead in that Van Fraasen's
method of supervaluations will play a central role in the
semantics used. The semantics differs quite a bit from
Thomason's, however, as the sorted semantics given by Thomason
was for a simple first-order extensional logic, while the
sorted semantics given here is for a higher-order intensional
logic.

The fragment given here is an extension of that given by
Montague in his article "The Proper Treatment of Quantification in Ordinary English" (1974) (hereafter referred to as
PTQ). The major revision proposed will be to the semantics
of that fragment. However, it is also necessary to extend the
PTQ syntax and translation rules to allow for the generation
of some paradigm sortally incorrect sentences. This change
amounts to adding adjectives and a 'be' of predication to the
fragment. In adding adjectives I have borrowed heavily from
Bennett's treatment (1974), ignoring a number of problems
which have to do with adjectives but which do not concern
sortal incorrectness. The addition of the 'be' of predication
is made necessary for reasons which are spelled out later.

Following tradition, I will first present an addition to
the syntax of PTQ. The resulting set of rules will generate
a subset of the sentences of English, a number of which are
sortally incorrect. I will then give a semantics for an
artificial language. Finally, I will give an addition to the
translation rules of PTQ which will allow us to map the
strings generated by the syntax to formulas in the formal
language. A final section is devoted to some examples which

show how the system works. Since this system is an extension
of PTQ, only those features which add to or replace features
of the PTQ system will be mentioned.

Syntax

In addition to the basic categories of PTQ we will add:

$$B_{adj} = B_{CN/CN} = \{shiny, breakable, big, bald, difficult\}$$

$$B_{IV/adj} = \{be_p\}$$

Further, the category of basic common noun phrases, B_{CN}, is
to be extended to include the lexical items 'theory of relativity', 'taste of lemon', 'king of France'.

One minor change is necessary in the existing syntactic
rules of PTQ:

S4. If $\alpha \subset P_{t/IV}$ and $\delta \in P_{IV}$, then $F_4\ (\alpha,\ \delta) \in P_t$, where

$F_4\ (\alpha,\ \delta) = \alpha\ \delta'$ and δ' is the result of replacing the

first verb (i.e., member of B_{IV}, B_{TV}, $B_{IV//IV}$, or

$B_{IV/adj}$) in δ by its third person singular present.

Two rules must be added to the syntax.

S18. If $\gamma \in B_{adj}$ and $\zeta \in P_{CN}$, then $F_5\ (\gamma,\ \zeta) \in P_{CN}$,

where $F_5\ (\gamma,\ \zeta) = \gamma\ \zeta$.

S19. If $\delta \in B_{IV/adj}$ and $\gamma \in B_{adj}$, then $F_{16}\ (\delta,\ \gamma) \in P_{IV}$, where

$F_{16}\ (\delta,\ \gamma) = \delta'\ \gamma$ where δ' is δ with the subscript removed.

It should be noted that rules S18 and S19 are both rules of
functional application, even though they are numbered in such
a way that they do not appear in that group of rules. This
numbering was done so that the numbering of rules in the PTQ
system could remain unchanged.

This extension of the syntax allows for the generation of sentences with both pre-common-noun and predicate adjectives. It also allows for the generation of a number of sentences which ought, on a Thomason-type semantic theory, to receive no truth value in the semantics.

Though Montague did not include adjectives in his system PTQ, he did include them in earlier grammars for fragments of English such as those presented in his articles "English as a Formal Language" (1974) and "Universal Grammar" (1974). The type assignment to adjectives of CN/CN follows his practice in those articles. The change in rule S4 is solely for the purpose of allowing the new verb, the 'be$_p$' of predication, to be tensed in the formation of sentences in which it is the main verb. Rule S18 follows the fragment given by Bennett (1974) and allows for the generation of adjectives in pre-common-noun position. Rule 19 is included to allow for the generation of predicate-adjective constructions. The reason for introducing the 'be$_p$' of predication will be discussed in the section on translation.

Semantics

Two notions which will be central to the following sorted semantics are those of a supervaluation and a partial function. Just as in the Thomason system, the value of a formula will be determined by a supervaluation. The notion of a partial function will be used to account for sentences which lack truth values.

If A and B are sets, a partial function f from A to B is a function such that for any $a \in A$, $f(a) \in B$ or $f(a)$ is undefined. We can consider all functions to be partial functions, and further distinguish two sorts of special cases of partial functions. One of these special sorts is the

null function from A to B, which is a function f such that
for all a $\in$ A, where A is the domain of f, f(a) is undefined.
The other special case is that of a *complete function* from A to
B, which is a function f such that for all a $\in$ A, f(a) $\in$ B.
It should be noted that for any partial function there is a
function f^c (possibly null) with domain A' = $\{x \in A: f(x) \in B\}$
which is a complete function from A' to B. In what follows,
such a function will be called the *complete subfunction* of f.

The set of types and meaningful expressions in our sorted
logic will be similar to that given for the intensional logic
in PTQ. Let A, I, J be any sets, which will be regarded as
the set of entities, the set of possible worlds, and the
set of times respectively. If a is a type, then the set of
possible denotations of type a with respect to A, I, J can
be given by the following recursive definition:

$$D_{e,A,I,J} = A$$

$$D_{t,A,I,J} = \{0, 1\}$$

$$D_{\langle a,b \rangle,A,I,J} = \text{the set of partial functions with domain}$$
$$D_{a,A,I,J} \text{ and range } D_{b,A,I,J}$$

$$D_{\langle s,a \rangle,A,I,J} = \text{the set of partial functions with domain}$$
$$I \times J \text{ and range } D_{a,A,I,J}$$

The sortal specification, E, is the function from the set
of partial functions to the set of domains of their complete
subfunction. More precisedly, if $\alpha \in D_{\langle a,b \rangle,A,I,J}$, E ($\alpha$) =
$\{x \in D_{a,A,I,J}: \alpha (x) \in D_{b,A,I,J}\}$ and if $\alpha \in D_{\langle s,a \rangle,A,I,J}$,
E (α) = $\{x \in I \times J: \alpha (x) \in D_{a,A,I,J}\}$.

We can now define an interpretation relative to E, UE,
as a quintuple $\langle A, I, J, \leq, F \rangle$ such that:

1. A, I, J are nonempty sets.

2. $\leq$ is a simple (linear) ordering on J.

3. F is a function having as its domain the set of all constants.

4. whenever $a \in$ Type and $\alpha \in \text{Con}_a$, $F(\alpha) \in S_{a,A,I,J} = D_{\langle s,a \rangle,A,I,J}$.

Suppose UE is an interpretation having the form $\langle A, I, J, \leq, F \rangle$, and g is a UE assignment of values to variables, that is, a function having as its domain the set of all variables and such that $g(u) \in D_{a,A,I,J}$ whenever u is a variable of type a. If α is a meaningful expression, we shall understand by $\alpha^{UE,g}$ the intension of α with respect to UE and g; and if $\langle i, j \rangle \in I \times J$ then $\alpha^{UE,i,j,g}$ is to be the extension of α with respect to UE, i, j, and g — that is, $\alpha^{UE,g}(\langle i, j \rangle)$ or:

a. If $\langle i, j \rangle \in E(\alpha^{UE,g})$ then $\alpha^{UE,g}(\langle i, j \rangle)$ is the value of the partial function which is the intension of α when applied to the point of reference $(\langle i, j \rangle)$.

b. If $\langle i, j \rangle \notin E(\alpha^{UE,g})$ then $\alpha^{UE,g}(\langle i, j \rangle)$ is undefined.

These notions can be introduced by the following recursive definition:

1. If α is a constant, then $\alpha^{UE,i,j,g}$ is $F(\alpha)(\langle i, j \rangle)$.

2. If α is a variable, then $\alpha^{UE,i,j,g}$ is $g(\alpha)$.

3. If $\alpha \in ME_a$ and u a variable of type b, then $[\lambda u \, \alpha]^{UE,i,j,g}$ is that partial function h with domain $D_{b,A,I,J}$ such that whenever x is in that domain, h(x)

is $\alpha^{UE,i,j,g'}$ where g' is a UE assignment of values to variables just like g except for the possible difference that g'(u) = x.

4. If $\alpha \in ME_{\langle a,b \rangle}$ and $\beta \in ME_a$, then $[\alpha(\beta)]^{UE,i,j,g}$ is:

   a. Undefined if $(\alpha)^{UE,i,j,g}$ or $(\beta)^{UE,i,j,g}$ is undefined.

   b. $(\alpha)^{UE,i,j,g} [(\beta)^{UE,i,j,g}]$ otherwise.

5. If α, $\beta \in ME_a$, then $[\alpha = \beta]^{UE,i,j,g}$ is:

   a. 1 iff $\alpha^{UE,i,j,g}$ is $\beta^{UE,i,j,g}$ and both are defined.

   b. 0 iff $\alpha^{UE,i,j,g}$ is not $\beta^{UE,i,j,g}$ and both are defined.

   c. Undefined if either $\alpha^{UE,i,j,g}$ or $\beta^{UE,i,j,g}$ is undefined.

6. If $\psi \subseteq ME_t$, then $[\neg \phi]^{UE,i,j,g}$ is:

   a. 1 iff $[\neg \phi]^{I^+,i,j,g^*}$ is $\langle 1, 1 \rangle$ for all $I^+ \in In^+$ (I^+, In^+, and g^* to be defined below).

   b. 0 iff $[\neg \phi]^{I^+,i,j,g^*}$ is $\langle 0, 0 \rangle$ for all $I^+ \in In^+$.

   c. Undefined otherwise.

7. If ϕ, $\psi \in ME_t$, then $[\phi \wedge \psi]^{UE,i,j,g}$ is:

   a. 1 iff $[\phi \wedge \psi]^{I^+,i,j,g^*}$ is $\langle 1, 1 \rangle$ for all $I^+ \in In^+$.

   b. 0 iff $[\phi \wedge \psi]^{I^+,i,j,g^*}$ is $\langle 0, 0 \rangle$ for all $I^+ \in In^+$.

   c. Undefined otherwise.

   Similarly for $\vee$, $\rightarrow$, and $\leftrightarrow$.

8. If $\phi \in ME_t$ and u a variable of type a, then $[\vee u \ \phi]^{UE,i,j,g}$ is:

a. 1 iff there exists some $x \in D_{a,A,I,J}$ such that $[\phi]^{UE,i,j,g'}$ is 1, with g' defined as above.

b. 0 iff there exists some $x \in D_{a,A,I,J}$ such that $[\phi]^{UE,i,j,g'}$ is defined, and for all such $x \in D_{a,A,I,J}$, $[\phi]^{UE,i,j,g'}$ is 0.

c. Undefined otherwise.

9. If $\phi \in ME_t$ and u a variable of type a, then $[\wedge u \ \phi]^{UE,i,j,g}$ is:

a. 1 iff for some $x \in D_{a,A,I,J}$, $[\phi]^{UE,i,j,g'}$ is defined and for all $x \in D_{a,A,I,J}$ such that $[\phi]^{UE,i,j,g'}$ is defined, $[\phi]^{UE,i,j,g'}$ is 1, with g' defined as above.

b. 0 iff there exists some $x \in D_{a,A,I,J}$ such that $[\phi]^{UE,i,j,g'}$ is 0, with g' defined as above.

c. Undefined otherwise.

10. If $\phi \in ME_t$, then $[\Box\phi]^{UE,i,j,g}$ is:

a. 1 iff $[\phi]^{UE,i',j',g}$ is 1 for all $\langle i', j'\rangle \in I \times J$.

b. 0 iff $[\phi]^{UE,i',j',g}$ is 0 for all $\langle i', j'\rangle \in I \times J$.

c. Undefined otherwise.

Similarly for W and H.

11. If $\alpha \in ME_a$, then $[^\wedge\alpha]^{UE,i,j,g}$ is that partial function h with domain $I \times J$ such that whenever $\langle i, j\rangle \in I \times J$, $h(\langle i, j\rangle) = \alpha^{UE,i,j,g}$.

12. If $ME_{\langle s,a\rangle}$, then $[^\vee\alpha]^{UE,i,j,g}$ is $\alpha^{UE,i,j,g}(\langle i, j\rangle)$.

If ϕ is a formula (a member of ME_t), then ϕ is true with respect to UE, i, j iff $[\phi]^{UE,i,j,g}$ is 1 for every UE assignment g.

To complete the valuation requires that we make explicit the set of extended valuations, In^+. What is needed is a set of valuations which will play a role analogous to that played by bivalent valuations in a more ordinary system of super-valuations.

Let A, I, and J be the same sets of individuals, possible worlds, and times that we used in the UE interpretation. The set of possible denotations for an extended interpretation, I^+, will be those of UE with the addition of:

$$D^*_{e,A,I,J} = A$$

$$D^*_{t,A,I,J} = \{0, 1\}$$

$$D^*_{\langle a,b \rangle,A,I,J} = \text{the set of total functions from}$$

$$D_{a,A,I,J} \text{ to } D_{b,A,I,J}$$

$$D^*_{\langle s,a \rangle,A,I,J} = \text{the set of total functions from } I \times J$$

$$\text{to } D_{a,A,I,J}$$

An extended interpretation, I^+, relative to UE will be a sextuple $\langle A, I, J, \leq, New, F' \rangle$ such that:

1. A, I, J are the same nonempty sets specified in the quintuple UE.

2. $\leq$ is the same linear ordering on J found in UE.

3. *New* is a function having as its domain the set of all denotations in UE, such that:

   (i) $x \in D_{e,A,I,J} \cup D_{t,A,I,J}$ then *New* $(x) = \langle x, x \rangle$.

(ii) $x \in D_{\langle a,b \rangle,A,I,J}$ then $New\ (x) = \langle x, f^X \rangle$, where:

    a. $f^X \in D^*_{\langle a,b \rangle,A,I,J}$.

    b. If $y \in D_{a,A,I,J}$ and $x(y)$ is defined,

       then $f^X(y) = x(y)$.

(iii) $x \in D_{\langle s,a \rangle,A,I,J}$ then $New\ (x) = \langle x, s^X \rangle$, where:

    a. $s^X \in D^*_{\langle s,a \rangle,A,I,J}$.

    b. If $\langle i, j \rangle \in I \times J$ and $x(\langle i, j \rangle)$ is defined,

       $s^X(\langle i, j \rangle) = x(\langle i, j \rangle)$.

4. Whenever a $\in$ Type, $\alpha \in Con_a$, $F'\ (\alpha) = New\ (F(\alpha))$.

Let $I^+ = \langle A, I, J, \leq, New, F' \rangle$ be an extended interpretation of UE, and g^* an I^+ assignment of values to variables relative to g, a UE assignment of values to variables, that is, where u is a variable and $g(u) = x$, $g^*(u) = New\ (x)$. If α is a meaningful expression, then by α^{I^+,g^*} is understood the intension of α with respect to I^+ and g^*, subject to the restrictions stated above. If $\langle i, j \rangle \in I \times J$, then α^{I^+,i,j,g^*} is understood as the expansion of α with respect to I^+, i, j, and g^*, again subject to the above restrictions. We will stipulate the following convention concerning functional application in what follows: where $\langle x, y \rangle \notin I \times J$, $\langle x, y \rangle (z) = y(z)$, and $z(\langle x, y \rangle) = z(x)$. Using this convention we can introduce the notions of an intension and an extension relative to an I^+ interpretation by the following definition:

1. If α is a constant, then $\alpha^{I^+,i,j,g^*} = New\ (F'(\alpha)$

                                       $(\langle i, y \rangle))$.

2. If α is a variable, then $\alpha^{I^+,i,j,g^*} = g^*(\alpha)$.

3. If $\alpha \in ME_a$ and u a variable of type b, then

    $[\lambda u \ \alpha]^{I^+,i,j,g^*}$ is $\langle h, h \rangle$ where h is a function from

    $D_{b,A,I,J}$ to $D_{a,A,I,J}$ such that, whenever x is in the

    domain, $h(x) = \alpha^{I^+,i,j,g^{*\prime}}$ where $g^{*\prime}$ is an I^+ assign-

    ment of values to variables just like g^* with the

    possible exception that $g^{*\prime}(u) = New\ (x)$.

4. If $\alpha \in ME_{\langle a,b \rangle}$ and $\beta \in ME_a$, then $[\alpha(\beta)]^{I^+,i,j,g^*} =$

    $New\ (\alpha^{I^+,i,j,g^*}\ (\beta^{I^+,i,j,g^*}))$.

5. If $\alpha,\beta \in ME_a$, then $[\alpha = \beta]^{I^+,i,j,g^*}$ is $\langle 1, 1 \rangle$ iff

    α^{I^+,i,j,g^*} is β^{I^+,i,j,g^*}.

6. If $\phi \in ME_t$, then $[\neg \phi]^{I^+,i,j,g^*}$ is $\langle 1, 1 \rangle$ iff

    $[\phi]^{I^+,i,j,g^*}$ is $\langle 0, 0 \rangle$, and is $\langle 0, 0 \rangle$ otherwise.

7. If $\phi,\psi \in ME_t$, then $[\phi \wedge \psi]^{I^+,i,j,g^*}$ is $\langle 1, 1 \rangle$ iff

    $[\phi]^{I^+,i,j,g^*} = \langle 1, 1 \rangle$ and $[\psi]^{I^+,i,j,g^*} = \langle 1, 1 \rangle$, and

    is $\langle 0, 0 \rangle$ otherwise.

    Similarly for v, →, ↔.

8. If $\phi \in ME_t$, and u is a variable of type a, then

    $[\forall u \ \phi]^{I^+,i,j,g^*}$ is $\langle 1, 1 \rangle$ iff there exists an

    $x \in D_{a,A,I,J}$ such that $[\phi]^{I^+,i,j,g^{*\prime}}$ is $\langle 1, 1 \rangle$, where

    $g^{*\prime}$ is an I^+ assignment of values to variables just

    like g^* with the possible difference that $g^{*\prime}(u) =$

New (x); and is $\langle 0, 0 \rangle$ otherwise.

Similarly for $\wedge$.

9. If $\phi \in ME_t$, then $[\square \phi]^{I^+,i,j,g^*}$ is $\langle 1, 1 \rangle$ iff

$[\phi]^{I^+,i',j',g^*}$ is $\langle 1, 1 \rangle$ for all $\langle i', j' \rangle \in I \times J$,

and $\langle 0, 0 \rangle$ otherwise.

Similarly for W and H.

10. If $\alpha \in ME_a$, then $[^\wedge\alpha]^{I^+,i,j,g^*}$ is $\langle h^*, h^* \rangle$, where h^* is

that function with domain $I \times J$ such that whenever

$\langle i, j \rangle \in I \times J$, $h^*(\langle i, j \rangle) = \alpha^{I^+,i,j,g^*}$.

11. If $\alpha \in ME_{\langle s,a \rangle}$ then $[^\vee\alpha]^{I^+,i,j,g^*}$ is *New* $(\alpha^{I^+i,j,g^*}$

$(\langle i, j \rangle))$.

If $\phi \in ME_t$, then ϕ is true with respect to I^+, i, j iff $[\phi]^{I^+,i,j,g^*}$ is $\langle 1, 1 \rangle$ for every I^+ assignment g^*. The set In^+, or the set of extended interpretations with respect to an interpretation UE, is the set of all I^+ satisfying conditions (1) - (11).

Intuitively, the system works like this. The UE interpretation assigns to each constant of type a in the language an intension, which will be a partial function with domain world-time indices and range members of the set of possible denotations of type a. So the value of α given a sortal interpretation applied to an index world and time will be either an entity of type a or undefined, depending on whether the partial function assigned by the interpretation as the intension of α is defined for the given index.

In our extended interpretation we have a function, *New*, which maps the denotations of the sortal interpretation to ordered pairs, the first member of which is the old denotation and the second member of which is either identical to the first (in the case of entities or truth values) or is a complete function (in the case of anything else). Note that if we have a partial function in the sortal interpretation, the second member of the ordered pair that function is mapped to by the *New* function is such that for any argument for which the partial function is defined, the full function applied to that argument gives the same value as the partial function applied to that argument. Thus if x is a partial function which is a possible denotation in the sortal interpretation UE and y is some argument for x such that x(y) is defined, the ordered pair which x is mapped to by the *New* function is such that the second member is a full function, but a full function such that when it is applied to y the result is x(y). The only time this new function will differ from x in the result it gives when applied to an argument is if x is undefined for that argument. When x gives no value, the new function will give some value as the new function is total.

The intension or extension assigned to any constant of the language will be the result of applying the *New* function to the intension or extension of what that constant was assigned by the sortal interpretation. Thus the intension or extension will be an ordered pair in the extended interpretation. The stipulated convention concerning functional application has the effect that if we are considering the ordered pair as a function applying to an argument, we ignore the first member of the ordered pair; and if we are considering the ordered pair as the argument of some function, we ignore the second member of the ordered pair. The effect of all this is that, given any functional application $x(y)$, the result of the function applied to the argument will differ in the sorted interpretation and the extended interpretation only when $x(y)$ is undefined in the sorted interpretation. Further, we have placed restrictions on the interpretations so that the only time the result of applying a function to an argument will differ from one extended interpretation to another will be when that function is undefined for that argument in the sorted interpretation.

These results serve the following end. Let α be a meaningful expression of any type. The way UE was set up, $\alpha^{UE,i,j,g}$ will be either defined or undefined, while α^{I^+,i,j,g^*} will always be defined. However, if $\alpha^{UE,i,j,g}$ is defined, α^{I^+i,j,g^*} will have the same value for all $I^+ \in In^+$. The only place that the values determined by UE and I^+ will differ is when $\alpha^{UE,i,j,g}$ is undefined. In such a case, α^{I^+,i,j,g^*} will be defined. But the value of α^{I^+i,j,g^*} may differ from that of α^{I^+',i,j,g^*} for $I^+, I^{+'} \in In^+$. So if α is undefined in UE, sentences in which α is a truth-functional component will get their truth value depending on whether or not the truth value of the whole varies as the truth value of α varies from member to member of In^+.

Formulas which have no occurrence of the truth-functional connectives can be evaluated without reference to the extended interpretations. A special note should be made of the satis-faction conditions for the quantifiers. A condition for the value of a quantified formula having a truth value is that there be some assignment of values to the quantified variable such that that assignment makes the formula either true or false. Further, if there are such assignments, the satisfaction

conditions depend only on them, and not on instances which
result in a formula which lacks a defined truth value. This
has the effect of limiting the domain of the quantifiers to
instances which are members of the set determined by the E
function, and further stipulating that, for the quantified
formula to have a truth value, the set determined by the E
function cannot be empty. In terms of sorts, this means that
quantifiers range only over entities of the proper sort, and
that for a quantified formula to be true there must be some
entities of that sort.

The notion of an extended interpretation comes into the UE
valuation only when assigning values to formulas containing
truth-functional connectives. The reason for this is so we
can avoid having to treat the value 'undefined' as a separate
truth value. Since the value of these formulas will be determined by their values in extended valuations, and extended
valuations deal only with the values 'true' and 'false' (or
0 and 1), we are never forced to make the decision, for example,
of what truth value to give to a disjunction one of whose
disjuncts is sortally incorrect.

Translation

To translate this fragment requires the translation rules of
PTQ, one of which is amended; two new translation rules
corresponding to the two new syntactic rules; and the introduction of a new abbreviatory sign for a variable. Let R be
the variable $v_{0,\langle s,\langle\langle s,\langle\langle s,e\rangle, t\rangle\rangle:\langle\langle s,e\rangle,t\rangle\rangle\rangle}$, which ranges
over intensions of relations in extension between individual
concepts and properties of individual concepts, the semantic
type corresponding to the intensions of adjectives. The
amended rule is T1, to which we add the following clause:

T1 (f). be_p translates into $\lambda R \, \lambda x \, \lor P \, [P \, \{x\} \wedge (\lor R)(^\wedge P)(x)]$.

The two new translation rules, corresponding to S18 and S19, are:

T18. If $\gamma \in B_{adj}$, $\zeta \in P_{CN}$, and γ and ζ translate into γ', ζ' respectively, then F_5 (γ, ζ) translates into γ' $(^\wedge \zeta')$.

T19. If $\zeta \in B_{IV/adj}$, $\gamma \in B_{adj}$, and ζ, γ translate into ζ', γ' respectively, then $F_{16}(\zeta, \gamma)$ translates into ζ' $(^\wedge \gamma')$.

It is now possible to explain why this fragment breaks with Montague's practice and introduces a 'be' of predication. Montague stated that this move is unnecessary — that all occurrences of the 'be' of predication happen in sentences which are logically equivalent to a sentence which uses the 'be' of identity. Thus, he claimed, a sentence like

(3) John is big.

where the 'is' is an occurrence of the 'be' of predication is logically equivalent to the sentence

(4) John is a big entity.

in which the occurrence of 'is' is a case of the 'be' of identity. Montague realized that such a strategy was questionable — for example:

(5) That flea is big.

might well be true, but the sentence

(6) That flea is a big entity.

will never, outside of science fiction, be true. Montague suggests that the reduction might still be accomplished by equating sentences like (5) with

(7) That flea is a big entity of its kind.

While a move to kinds might get one out of the problem posed
to the reduction by big fleas and small stars, no such move
can be made if we want to get the result that sortally incorrect sentences have undefined truth values. For consider a
paradigm sortally incorrect sentence:

(1) The theory of relativity is shiny.

If the 'is' here is the 'be' of identity, this statement will
translate into the intensional logic as an identity statement,
claiming that identity holds between the theory of relativity
is some shiny entity. Since there is no entity which is both
shiny and identical to the theory of relativity, such a
sentence will turn out to be false rather than lacking a truth
value. The problem is that we can never get some identity in
our translated statement between the property set which is
our translation of 'the theory of relativity' and the function
of property sets to property sets which is the translation of
'shiny'. By introducing the 'be' of predication we gain such
a relation, allowing us to give the sentence a truth value of
undefined.

Examples

As the system given in this paper is an extension of PTQ,
it differs in generating capacity only in that it generates
more sentences than does the PTQ system. Thus all the sentences
of PTQ will be sentences of this fragment. Further, there are
sentences which can be generated by the rules of PTQ which
one might well want to consider sortally incorrect, such as

(8) Ninety loves Mary.

All sentences generated by the PTQ system which are not
sortally incorrect or deviant for some other reason will be

given the same semantic interpretation as given by the PTQ
semantics.

The extension was put forward to allow for the generation
of sentences which are sortally incorrect in an obvious way,
such as our paradigms:

(1) The theory of relativity is shiny.

(2) The taste of lemon is breakable.

both of which are now generated in the fragment. These will
translate into the intensional logic as

(1') $\wedge$y [theory of relativity' (y) $\wedge$ $\vee$P [P {y} $\wedge$ shiny'

$$(^\wedge P)(y)]]$$

(2') $\wedge$y [taste of lemon' (y) $\wedge$ $\vee$P [P {y} $\wedge$ breakable'

$$(^\wedge P)(y)]]$$

Both (1') and (2') are of the same general form, and will
be given their truth values on analogous grounds. Both will
be defined iff there is some instance which is either true
or false, and both will be true iff all such instances, if
there are any, are true. So they will turn out to be defined
only if the conjunction is true for some instance. This
requires evaluating the conjunction on the level of the
extended valuations. The crux of the matter in (1'), for
example, is going to be whether there is any property which
can be in the property set of an entity which also has
'theory of relativity'' in its property set such that that
property is in the sortal specification of 'shiny''. On a
sortal specification which takes English seriously, I think
that we can reasonably assume that there is no such property.
Therefore the truth of the second conjunct will vary from
extended interpretation to extended interpretation, and thus

the value of the conjunction as a whole will also vary from some of those extended interpretations to others. Thus the conjunction is undefined. Thus there is no instance for which the formula is defined, and the existentially quantified formula we started out with in (1') is undefined. (2') will receive an undefined value for analogous reasons.

A more interesting case is that of

(9) Every shiny theory of relativity is shiny.

which will translate into

(9') $\wedge x$ [shiny' (^theory of relativity') (y) $\rightarrow$ $\vee P$ [P {y} $\wedge$

shiny' (^P)(y)]]

Again, this will be defined only if the conditions which are instances of the quantified formula are such that at least one of them is defined, and true only if all the conditionals defined are true. To evaluate the conditional, we must again go to the set of extended valuations. In each of these valuations, the antecedent of the conditional will be either true or false, since all extended valuations are bivalent. If the antecedent is false, the conditional is true. If the antecedent is true, then the consequent will be true, for there will be a property in the property set of y which is such that the consequent is true — namely, 'theory of relativity''. So if the antecedent is true, the conditional is true. Thus on all extended interpretations the formula is true: therefore the conditional is true. So the translation of (9), (9'), tells us that (9) is true, corresponding to our intuitions.

A final example to be considered is

(10) The king of France is bald.

read as referring to the present king of France. Such a sentence is not sortally incorrect. However, the method of

supervaluations was first proposed by Van Fraasen in the
context of attempting to solve problems caused by sentences
like (10). Thus it should not be surprising if the present
theory can give an adequate account of (10).

The present fragment will translate (10) as

(10') $\wedge y$ [king of France' (y) $\wedge$ $\vee P$ [P {y} $\wedge$ bald' (^P)(y)]]

The key to interpreting (10') is realizing that our interpretation assigns an intention to the constant 'king of France''
a partial function from world-time indices to property sets.
This intention will be defined for some world-times and not
others; specifically, the function will be defined for worlds
and times at which the king of France exists, and undefined
for worlds and times at which the king of France does not
exist. Thus, if the king of France exists, (10') will be true
or false depending on the condition of his head; but if no
king of France exists the sentence will be undefined in truth
value.

A residual problem concerns sentences with undefined truth
value in belief contexts. It is unclear to me how to treat
sentences like

(11) John believes that the theory of relativity is shiny.

We could decide that such a sentence also has an undefined
truth value, justifying such a treatment on the grounds that
a function with an undefined argument yields no value. This
is the course taken in this fragment. But it could also be
that we want to allow sentences like (11) to be true — after
all, there is no accounting for the range of beliefs open to
people. This could also be accounted for in the theory, by
allowing the sortal range of 'belief' to include null functions like the proposition expressed by 'The theory of
relativity is shiny.' A problem with this solution, however,

is that, because propositions are functions, the null function will be the proposition corresponding to all sortally incorrect sentences. Thus, if we allow for the belief of sortally incorrect sentences, a belief in one sortally incorrect sentence will be a belief in all sortally incorrect sentences. It should be noted, however, that Montague's system already has an analogous problem concerning belief in tautologies and contradictions, since all tautologies share the same intension, as do all contradictions.

References

Bennett, Michael. 1974. "Some Extensions of a Montague Fragment of English." Ph.D. dissertation, UCLA; available from the Indiana University Linguistics Club.

Cooper, Robin. 1975. "Montague's Semantic Theory and Transformational Syntax." Ph.D. dissertation, University of Massachusetts, Amherst.

Montague, Richard. 1974. *Formal Philosophy: Selected Papers of Richard Montague*. Ed. Richmond H. Thomason. New Haven: Yale University Press.

Thomason, Richmond. 1972. "A Semantic Theory of Sortal Incorrectness." *Journal of Philosophical Logic* 1: 209 - 258.

van Fraasen, Bas. 1968. "Presuppositions, Implications, and Self-Reference." *Journal of Philosophy* 136 - 152.

Index